HISTORICAL INQUIRY IN EDUCATION
A RESEARCH AGENDA

HISTORICAL INQUIRY IN EDUCATION

A RESEARCH AGENDA

Edited by
John Hardin Best

American Educational Research Association

The American Educational Research Association
1230 17th Street, N.W.
Washington, D.C. 20036

Copyright, 1983, by the
American Educational Research Association
All rights reserved
Cataloging in Publication
Library of Congress catalogue card number 82-74458
ISBN 0-935302-03-4

CONTENTS

INTRODUCTION

John Hardin Best
The Pennsylvania State University

This group of speculative essays offers a variety of views on issues that are developing, or that should develop, in the field of history of education today. The authors build on present work of course, but the essays are not intended to form a comprehensive review of literature that leaves no research stone unturned. Instead, they offer a review of thinking in the field today, of where we are and where we can expect to be in the next decade or so in history and education. It is a speculative agenda for research to come.

The essays are intended to be useful to educational historians, other educational researchers, and those interested in better understanding American society through its educational development. It is clear to historians that such a collection of essays is an effort to clarify trends of thinking in this diverse field. But the volume is also intended to be used by other educational researchers to suggest ways that historical study may inform this broad area of research, and to assist researchers in formulating studies and analyzing the findings in greater depth.

The volume also may be useful to any reader who looks for understanding of today's society through the history of education and schooling, an essential element in how our world is formed. Let me further explore these three uses of this volume.

First, historians, as everybody knows, have a strong tendency to revise, to continually (even compulsively) reinterpret and reanalyze the past. Some say that it is the historians' nature to do so; others suggest that it may be a learned behavior. In either case they relentlessly rework the past so that it never seems to stay put. In the field of education, for example, many of us are just beginning to get used to the idea that everything we learned in graduate school a decade or so ago--about how the Great American Public School had opened the door of opportunity to us all--was at the very least a romantic myth if not a deliberately malicious lie. But now all that seems to be overturning. Now it appears that various ethnic groups, minorities, and others all over the country were defining their world without the ministrations of the public school, perhaps even rejecting what it represented in opportunity and success and were looking to other institutions, other means, and other directions. But what does this overturning mean? It means that all of us will need to look at this history one more time. And in light of this new interpretation of what the school has meant and how it has related to other institutions in our society, we may come to understand this part of our history better. I exaggerate and oversimplify these overturnings, of course, in order to suggest something of the process of the historians' revising, of every new revision revising an earlier one.

Each generation tends to reappraise its past to understand it in light of present reality. In the study of history of education in recent years the process has been lively. New interpretations and methodologic developments of varying circumference have been presented in books, monographs, and journals in the field. They have been reviewed and discussed, replied and rejoined to, fought over up and down the country at conferences and meetings for years. In fact, the field of history of education over the past two decades has had a remarkable vitality of revision and re-revision which has stimulated continual exploration and study. New positions have been defined and defended, and, as the process goes on, these positions become assimilated to create the departure point for yet further study. This volume of essays brings together the thinking of this process now and speculates on what it will be in the future. For the historian these essays can introduce important directions for study.

Second, these essays offer researchers in education and related fields the advantage of historical insight, that is, the dimension of time in analyzing research issues. In this case the volume's applications are those of history in general.

Gertrude Stein, surrounded on her deathbed by her close friends, turned to them and asked, "What is the answer?" Met with silence, she said, "In that case, what is the question?" Now this may simply reflect a whimsical turn of mind to the end, but I think it is more than that. It was the Stein wisdom to point out that the great question at issue is always the question itself. And so it is in any field of study and research: a grasp of essence, basic assumptions, frame, and implication must determine what questions are to be posed and what meaning may lie in the answers derived. Excellence in research, empirical and otherwise, seems to rest ultimately on such a fragile foundation as that of historical context. Such perspective is indeed essential to the whole enterprise of educational research.

Finally, these essays should be useful and valuable not only to the professionals in history and in educational research but to a broader population of readers, that is, to anyone who wishes to better understand American society. The work here offers fresh thinking on a range of topics relevant to analyzing today's society. From one context to the next the reader will find a play of ideas that is enlightening, lively, and stimulating.

And so, to scholars and professionals, as well as to an aware public, here is a speculative agenda for research in history of education, fifteen essays of many dimensions and many uses.

As to the volume's organization, each essay stands independently in focusing on a particular topic. The fifteen essays were not made to fit into a grid to see that a set of predetermined concerns be systematically addressed. Instead, each author explored directions of study with his or her own special genius. Hence, a fine variety and spice: some of the essays follow a review format with full historiographic exposition; others offer a more illustrative approach by outlining ongoing research to suggest the state of the area and its directions. The principle was to encourage many flowers.

The Editor and Editorial Committee developed the fifteen topics so that the major disciplinary aspects, methodologic matters, and important issues that are central to the history of education would be addressed and represented by a scholar cum advocate. The sum of these many differing perspectives offers an unparalleled view of an agenda for research. And indeed, the essays do interrelate, augmenting and complementing one another with excellent effect. The result is a coherence that creates an impressive whole while maintaining the independent interest of each topic and author.

A broad plan for a project of this sort originated several years ago with a publications committee chaired by Irving Hendrick of Division F of the American Educational Research Association, the "History and Historiography" Division. The plan was presented to the AERA Publications Committee, who endorsed it as an AERA sponsored monograph and directed that the historical writing relate to educational research in general. In June, 1980, the AERA Board, under then President Frank Farley, approved the project and appointed the editor to proceed with the work.

Many people contributed to creating this monograph, and they deserve grateful acknowledgement for their work. First and fundamentally are the authors, the ultimate contributors to this volume. They worked with dispatch and good spirit through the Editor's alternating cajoling and badgering. The nine members of the Editorial Committee, who represent a range of disciplines and interests, were invaluable from the very beginning, from consulting on the original plan, to the final critical review of manuscripts. Penn State colleagues in several academic areas, William Boyd, Joseph Flay, Henry Johnson, Harold Mitzel, and Edmund Short generously contributed more reviewing and consulting time. Several graduate student assistants, particularly Teena Villarroel, contributed in good graduate student ways. Deborah Stahl and Judy Leonard, masters of the System 6 at the Penn State office, were invaluable in preparing the manuscript for publication. Anita King and the publications staff at the AERA offices also did essential editing work along the way. And finally, Charlotte Best should be acknowledged as the person who listened to more talk about this project than anyone should ever have been expected to do.

1

RESCUING CLIO
PHILOSOPHY OF HISTORY

Henry C. Johnson, Jr.
The Pennsylvania State University

Propelled by the popular disaffection with our
institutions that arose in the late fifties,
"radical" social critics and historians proposed a
thoroughgoing reconstruction of our past and the
historiography that produced it. (1) Their
perspective posited the virtual failure of the
American experiment rather than its success. For
some, the engine of change was a new
psychometaphysical process. We were witnessing the
"Age of Aquarius," the birth of a new
"consciousness" that signified a transcendental leap
into something so novel that we would, by 1980 or
so, scarcely recognize the world we inhabited. More
plausible accounts rested on some sort of
"liberation" process, inspired by parallels with
racial struggle or drawn from classic notions of
class conflict. Many called for the rejection of
"colonial" models of social organization grounded on
economic exploitation and an accompanying "cultural
imperialism," often repudiating rational reform
itself. (2)

Treatments by "revisionist" educational
historians followed in due course and mirrored the

approaches used elsewhere. Their nearly unanimous conclusion was straightforward: schooling had at best failed to keep its promises; at worst it not only had become but (as historians were particularly fitted to prove) had always been an active agent of oppression and exploitation. In explanation, they invoked their own elaborate array of psychological and socioeconomic concepts and theories: bureaucracy, modernization, status-envy, or intergenerational conflict, for example.

The literary power, timeliness, and tight focus of many of these critiques guaranteed that they would not be entirely bereft of benefit, of course. The ensuing discussion has forced all to grapple with fundamental issues and to face the possibility of unpleasant conclusions. But it has largely failed to give birth to any significant reconstruction, let alone provide the radical alternatives that were purportedly waiting just over the horizon. Why? Much of the reason for this sterility may lie in the fact that, although the allegations appeared to be novel, the conceptions of education and schooling involved were not. Their source was an educational historiography that, far from being a radical departure, was essentially similar to the conventional logic of educational argument. However valuable as a provocative professional literature, the work of too many recent educational historians has produced not an enduring revitalization but some general conclusions that are logically dubious, frequently misleading, and possibly empirically false. Much of the poverty of these conclusions has already been exposed, and an apology may be required for reopening what have already become ritualized arguments. (3) My purpose is, however, to push the critique to a different level, so that not only will our fruitless historiographical fugue be terminated but the foundation laid for a fresh start.

The procedure employed by the new critics has customarily been two-stage: The first stage has been to accept (not on the basis of compelling evidence, but largely by deduction) the notion of radical and virtually universal school failure as a starting point. That is to say, the tendency has been to accept the more general radical critique of institutions rather than to make the first order of business the probing of its adequacy in respect to schooling. Having accepted a questionable critique, the second stage has been to explain the phenomenon created by the critique, and only then to illuminate and interpret it in historical terms. The logical defects of the critique itself, however, have seriously restricted the empirical studies that ought to occupy the attention of historians and have consequently disastrously limited the resulting evidence. This evidence is taken as confirming a negative judgment about education and schooling, not because it has been shown to do so but because it fits the explanatory theory it was designed to prove.

The problem begins, I believe, with Horace Mann and what I will call the Yankee School Platform. We must take a moment to provide that notable apologist with an intelligible setting for his arguments. When, in 1837, Mann became the first Secretary of the Board of Education for the Commonwealth of Massachusetts, he already regarded it as axiomatic that a republic that had no "sectarian" commitment would necessarily rely on education for its principles of cohesion and direction, since it perforce eschewed government by preformed elites, most particularly hierarchy and/or royalty. The "Friends of Education" appear largely to agree with such principles. They further agree that common schooling is the instrumentality of choice for achieving this goal. Common beliefs and values are available, out of science, political philosophy, and a minimal natural theology. To the principles derived from such sources, rational assent can be freely given by both teachers and students, issuing in a "voluntary self-government" that will maximize individual liberty within the necessary social constraints, and at the same time produce both the potential for individual growth and social harmony and progress. This subject matter, together with the necessary academic and technical skills, constitutes the stuff of which an effective republican education is to be made. (4)

As has frequently been pointed out, when Mann took office, there were already many schools, and a considerable portion of the eligible population was attending them. The real problem was that the schools were not "common." They also varied enormously in their nature and quality. Hence, Mann saw his task as twofold. First, their individual quality had to be improved, chiefly by the provision of a new, professional teaching force. The second problem was their organization: the vast differences and inequalities which met the eye as he inspected them could only be done away by equalizing their support across district lines. Here, however, Mann encountered important resistance under the color of the same principles he invoked: if the purpose of a republic is to "free" the individual, why should anyone be compelled to support even his immediate neighbor's children, let alone those in remote districts?

Mann's response generally is that people who do not understand their obligation in the premises simply do not understand either education or its relation to a republic. Consequently, although his arguments are chiefly practical, concerned with money and organization, they are attempts nevertheless to demonstrate what education and schooling ought to be in a republic. Mann relies for this purpose on three chief sources. Two are moral. Political moral principles such as justice comprise the first. Equally important are his theological moral principles. Here Mann makes use of an interesting argument previously articulated by John Winthrop. "Natural" justice is necessary but not sufficient for a good state or community because it assumes that men are friends when they are not! That is, while conceptions of justice may tell us what ought to prevail, they do not furnish a sufficient motive for doing it, especially across the differences and enmities that are actually present among persons. The religious notion that all men are brothers, Mann (like Winthrop) believes, compels a positive duty to care for others in a manner not required by simple political justice. (5)

The third source for Mann's Platform is empirical. It is the case, Mann believes, that both individuals and societies now get on, and always have gotten on, much better as a consequence of schooling. What that means, Mann does not hesitate to define. In his Fifth Report, he tells us that there are four criteria of individual benefit: "worldly fortunes," "health and length of life," "manners and tastes," and "intellectual and moral character." In respect to the state, there are three criteria: "wealth," "social standing," and the "number of distinguished individuals produced." In sum, the individual's interests and the state's interests naturally coalesce in this "utilitarian view of education, as it may be called, which regards it [education] as the dispenser of private competence and the promoter of national wealth." (6)

It is important to note that in the Fifth Report (as frequently before and after) Mann adopts a strategy that will be crucial in future arguments about schooling. The moral-political principles are commended, not established; they are simply assumed to hold. The practically important task is to convince his hearers of the third principle: that education through schooling is productive, on empirical grounds, of just those effects that our moral principles call for and justify. That is what will move them to political action. Hence, Mann devotes the greatest part of his argument to providing empirical evidence that various towns provide different levels of support and, most importantly, that where support is low, the individual (and social) consequences are counter-productive. In evidence for the last, he summons to the bar "many of the most practical, sagacious and intelligent business men amongst us, who for many years have had large numbers of persons in their employment." "My object has been," Mann says, "to ascertain the difference in productive ability,--where natural capacities have been equal,--between the educated and the uneducated. . . ." These employers have examined the record "for a series of years" respecting both "quality and the amount" of work done. From this "mass of facts,"

Mann says he can "prove incontestably that education
is not only a moral renovator, and a multiplier of
intellectual power, but that it is also the most
prolific parent of material riches." (7)

The point to be drawn from this discussion of
the Yankee School Platform and the arguments used to
sustain it is that while the content changes
importantly over the succeeding decades, its
crucial, logical form remains substantially
unchanged even at the hands of the so-called radical
educational historians. To show that, the argument
must now be cast in more formal terms. Reducing
rhetorical statements to pristine logic furnishes
many potential pitfalls, but I shall call this
formulation the "Old Conventional Wisdom."

First, there is a preliminary deductive
argument, the truth of which neither Mann nor anyone
else at the time seriously doubts:

> If [P] any enterprise is individually and
> socially beneficial, then [Q] we ought to
> engage in it.
> [P] Schooling is an enterprise which is
> individually and socially beneficial.
> Therefore, [Q] we ought to engage in it.

This argument establishes the essentially moral
framework of all his subsidiary arguments, whether
they are cast in expressly moral terms or not.

Mann himself claims a general logical force for
his arguments as well as an empirical agenda
following from them. Take, for example, this first
order enthymeme: "Considering education as a
producer of wealth, it follows that the more
educated a people are, the more will they abound in
all those conveniences, comforts and satisfactions
which money will buy; and, other things being equal,
the increase of competency and the decline of
pauperism will be measureable on this scale." (8)

It seems fair to cast Mann's appeal, including
the missing major premise, as follows:

> (Education [i.e., schooling] will produce
> wealthy people.)

These people have been educated.
Therefore, these people will be wealthy
(and, mutatis mutandis, the more educated,
the wealthier they will be).

The context makes it clear, however, that Mann does
not wish us to draw strict conclusions but rather to
believe in the necessity of school improvement.
Mann's argument has a particular content here,
but we can, on the basis of a more extensive survey
of his writings and actions, provide a more general
form and content. As in the quotation above, there
is almost always an implicit double claim: both the
individual and the state will benefit (as in the
example, by the "decline of pauperism"). Time and
time again, Mann argues as follows:

If [P] children are schooled, and
If [P'] that schooling is successful
[i.e., if that schooling is adequately
funded and competently staffed, in which
case it presumably will be successful],
Then [Q] the life consequences to those
children will be beneficial and
[Q'] The life consequences to the state
will be beneficial.

Mann's concluding argumentative strategy varies
from audience to audience, but it usually takes one
of two paths. The first appears to be a classical
example of the fallacy of affirming the consequent.

[Q] For the most part, in the cases I have
encountered, these children have enjoyed
beneficial life consequences, and
[Q'] The states/communities I have
examined have enjoyed beneficial life
consequences.
Therefore, [P] these children and [P']
these states/communities must have
experienced or provided good (i.e.,
successful) schooling.

The second strategy appears to be a valid but

factually questionable example of <u>modus</u> <u>tollens</u>:

> [Not Q] For the most part, in the cases I have encountered, these children have not enjoyed beneficial life consequences, and [Not Q'] The states/communities I have examined have not enjoyed beneficial life consequences,
> Therefore [not P] these children and [not P'] those states/communities did not have/provide good (successful) schooling.

In both cases, the results are attributable to schooling. And, the rhetorical force is, of course, if you wish the same consequences, do likewise. Clearly, Mann believes that by being able to make his case both ways, his arguments establish that education/schooling is both a necessary and a sufficient condition for individual and social well-being.

There are, in fact, a host of logical problems here that we can neither define nor settle at the moment. Note, however, that Mann slides from deductive to inductive argumentation, while conveying the impression that his inductive arguments have the universal authority he can claim only for his deductive arguments. Note also that, because of his practical agenda (school improvement), he has carried us into that tendency which persists to this day: to identify schooling with good (successful) schooling. His aim is in fact to reform and expand the school system, not simply to define and justify it. He therefore insists that it is only good schools that will be successful, that is, schools with adequate funding and competent personnel, competent personnel being teachers and administrators whose activities bring about successful life consequences for their students. But this is at least faintly circular. (His conclusion, of course, might still be true; and in that case we might fault him largely for using the color of logic when the case rested on quantitative empirical demonstration, which he tries to supply anyway.)

Yet, however important these problems may be, the chief point is that an empirical agenda does follow from arguments of this sort, and that agenda takes its shape and direction from the arguments underlying it. You may have noted that Mann's argumentative strategy focuses on the logical consequent. His arguments involve the real world. Hence, there is both a deductive and an inductive task at hand. Mann is satisfied that the deductive task has been successfully accomplished. The crucial point is the inductive task. Hence, he and his friends and colleagues busily go about finding successful and unsuccessful instances of the conjunction between schooling and beneficial social and individual life consequences. And so do their successors. Like Mann, educational historians "old" and "new" have (as we shall see) too frequently defined their activities in relation to the original argument when, in fact, their appropriate goal and activity is to investigate the premises in a more adequate manner.

Thus, it should not surprise us that school apologists in subsequent decades, including the early educational historians, essentially follow a similar deductive and inductive agenda. As the "radical" historians have made notorious, the case of the "infamous" Ellwood Patterson Cubberley is particularly instructive. It can be shown that Cubberley offers simply a grander version of the same Yankee Platform, and he claims to offer it on large-scale, speculative, historical grounds. Enlarging Mann's original vision, Cubberley sees education and common schooling as a "phase of the history of civilization" itself. There is, he says, "a close connection" between "the history of the civilization of a people and the ideas on and progress of education among them." (9)

By 1919, Cubberley believed that educational history-making should be recast in terms of the problems of the twentieth century, and in light of "the great social, political, and industrial changes which have given the recent marked expansion of state educational effort its entire meaning." The progress of education and schooling may now be seen as a virtually cosmic "battle" or "struggle" (his two favorite terms), but the Yankee faith is still undimmed: "education is our Nation's [Cubberley almost always capitalizes Nation and State] greatest constructive tool." This is true even though "the many problems of national welfare which education alone can solve are far greater than the schoolmaster [Mann?] of two or three decades ago dreamed." (10)

There are, however, a variety of interesting and sometimes important changes that have transpired between Mann and Cubberley. Mann's naive nonsectarianism has now become deliberate secularization--a process that Cubberley, curiously, finds implicit in Protestantism and its individualistic, ostensibly open, frame of mind, now emptied of its traditional theological content. It is also implicit, he thinks, in the basis of the modern state. The inductive task, then, is to show instances of victory in the battle, a direct parallel with the instances developed by Mann. History is now the searching of our "historical evolution" (Darwin has, of course, spoken) and what it reveals demonstrates not only Mann's less bold claim to satisfactory concrete results from the schools but a hint as to "probable lines of their future development." (11) Hence, most of Cubberley's work frankly catalogues instances of providing or failing to provide the free, secularized, tax-supported, state-controlled, and professionally supervised education and schooling (seen as a corollary of "the improvability of the race") that are requisite for the "emancipation of the individual." (12)

I will turn now to the new historians and what I will call the "New Conventional Wisdom." Assuming that you are more familiar with their arguments and claims, I shall move directly to the logical formulation that, in my opinion, most generally characterizes their efforts. There are, I believe, two major sorts, which I will refer to as "soft" and "hard" revisionism.

In the "soft" form, the argument usually runs as follows:

If [P] schooling produced beneficial life consequences for individuals, and
If [P'] schooling produced beneficial social life consequences (given: longer, costlier, and more widespread schooling),
Then [Q] the lot of those individuals who were schooled would have shown improvement over time, and
[Q'] Society would have shown a parallel improvement.
But, [not Q] those who were schooled did not, on the whole, improve their relative lot--that is, did not enjoy beneficial life consequences (here there are called to witness, <u>inter alia</u>, the hard cases, namely the subsequent careers of the blacks, the working class, and the immigrants, all of which are usually presented categorically),
And [not Q'] society is no more open, just, equitable, or peaceful, than it was before--that is, has not enjoyed beneficial social life consequences (as witness, again, <u>inter alia</u>, the oppression, exploitation, and disenfranchisement, which still abound in our society).
Therefore, [not P] schooling did not [and, it is usually claimed or suggested, does not and possibly cannot] produce beneficial individual life consequences, and
[Not P'] Schooling did not [does not or cannot] produce beneficial social life consequences.

In the case of "hard" revisionism, the logic is similar in form and substance, but it is usually cast in personal terms and at least borders on the conspiratorial. For brevity I shall put it simply as follows:

If [P] schoolmen had <u>intended</u> to make schooling an instrument of social and

individual benefit,
Then [Q] the relative lot of individuals
and of society would be improved.
But, [not Q]
Therefore, [not P] schoolmen <u>did</u> <u>not</u>
<u>intend</u> that schooling should be
beneficial.

A further practical leap is sometimes made, namely,
that if school people did not intend schooling to be
beneficial, they must on that account have had
malevolent designs, and so on. It seems unnecessary
to examine this obviously illicit extension,
however, except to note that it throws into even
sharper relief the psychologizing that marks much of
the work of the more extreme critics.

Thus, in light of Mann, Cubberley, and the
logic of the Yankee Platform--and precisely because
that Platform has been accepted by both critics and
the criticized--either case appears persuasive. And
the empirical agenda is straightforward: show that
the subsequent (i.e., postschooling) careers of
blacks, the working class, and the immigrants were
unsatisfactory and either the hard or the soft case
can be presented persuasively, though perhaps not
quite rigorously demonstrated. What seems difficult
to doubt is that it is the same argument. Perhaps
the most prestigious of the new historians has
articulated the conclusion of such "demonstrations"
quite explicitly, and is frequently quoted with
approval: "In any event, the burden of proof no
longer lies with those who argue that education is
and has been unequal. It lies rather with those who
would defend the system." (13)

For the present, my purpose is not to challenge
either side, but to suggest that not only is the
argument essentially unchanged both in its form and
its presuppositions, but that the empirical agenda
to which it gives rise is also substantially
similar: as the "old" historian must look for
confirming evidence, the "new" searches for
disconfirming evidence. But there is one crucial
difference: the new historian, believing the
negative case to have been easily made, now presses

on for an explanation of the failure. These
"explanations," however, are likewise the
consequence of the original general logic of the
Yankee Platform. These "new" arguments are still
imprisoned in a logic that presupposed two vital
components: an argument for a notion of schooling
that entailed successful results (or the argument
would not work) and a notion of the educational
process that empirically implied a causal connection
between attempting to school and gaining success.
Thus, both the old apologists and the new critics
are compelled to confirm or disconfirm the
productivity of education and schooling on empirical
grounds outside schooling itself. In both cases
they look at life careers and attribute their
results to schooling, when (it is crucial to note)
the issue is what, if anything, schooling really
does. For the latter, the disconfirmation of an
effective schooling proves relatively easy to
accomplish; the problem is explaining it. The
discussions and observations are then further
removed: the critical historians now argue neither
about schools nor their (presumed) effects, but
about the explanations of the effects of a failure
that is now simply presumed to exist on the shakiest
of logical and empirical grounds.

We must turn now to more general difficulties
raised by the whole "new" enterprise in American
educational history as it has been practiced in the
last two decades. One of the events precipitating
the "revolution" in American educational
historiography was the publication of Bernard
Bailyn's   Education in the Forming of American
Society. (14)   The chroniclers of American
educational historiography point (tiresomely, in
fact) to Bailyn's work as the impulse that liberated
the educational historian from the straightjacket
inherited not only from Mann, and that object of
particular scorn, Ellwood Patterson Cubberley, but
also from the social foundations people of the
thirties and forties who were confused about whether
the task of educational historians was to tell the
truth or to work for a particular brand of school
reform. (15) To do Bailyn only slight disservice,

the liberating (though surely less than oracular) proclamation he made was that education was more than schooling. Thanks to this timely clarification, "real" historians were freed at a stroke to talk about education in general and the effects of schooling in particular--matters which, of course, they had ignored for years, and about which many of them are still largely illiterate--without the painful necessity of paying much attention to schooling in concrete, individual cases. Likewise, educational historians were now back in the mainstream, provided, of course, that they accepted the new rubrics and canons for their craft. They, too, were now free to talk about education, but without paying much attention to schools or what actually went on inside them: the thoughts and conversations of school people over the long decades since Mann could be categorized simply as "rhetoric" or "ideology," for example, and there were established rules for dealing with such epiphenomena. So also with matters such as the normal school (that too painful symbol of the schoolman's benighted past). The work of the county superintendent, as a person who acted with certain intents and purposes in, say, McLean County, Illinois, in 1879, could be dismissed by reducing it categorically to an instance of nascent bureaucracy. Teachers all but disappeared from view except in the aggregate, or perhaps as test cases designed not to render teachers and their actions understandable in themselves but to prove the methodological rule. The dirty, day-by-day details of how the "system" worked, who ran it, who they were that (presumably) peopled it--all such considerations were cleansed, swept up into vast hypotheses generated not out of educational inquiry but by approved social scientists who had not been tainted by plunging into actual inquiries about schools.

On the conservative wing of the "revolutionary" new history, a new, magisterial volume has been released in which schooling in the concrete almost entirely slips from view underneath the broad waters of education as general culture. There are a scattering of illustrative cases of school activity

to "document" the life of school people across a
hundred years. Parts of two pages suffice for the
"Normal School Movement." Whole chapters, however,
expatiate on grander themes. (16) These are flowers
of scholarship (for which I myself have a certain
fondness) but entirely cut off from their roots in
the dusty soil of American schools.

On the radical wing, the case is again similar
in form, though different in content. It resembles
even more the work of Mann and Cubberley! Examine,
for example, one of the seminal works of the
revolutionary movement. The whole argument begins
with a myth--the myth that American social and
cultural development has been continuous and
successful (in the sense of admitting new groups to
participation and to the enjoyment of its benefits
and in the sense of lessening class, racial, and
ethnic distinctions in line with its proclaimed
republican or democratic goals) and the myth that
the public school has been the chief agency in this
accomplishment. As the author puts it, in the
familiar language of fairy tales, "Once upon a time
there was a great nation which became great because
of its public schools." (17) This purported
accomplishment has existed only in the imagination,
created and fostered by the early in-house
educational "historians" who were simply
institutional apologists, primarily concerned with
proving their own effectiveness. (18)

The facts belie the myth. By examining the
parallels between blacks and immigrants, we can see
the problem that is still with us. The question is
how to explain it? The author under consideration
has little patience with psychological and
sociological theories. His choice is for
explanatory constructs drawn from the political and
economic realm (seen, incidentally, as virtually
identical) because the problem stems from primitive
capitalist linkages between the Puritan theological
commitment to the scarcity of grace and the scarcity
of wealth. (19)

How do we know that all this is true? We
examine the school performance of children via the
statistical studies that became popular at the turn

of the century, particularly those respecting retardation, IQ by ethnic group and social class and by occupation. From this (and similar examinations) we first deduce what went on in schools and then conclude that schooling not only did not assist the process but may have forestalled or at least seriously limited it. Since, the argument appears to run, we know the results, we can interpret the actions and intentions of the teachers, administrators, perhaps even those of the students. We can assume that the games they were taught were surely not innocent recreation but in fact clever indoctrination in rule-keeping of the sort required by the mindless occupations to which they would inevitably be assigned by the new industrial enterprise. We can conclude, for example, in the case of that paradigmatic reformer and para-schoolteacher, Jane Addams (this time contrary to her expressed interpretation of her own acts, of course), that rather than respecting, liberating, and caring, she was willy-nilly demeaning, exploiting, and oppressing her apparently docile subjects at Hull House. (20) True, there were some immigrants who wrote about their experiences for themselves, and those who did were largely benevolently disposed to their teachers and schools, but they were the successful ones. The voiceless were the unsuccessful (by deduction) and the unsuccessful were voiceless, speaking the real truth only through the mute statistics we have at last learned how to interpret.

As I turn now to the next phase of my argument I must again enter an important caveat: I am defending neither the old conventional wisdom nor either variant of the new. Nor am I convinced that we are now doing well enough in our schools or that we ever have. And I want to know why. My point is that I do not believe any answer will come to us if we proceed in this fashion. We are simply rehashing the same, long-exhausted, logical and empirical argument with new tools, shifting from mode to mode. The problem lies, I am beginning to suspect, both with the original argument and with the restricted historiography it has produced. Mann set the agenda by insisting that the justification for schools lay outside them in what they produced: prosperity, respectability, and honor. Consequently, the test of their success lay outside them. The revisionists are, I think, quite right in pointing out the failure of schooling, or at least the curious unevenness in its advertised "success." What I find difficult is to leap from the outer failure to the inner "reality" of schooling in such a way as either to understand it adequately or to correct it. (That sounds dangerously like reformism, but one must sin bravely, I suppose.)

Notice, if you will, several things. What is palpable fact is that there has never been a "common school system." That is, I think, the real myth or legend. Mann and his disciples were intent on creating it, but they never succeeded. The revisionists assume the existence of this monolithic process and that it has produced our inequalities. What do we know about the intents and values of teachers and students, from then until now? Is it idle to suggest that the goals, and especially the criteria of success for the system and for the society and culture, may not have been quite so unitary as Mann felt free to suggest--largely as a consequence of his arguments to a particular audience at a particular time for a particular purpose? That possibility gives rise, in turn, to another unthinkable thought: perhaps Frederick or Mehitabel did not go to school, at least not exclusively, to "get ahead," whether on Mann's terms, or Cubberley's, or those of the equally ethnocentric contemporary revisionists, who have their own notion of what satisfactory social or individual benefit would be.

If we turn to one aspect of the argument (or rather the lack of it) the house falls down, I believe. The test cases always include "the immigrants" and "the working class." Brushing aside the problems raised by such crude and bloodless abstractions, ask yourself, what were the educative "forces" impinging upon these folk--especially those who came at the peak, from eastern and southern Europe--and where did they go to school? In

considerable proportion they attended the incredible
variety and number of parochial schools, broadly
defined--Catholic,   Orthodox,   Protestant,   and
Jewish--and a host of other contextual agencies.
What were they taught there? Why were they taught
it? Who taught them? What did they intend, expect,
require? We do not know, and we will not learn that
from public school surveys or government census data
or from the apologists for, or the critics of, the
public schools. It is true that by no means all
Catholics (again, a crude category, and only one
possible example) attended parochial school, or even
frequented their churches. The total number in such
schools or even in all the contextual groups,
communities, and organizations, was not a majority
of the population. But, such attenders and
participants did constitute a highly significant
portion of just those "hard cases" whose "failure"
to advance themselves is now taken as determining
the issue. In spite of this fact, one of the major
works already mentioned devotes a scant half-dozen
pages to parochial schools, of which only two
paragraphs deal with developments other than the
Hughes-Seward affair in New York. (21)
    Such schools, and other educative associations,
may have had quite different goals from those of
Horace Mann or his mirror images in the present.
Although we know little about this, we do know that,
for example, in the pastoral letters of the American
Roman Catholic hierarchy, which led up to the
determination to create a parallel elementary school
system, defense of family and tradition from
intrusion by the state stood out as a compelling
motive. For many, bambini rather than bachelor's
degrees (or even high school diplomas) were the
important ends in life, for a host of reasons too
complex to comprehend in simplistic aggregates
masked as rigorous inductive generalizations.
    Having shown Mann's conclusions to be false,
the revisionists must account for the apparent gap
between the whole argument for schooling that has
determined the form of the debate and the implied
practical agenda on the one hand and the falsity of
its empirical claims on the other. The debate, as I

have pointed out, slides then to the explanatory
theories. These theories, asserted to be true and
of unquestionable applicability to questions of
education and schooling, are then used to
manufacture a new "realism" about schooling. These
theories do not arise out of an adequate empirical
investigation of education and schooling, however.
They instead substitute for it.

I will conclude with two more illustrations.
Take for example, the following characterization of
(by implication) "all" American education in the
mid-nineteenth century. It is based on an inquiry
of a particular sort, in a particular community but
(thanks, apparently, to an interesting set of
"covering laws") it enables us to determine reality
universally.

> The extension and reform of education in
> mid-nineteenth century were not a
> potpourri of democracy, rationalism, and
> humanitarianism. They were the attempt of
> a coalition of the social leaders,
> status-anxious parents, and status-hungry
> educators to impose educational
> innovation, each for his own reasons, upon
> a reluctant community. (22)

Or, let us, in the words of two other historians,
picture (all) the teachers of nineteenth-century
America practicing "pedagogy as intrusion." They
were, say these historians, acting as

> the authoritative conveyor[s] of the
> knowledge, manners, and morals most highly
> approved by the dominant society. And
> they did it in a "rigid and highly
> controlling manner." Teachers almost
> everywhere pressured students to learn the
> value of conformity to law and regulations
> and stressed obedience and submission to
> authority. (23)

To save time, look only at the latter claim.
Did teachers say, "Now, children, you must conform

to law and regulations of this capitalist,
industrial society of which you are a part"? Only
infrequently, one suspects. What they said was,
"Children, you must hang up your coats" or, "Raise
your hands!" But, we are told, what they were
really doing was pressuring students into
conformity. Whence this new layer of reality, in
the iron grasp of which lay all teachers and
students and (especially) administrators? It's what
we already know "schooling is all about." If we ask
this student or that, this teacher or that, what
they are doing and why, they will not answer us that
way. But, they do not, you see, really understand
their own acts and the intents that shape them. But
since we do, it is all right. In fact we need ask
them no further!

Surely there is something wrong here. To put
it briefly, in such "histories," individuals and
events are accounted for by reference to the "laws"
of social or behavioral science. Presumably these
laws are in some sense "true." Having accepted (on
entirely prior grounds, of course) their truth, and
having shown (often in some minimal way) the
appropriateness of so categorizing any particular
individual or event (note that I do not say "person"
or "act") we may assure ourselves that we have
accounted for things, found a satisfactory
explanation. We have, as it were, gotten to the
bottom of things--or, perhaps better, on top of
things. But it seems to me that we have in this
case not done poor history but no history at all.
We have, of course, done a certain kind of "science"
on the past, and that, though often a shaky process,
may sometimes be useful. But it is also dangerous,
particularly when (as is so often the case) it
absolves us from the duty of going further. Having
caught William T. Harris reading Hegel, we need, at
least in the crudest of these cases, look no
further. We already know what he will do in the St.
Louis schools, or as Commissioner of Education, and
at best we need only look until we find "it."
Sometimes we do find "it," and then we have the very
worst sort of proof-texting mascarading as
scholarship.

Now I hope that it is clear that I am not
maintaining that social or behavioral science (or
any other kind of science) is illegitimate, or that
when we find Charles William Eliot thinking, or
saying, or doing "elitist" things (provided, of
course, that we can construct a fair meaning for
what that would be, not only in general but in this
particular case) we should not pay attention to such
a historical fact. We should indeed pay attention,
and, as Thomas Huxley once said, follow truth "as a
little child," to see where it actually leads. The
problem is, that we have here the substitution of
relevant and useful modes of knowledge in one
enterprise for those appropriate to another, usually
to the detriment of both. In this case the effect
is, I believe, doubly pernicious, because in doing
purportedly educational history, this sort of
category transference and imposition not only
produces curious history but often renders the
education and schooling under examination virtually
unintelligible. That is why we find books about
schools that have no content, because what is
taught, and how it is taught, is (I suppose) simply
reducible to, and explainable by, some law of
"class" or "personality," which makes inquiry
unnecessary. We can, for example, see subject
matter as "imperialistic," methodology as
"oppressive," and so on, without carefully looking
at what was thought or done, in this setting, for
that purpose, as the case may be.

We need pay little attention to thoughts, or
words, or particular deeds, except insofar as to
spot something that enables us to assimilate that
person or event (by ignoring the details, the
concrete particulars that render persons or acts
unique) to some already existing conceptual and
explanatory structure, likely drawn from some other
universe of discourse and activity. When we catch
Dewey saying some curious things to the Poles about
their schools, we see the hand of western industrial
imperialism at work, and we conclude that everything
else Dewey thought or said or did must be
reinterpreted, revised, in light of just that sort
of evidence because it fits handily under some

principle or law which has, we are assured, real explanatory power. But, when we have done all that, what have we accomplished? A revolution in historiography or a cartoon of the past? When we discover that some hard-working county superintendent is gathering the teachers into a reading circle because they have had little education and practically no professional training, and we say: "Aha! There it is--the bureaucratization of American life clearly shown to have penetrated the schools,"--when we have succeeded in that way at getting the particulars neatly stripped of their particularity (the very particularity that, it seems to me, it is the business of history to provide) what have we done? Landed ourselves in a simple-minded and particularly pernicious historicism, perhaps, but probably little more.

Furthermore, if we assume that we inquire into and think about educational matters in order to maintain them or improve them, what will happen if we accept the truth of such structures and are guided by them in our actions? Will we alter the sweep of these great tendencies which lie behind (in fact, create) the instances we have happened upon, and then proceed to remedy the ills of the schools, the lives of children, or the lot of teachers and administrators? I think not, because what comes most readily from such abstract analyses are counsels of despair. What can be done, after all, by you or me, or Ms. Jones or Mr. Smith, to reverse the tide of bureaucratization? Probably little, if anything. What we gain from such despair is largely cheap grace and easy absolution: we are caught up in (and hence given some meaning by) something larger than ourselves, larger even than "life," but we are consequently powerless to alter it.

The question is, what alternative is there? The problem is an ancient one: how are we to handle, to keep in relation, the universal and the particular, the continuities and the discontinuities, the singular and the plural? That is the problem William James approached in A Pluralistic Universe. (24) James's problem in that work is not of course precisely ours, though I think what he is doing is relevant both to education and to our particular historiographical quandary. He is concerned largely with the adequacy of the then reigning monistic and intellectualist idealism in giving any account of ordinary experience that we could, as human beings, find in any sense "real" or fruitful. Monism, by abstracting and unifying everything through some vast, single, all-encompassing absolute principle, can get the unity which human beings appear in some sense to seek, but only at the cost of the irreducible "thisness" and "thatness" of things and persons, as we encounter them. And that cost is too high a price, James insists.

I am not pleading for an uncritical acceptance of James's general philosophical viewpoint, though I think it has much to recommend it, especially for educators. Rather, I am using it to provide a critique of the way we have approached a good deal of recent educational history. If we have not become adherents of any substantive monism, we have surely fallen victim to a debilitating methodological monism which threatens to empty both education and history of any recognizable and useful content and meaning. James proposes that we adopt instead a "radical empiricism" that adequately confronts the varieties of thought and experience evident in concrete human existence. I think he is correct, at least in this case.

For James, concepts lay out "points," which are not necessarily grounded in the nature of things but more commonly reflect the intents and goals of those who construct them. Such abstract points are the result of flying over the surface of reality on the wings of abstractions, "skipping the intermediaries." "Skipping" and an occasional "perching" can be useful, but that sort of procedure is dangerous when the theoretical formulations that result are virtually reified. Life, meaningful human experience, is continuous, not merely an aggregation of points. To grasp adequately its meaning, we must patiently plough or wade through the intervals, not falsify reality for our purposes,

however beguiling that temptation is. (25) And
James himself illustrates his argument by
application to history making. We must, he says,
also eschew linear and crudely causal historical
development (which substitutes neat formal logics,
applicable to concepts, but not to persons and real
events), because such a history falsifies what James
sees as the continuous, interactive pluralism which
is the chief feature of our experience. (26)

The upshot for all of us who hope to be
educational historians is sufficiently patent not to
require elaborate treatment. When we are dealing
with reality in terms of concrete human
experience--as surely we must do in respect to both
history and education--the most dangerous thing we
can do is "thin" it out, says James. That is, to
falsify it by the indiscriminate use of theories
that draw from real persons and events all the
numberless connections and particularities that we
encounter when we wade through the actual "thicket
of experience." Because real experience is "thick"
and "burly," what we must have are thickened
historical and educational theories, theories which
come from experience rather than merely being about
experience. (27) To achieve them, we must also make
use of all the modes of knowing and making sense of
things, not substitute (because of its neatness and
efficiency) some single epistemology or method of
inquiry. Adequate educational thinking, because it
must be reflectively bound to the wholeness of human
life, cannot put aside the complexity of thought
forms that parallels that complexity and remain
either meaningful or useful.

As James himself sums the matter up, in the
final paragraphs of A Pluralistic Universe:

> I have now finished these poor
> lectures. . . . My only hope is that they
> may possibly have proved suggestive; and
> if indeed they have been suggestive of one
> point of method, I am almost willing to
> let all other suggestions go. That point
> is that it is high time for the basis of
> discussion in these questions to be
> broadened and thickened up. (28)

Like the philosophers of James's day, too many "historians" in our day proceed "as if the actual peculiarities of the world that is were entirely irrelevant to the content of truth." "But," as James says, "<u>they</u> <u>cannot</u> <u>be</u> <u>irrelevant.</u> . . ." (29)

If we need thickened educational theories, only a thickened history can be of much help in providing them: a history which takes full acount, not simply of trends and forces, but of particular events and places and singular persons, including the thoughts, words, and deeds, which are the conclusion to their beliefs and values. In short, we require a history that can examine our failures freed from the constricting demands of the curious "educational" logic which has in large measure, and for so long, created them, and can thus make possible a genuinely different future.

NOTES

1. An earlier version of this paper was delivered as the 1981 Presidential Address at the Mid-Atlantic States Philosophy of Education Society, Albany, N.Y.
2. Frantz Fanon, <u>The Wretched of the Earth</u>. Pref. by Jean-Paul Sartre, trans. Constance Farrington (New York, 1966). Fanon saw the demand for rational analysis as only one more instance of the illegitimate social and political triumph of the Greek way of life.
3. The most extensive and penetrating analysis of the revisionist stance is Diane Ravitch, <u>The Revisionists Revised--A Critique of the Radical Attack on the Schools</u> (New York, 1978). Professor Ravitch's conclusions (and sometimes her fairness and accuracy) are vigorously disputed by Walter Feinberg, Harvey Kantor, Michael Katz and Paul Violas, in <u>Revisionists Respond to Ravitch</u> (Washington, D.C., 1980). Also see Marvin Lazerson, "Revisionism and American Educational History," <u>Harvard Educational Review</u> 43, no. 2 (May 1973):

269-83. The views (and the efforts) of David Tyack represent a significant, though somewhat timid, exception. See his "Ways of Seeing," Harvard Educational Review 46, no. 3 (August 1976): 355-89.

4. Horace Mann, "Report of 1845" (the ninth) in Annual Reports on Education (Boston, 1868), pp. 454-55.

5. Fifth Annual Report of the Board of Education Together With the Fifth Annual Report of the Secretary of the Board (Boston, 1842), p. 78. John Winthrop, "A Modell of Christian Charity" (1630) in The Winthrop Papers (Boston, 1931), 2: 282-95.

6. Fifth Annual Report, pp. 78, 80, 82.

7. Ibid., pp. 83, 100. (Italics added.)

8. Ibid., pp. 101-2.

9. Ellwood P. Cubberley, Syllabus of Lectures on the History of Education with Selected Bibliographies and Suggested Readings, rev. and enl., 2 vols. (New York, 1904), 1: iii.

10. Ellwood P. Cubberley, A Study and Interpretation of American Educational History-- An Introductory Textbook Dealing with the Larger Problems of Present Day Education in the Light of Their Historical Development (Boston, 1919), pp. viii, x.

11. Ibid., pp. viii, xiii.

12. Ellwood P. Cubberley, A Brief History of Education--A History of the Practice and Progress and Organization of Education (Boston, 1922), pp. v, 456.

13. Michael B. Katz, Class Bureaucracy and the Schools, expanded ed. (New York, 1975), p. 185. For an example of its application, see Sol Cohen, "The History of the History of American Education, 1900-1976: The Uses of the Past," Harvard Educational Review 46, no. 3 (August 1976): 328.

14. Bernard Bailyn, Education in the Forming of American Society: Needs and Opportunities for Study (Chapel Hill, N.C., 1960).

15. Cohen, History of American Education, pp. 298-330, provides a useful example in this case.

16. Lawrence A. Cremin, American Education, The National Experience (New York, 1980).

For normal schools, see pp. 146-47. Of the 520 pages of text, perhaps 60 or so deal with schooling activity in concrete cases.

17. Colin Greer, The Great School Legend--A Revisionist Interpretation of American Public Education (New York, 1972), p. 3. Admittedly, Greer is an egregiously strident example, but (unfortunately) his logic differs little if at all from that of his colleagues.

18. Greer, Great School Legend, chap. 3. This chapter also includes Greer's attempt to show that both Bailyn and Cremin are really "old school."

19. Ibid., p. 46 and chap. 7, passim. The "scarcity" argument is also central to Samuel Bowles and Herbert Gintis, Schooling in Capitalist America: Educational Reform and the Contradictions of Economic Life (New York, 1976).

20. The origins of this widely discussed assessment lie in Paul C. Violas, "Jane Addams and the New Liberalism," in Roots of Crisis, ed. Clarence J. Karier, Paul Violas, and Joel Spring (Chicago, 1973), pp. 66-84. Also see Violas's later The Training of the Urban Working Class (Chicago, 1978).

21. Cremin, American Education, pp. 166-69. Cremin's work covers only the period roughly to 1876, but, as James Sanders records, even at that point the number of Roman Catholics and the number of their schools in Chicago was significant. In 1880, e.g., there were 29 elementary schools with 17,000 pupils. See James W. Sanders, The Education of an Urban Minority: Catholics in Chicago, 1833-1965 (New York, 1977), p. 4. Lila Van Planck North, in discussing Roman Catholic parochial schools in Pittsburgh, notes that "in nearly every residence section in Pittsburgh, the most prosperous not excepted, the Roman Catholic church is to be found; but here, as everywhere, it is the special companion of the poor and the working classes," yet the "character and influence" of these schools, "significant as they are, are little known to non-Catholics." In 1907-1908, she claims, 26 percent of all the school children in Pittsburgh were in parochial schools. See her chapters on

"Pittsburgh Schools" in The Pittsburgh District Civic Frontage, ed. P. U. Kellogg (vol. 5 of Pittsburgh Survey--Findings, in 6 vols.) (New York, 1914), p. 228.

22. Michael B. Katz, The Irony of Early School Reform--Educational Innovation in Mid-Ninteenth Century Massachusetts (Boston, 1968), p. 218. For an even more psychologized interpretation, see Robert L. Church and Michael W. Sedlak, Education in the United States--An Interpretative History (New York, 1976).

23. R. Freeman Butts, Public Education in the United States--From Revolution to Reform (New York, 1978), p. 106. The internal reference is to Barbara Finkelstein, "Governing the Young: Teacher Behavior in American Primary Schools, 1820-1880" (Doctoral diss., Teachers College, Columbia University, 1970) and (the source of the quotation) idem, "Pedagogy as Intrusion: Teaching Values in Popular Primary Schools in Nineteenth Century America," History of Childhood Quarterly: The Journal of Psycho history 2, no. 3 (1975): 369.

24. William James, A Pluralistic Universe, vol. 2 of Essays in Radical Empiricism (New York, 1943).

25. Ibid., pp. 217, 245-52. Cf. pp. 349-50.

26. Ibid., pp. 347-53.

27. Ibid., pp. 135-39, 232-241. Also see pp. 312, 331.

28. Ibid., p. 330. (Italics original author's.)

29. Ibid., p. 331. (Italics added.)

2

STRUCTURES OVER TIME
INSTITUTIONAL HISTORY

Paul H. Mattingly
New York University

During the 1960s and 1970s the general clamor for decentralization had a curious impact on the historical study of educational institutions. In some sectors institutional criticism seemed to broaden and confirm Bernard Bailyn's earlier complaint that educational historians were preoccupied with and defensive of formal instruction and its institutions. Bailyn had deplored the study of institutions in isolation, which, in effect, distorted their significance. He argued for a broader conceptual framework, one which placed formal, educational institutions within the mainstream of American historiography. The proper object of study thus became "the entire process by which a culture transmits itself across the generations." (1) His criticism and the increasing political demand for decentralization sought new contexts for understanding social institutions. Bailyn's essay received an enthusiastic welcome, even from practitioners in the field he criticized; his reinterpretation, however, led more to soul-searching than to a genuinely new brand of historical or educational scholarship. Bailyn sought to make formal schooling one element of a larger cultural mainstream. Significant change became necessarily slow and gradual, downplaying revolution and its discontents; it qualified as well the role of charismatic individuals, pivotal decisions, and historical causation. Where individuals and dramatic events played serious roles as historical agents, they necessarily illuminated deeper processes of change. All protagonists tended to be subsumed into an expanded matrix, and their actions became seemingly more comprehensible in light of an entire historical process. The overall effect of Bailyn's essay reinforced many of the most conservative traditions in American education and in American historical writing.

The rush to accommodate Bailyn's viewpoint led to several confusions, which have affected educational history dramatically in recent years. It is perhaps worth noting that these confusions also extend to much of American historical writing generally, but here, where our focus is on recent trends in educational history, one might argue that these collectively shared confusions are evidence that educational history was never as separate from the historical mainstream as Bailyn and others tried to make it. In any case, the confusions rooted themselves in the approach to educational institutions: was it any longer legitimate to study them as voluntaristic acts, the relatively conscious emanations of particular group or individual designs? Or, by contrast, could institutions be considered only integers in the longer sweep that the Annalistes have called la longe durée? (2)

Lately historians have agreed that institutions could no longer be studied as self-contained exercises of human will, and they have also experienced considerable difficulty in establishing newly coherent contexts for discussing institutional significance. In the hands of Lawrence Cremin the logical consequence of Bailyn's scenario has become a two-volume study, American Education, an encyclopedia of institutional experience from 1607 to 1876. This massive sweep has accounted for circuses, museums, and religious revivals, as well as traditional schools in its broad panoply. (3) In the hands of equally capable scholars like Patricia Graham (Community and Class in American Education) or Carl Kaestle and Maris Vinovskis (Education and Social Change in Nineteenth Century Massachusetts) Bailyn's influence has led to a partitioning of educational change into town and state-bound history. (4) Both the exhaustive survey and the thorough study of a geographical locale reflect a loss of contextual significance, a confusion about the nature of a mainstream culture used to assess particular educational experiences. Bailyn himself recently testified that current American scholarship has not witnessed new and fascinating reconceptions of the American past but a proliferation of disconnected studies and fragmented insights. (5)

This essay contends that historical thinking about American institutions has become one of the most serious casualties of this turn of events, serious because the ongoing shaping and reshaping of institutions represents one of the distinctive features of modern life. The study of these institutional sectors over time--a morphology of institutional culture--would clear the stage for research somewhere between la longe durée and geographically specific policies or behavioral patterns. The morphology of educational institutions becomes more than a powerful historical subject; it builds a framework for reconstructing the historical context of significant educational experiences. The immediate need of historical scholarship is not merely a "broader" framework but a reconceptualization of the place of institutions in our culture. In part, Bailyn's essay contributed to the historiographical devaluation of educational institutions. To allay this devaluation, astute scholars like Laurence Veysey experimented with an amalgam of history and social science and produced studies of institutions as delineable "structures." (6) In the final section this essay argues that the adoption of "structure" as a historical subject has frozen our institutional thinking at Bailyn's stage and has made doubly difficult the development of a genuine morphology of educational institutions in our scholarship. The essay concludes with a discussion of studies that have avoided the pitfalls of the prevailing pattern.

The reception of Bailyn's <u>Education in the Forming of American Society</u> was not entirely a function of its intellectual power. Like many other seminal documents, several latent values later became more important than those he stated overtly in the essay. For example, Bailyn never discussed his central interpretive ideas, the notions of "process," "culture," "generation," and "education." The absence of these theoretical discussions left impossibly vague the methodological and conceptual implications of his commentary. His assumptions and meaning would have become more explicit had his essay been a history of educational historiography rather than a critique from an unstated perspective. Had Bailyn attempted a broader conceptual discussion, he would necessarily have had to explore the institutional and social contexts of educational history. (7) His unspoken standard of historical quality seemed to require some interaction between the intellectual and institutional forces of social change. For his part, however, he quickly charged educational historiography to be anachronistic, parochial, and evangelical; he lamented its simplistic assumptions about institutional evolution, from small to large, from voluntary to organized, from private to public.

In place of these facile, linear transitions, Bailyn appealed for a more complex mode of analysis. The central thrust of his critique concentrated on the transfer of authority from the family to schools and other institutions. This transfer clearly involved complex interactions and promised a richer sense of cultural transformation. Bailyn elaborated his argument with an ingenious commentary on premodern, eighteenth-century institutional patterns. In the end, he had defended well the study of institutions as inquiry into shifts of social power. His case rested, however, on a substitution of one institutional progression for another. Instead of the school-to-school progression that suffused the literature of educational history, Bailyn offered the transition from family to school. If he had corrected a habit of viewing the colonial period through twentieth-century lenses, he clarified little about the process of institutionalization as it became the predominant factor of American education and culture. Indeed, the most obscure idea in Bailyn's essay was the notion of "institution" itself.

Bailyn's contribution centered on his use of institutions, particularly the family, school, and church. The social arrangements and relationships among these institutions established their mutual limits of power and influence. The rise and fall, the expansion and contraction, say, of the church over the school or the school over the family suggested strategic areas of further research. At no point did he venture tentative lines of historical interpretation, only the loci from which reconceptualization might begin. His notation of further areas of study left and continues to leave his audience with their existing methodological assumptions in place. In fact, many studies that profess to have changed because of Bailyn's essay remain as methodologically conservative as their predecessors.

Selectively, Bailyn drew attention to strategic points in American history, particularly where educational institutions began their move from the social periphery to the center of American capitalistic development. His primary concern remained the period before the common school movement; his critique ended dramatically at the moment the "public" school began its monopoly of the acculturation process and became a metaphorical standard of modernization. It was no small corollary for Bailyn to insist that America's institutional experience conditioned its intellectual life, that properly understood, the historian needed to examine the interactions between ideas and their host organizations. It should be said that Bailyn understood this interaction far better for eighteenth-century than he did for twentieth-century historiography of American education. That historiography reflected two central features, which Bailyn ignored in his summary dismissal of educational scholarship: first, the necessity to reinterpret the ongoing impact of educational institutions and, second, the analysis of process as it connected with a definable form of mainstream American culture. For all its historical limitations, the singular virtues of that literature were made to be its vices. The twentieth-century school of education in Bailyn's eyes represented a far greater impediment to modernization than the eighteenth-century family.

Bailyn's focus on the premodern period dramatized the centrality of modern institutions, which actually went undiscussed. So completely have subsequent historians taken institutional dominance for granted that few have bothered to examine the nature of institutionalization itself. (8) Particularly in the last two decades, which have witnessed the emergence of a new social history, historians have understandably addressed themselves to the rise of centralized, bureaucratic institutions. Somewhere between the 1830s and the 1870s institutions became something more than the stabilizing orders of local and regional cultures. Virtually all institutions, local and nonlocal alike, changed due to the hierarchical and stratified organization that industrial capitalism required. By the 1870s it was impossible to credit statements like those of Ralph Waldo Emerson and his peers, who believed that an institution was the lengthened shadow of a man.

The Civil War and its aftermath reversed a process of thought that made voluntary networks and associations the preeminent engines of social benevolence. Permanent institutions, like normal schools, were no longer thought to be "auxiliaries" of the educational system; rather, they became the center of professional educational work for a full, postwar generation. The normal schools ultimately lost out in the turn-of-the-century competition for dominance, and two new institutions, the high school and the university, absorbed their functions. The competitive pattern repeated itself in other forms of work and made the moment of institutionalization

in the nineteenth-century a transformational
experience. The generation of Thorstein Veblen
(1857-1929) made an institution "a prevalent habit
of thought," self-interested, and coercive in behalf
of particular sets of values and narrow behaviors.
Between the generations of Emerson and Veblen the
process of institutionalization had gone from a
desirable goal to a ubiquitous fact of life. (9)

The trajectory of this change has impressed
itself on the imagination of historians; it also
underlay Bailyn's assumptions about institutional
change.   However, in the few seminal studies
comparing the institutional experience of, say,
different occupations or cities, the moment when an
organized effort transcended local pressures or
abandoned an exclusively voluntary course of
endeavor was seen to vary widely.   The actual
trajectory was less clean and vertical than was once
thought.   During the nineteenth century some
occupations, such as teaching, created national
organizations early on, only to have them break
down, reestablish new configurations on state and
regional levels, before once again establishing
national educational organizations. (10) Similarly,
some professions institutionalized earlier than
others; medicine, for example, did so almost two
generations before lawyers developed comparably
formal and permanent institutions for training,
selecting, and legitimating its members. (11) Then,
too, some institutions, like the university, so
changed that they transformed the society and
culture within which they had originally operated.
One of the most compelling issues for future study
of institutional life is that posed by Thomas
Bender: did institutions become separate cultures
as opposed to being institutions within a
culture? (12)

The overall process of institutionalization has
been far more erratic and irregular than our general
historical knowledge has admitted.   Indeed, the
actual timing and fluctuating scope of social change
has come to be as significant as the established
fact of an emergent institutional culture.   It is
precisely to these issues of timing and scope that

the newer methods of quantification have served so
well. The introduction of quantification has
shifted our current attention from the origins to
the duration, life span, and demise of institutions.
Indeed, the issues of failure or mere survival of
organizations have contributed as much to our
understanding of the essential cultural context as
the history of successful and flourishing
institutions. (13)

The inner dynamics of institutional development
have modified somewhat our earlier sense of the
overall trajectory of American institutional
development. The voluntary association, for
example, must in the future become less and less the
paradigm of the premodern stage. It can no longer
be used as the backdrop for succeeding permanent
organizations; rather, it will serve as an essential
order of both premodern and modern institutional
life. Only by reinterpreting the contexts and
meaning of voluntary organizations in modern life
can one account for the unsung and often unnoticed
strategic place of the nonprofit sector whose role
and authority so mightily influences the profit
sector. Attention must be paid to other voluntary
groupings, the so-called "mediating" institutions
like the American Council on Education, the
proliferating professional associations and lobbying
organizations, which now continually involve
themselves at every level of public policymaking but
which have no formal authority to engage in that
process directly. The very insistence on the role
of voluntary organizations underscores how
emphatically our institutional consciousness has
been shaped by presentist assumptions of
specialization, hierarchical structure, and
centralized control. A historical analysis of the
ongoing power of voluntary associations in modern
life calls in to question the myopic and ahistorical
habits of thought which have up to now largely
characterized the social science approach to this
subject.

The finest studies of American institutions
since Bailyn's 1960 essay have incorporated one or
more of these historical considerations. They

attend to the broader cultural context within which organizations function; they refine the limits of institutional authority by examining adjacent or analogous organizations; they depict the strategic moments of change together with the shifts in scope as prerequisites to the more taxing work of historical interpretation; they avoid the pitfall of an easy, linear evolution of bipolar development; their institutional assumptions accept that historical perceptions interact with particular structures and that both act on each other to change in unexpected ways. An institution becomes a system of collective behavior and thought with internal dynamics as well as external pressures. It is a device for illuminating broader and deeper issues of its own cultural context. An institution's membership often establishes the particular interconnection of distinctive power relationships and the immediate parameters of its impact over time. Virtually all these considerations would elaborate Bailyn's framework. It is striking that this elaboration has come about largely through the study of towns and institutions in the eighteenth and nineteenth centuries, particularly those rooted in the antebellum period where Bailyn ended his commentary. Like Bailyn, students of institutions continue to halt their inquiries in the nineteenth century, as if they sensed that the language and assumptions of their discipline would become clearly inadequate in depicting the institutional experience of the twentieth century.

In a very real sense, the central problem of institutional history is one of conception, of carrying our discourse beyond the canons of structuralism and pragmatism. The central flaw of both these late nineteenth-century ideologies rests with the compartmentalization of history. From Dewey to Parsons, scholars of the social sciences have subordinated historical interpretation to other values; they have made history an idea rather than the fundamental condition of analysis. They introduce and withdraw the dimension of time at will, giving a sense of analytic control and a power to the analyst that never obtained in the face of serious issues. History cannot be introduced, as is so common in the educational literature, with a "background" first chapter; it cannot be sustained by mere illustration from the past. The social functions of any institution will never be clear through studies of formal structure alone.

The most distressing impact of social science research on historical writing over the past two decades is one that Bailyn attributed almost exclusively to educational historians: the practitioners of history themselves have regularly diluted the value of historical interpretation. Far too often they have deferred to macro-studies of society and reserved for themselves the role of the acolyte. (14) Short-term, delimited studies of manageable topics abound; bold interpretations receive criticism for their small bases of evidence or for their prematurity. The very habit of reconceptualization, the essential equipment for historical interpretation, becomes increasingly rare; it is seldom thought to be a primary skill developed by graduate history programs, which nevertheless have tried to support the "new social history" in courses and seminars on historical statistics and oral history. Few departments have made these important numerical and interview skills systematic opportunities for cultivating a broader interpretive discipline. The most important advance of the next decade will rest on whether or not the historical profession can develop a working redefinition of its own work. (15) Most efforts to redefine ironically have preferred the delineation of structure to the interpretation of historical change.

In the field of educational history no better example of the problem exists than in Laurence Veysey's The Emergence of the American University, generally considered the established word on this subject. (16) There is no doubt as to the authenticity and mastery of data in this book. However, there are important conceptual problems with the book, which limit its service as historical analysis, and its depiction of the university as a powerful, social institution. The most serious conceptual problem is that the meaning of the university is taken for granted. Veysey explains that there is a diversity within the institution, certainly among the faculty, frequently among administrators and presidents. Nevertheless, at a middle level one can describe three reform traditions emerging by 1900: one devoted to "Utility," one devoted to "Research," and one committed to "Liberal Culture." Between 1876, the founding of Johns Hopkins University, and 1910, these three traditions contributed a new and overarching genre, the university, to American educational institutions. This creation displaced the older collegiate tradition of "Discipline and Piety." In spite of these categories and the variety within each, the idea of the university remained both cohesive and undefined throughout Veysey's analysis.

The problem of this historical study goes beyond mere definition; it rests with an issue of interpretation. How do these three reform traditions gravitate toward each other in their first generation? To what extent did they rely on roots in the earlier collegiate period? In their integration by 1910 did one tradition benefit more than others? What precise role did all the discussion about "the university" play in its formation? Did some individuals among the university leadership lead more than others? The list could go on. The point is that all these questions insist on sharper contextual judgments and historical distinctions than those found in the book. Emphatically, those sharper discriminations require a conscious dimension of time as well as structure.

The fundamental problem of Veysey's study lies with the static nature of his "university." The many changes that Veysey accounts for in his study gradually build the institution of the university into a thing. The extensive documentation of emerging hierarchical roles and attendant policy statements merely organizes the facts of the case; it does not clarify how the university came to be what it was when it did. The artifacts and participants within the university change; the "university" does not in any explicit sense. If three university traditions come together in 1910, the integrated university is not a different institution than it was a generation earlier. It is simply more a university.

These interpretive problems open Veysey to the charge of writing an ahistorical study. They certainly lead to assumptions that delimit the university as a social institution. For example, his study remains predominantly within academic walls, as if one could account for the external social pressures with a precise delineation of internal structural and policy responses. In addition, the study represents data on the dozen major institutions that the scholarly literature acknowledges as seminal in the creation of the university. But seminal in what sense? Can one understand the social forces producing the university by examining only those that dramatically survived? It is a confusing idea, precisely because so many higher education institutions in the nineteenth century failed to reach 1910. One might productively inquire about the meaning of "university" based on the oldest and best endowed. Distinctive cultural and social forces worked to create and suffocate such institutions with ease in America, just as in England comparable forces worked in opposite ways. (17) "The university" simply cannot mean the same thing for both sides of the Atlantic without some interpretation of extramural forces. Similarly, as those external forces worked, the relationships between, say, untutored benefactors and learned presidents necessarily changed. So did the nature of the university's service to its heterogeneous student clienteles, or in some cases it failed to respond at all to those it supposedly served. At the very least, these group changes assuredly have as much to do with the creation of academic policy as did policy debates. A more time-bound analysis of the rhetoric of new university presidents would have shown their arguments at times to have inflated the college's limitations for the sake of political leverage. The

changes Veysey does discuss are never as important
as the unchanging subject of his study, the
University. Its historic meaning goes undiscussed.

Beyond Veysey's particular treatment of the
university as a static phenomenon, there is the
broader problem of conceiving institutionalization
in the nineteenth century. The idea "institution"
is so basic to a notion of social composition that
analysts often confuse the two. Sometime during the
nineteenth century (indeed one of the major cultural
contributions of that century) was the emergence of
a new sense of institution building. This new sense
arose from a host of factors that were initially
thought to be different from, but not necessarily
hostile to, the family, the church, and the school,
which were themselves undergoing fundamental
reformulation. The very notion of reform, so
prevalent in the antebellum period, carried with it
this new sense of institutionalization, the creation
of new and limited jurisdictions for orderly
collective behavior. Educational institutions that
later became women's colleges, schools for the
liberal arts, universities, high schools, scientific
associations, and the like, were in this novel stage
most often referred to as "institutes." (18) New
institutions outstripped popular abilities to grasp
their distinctions conceptually. For the first half
of the nineteenth century the distinguishing
historical feature of this phenomenon was the
indistinctness of institutional categorization. The
second half of the nineteenth century must be
understood as the period of conscious debate over
the meaning of institutional designations. For the
historian of the academy, the high school, the
university, or whatever educational or social
institution, in this period the generic
institutional designation must remain problematic,
that is, its emergence must illuminate an ongoing
and often provocative process, not a static
structure, one whose own policies were never as
clear to their agents as they seem to be
retrospectively. The actual and perceived sense of
dissonance between words and experience must become
a central focus of historical analysis.

This sensitivity to generic categories of interpretation is a feature of the more important histories of institutional genres of the past decade. For example, James McLachlan's American Boarding Schools documented and reinterpreted the transition from the ubiquitous "public" academy of the antebellum period to the private, selective, boarding school for the rich at the end of the nineteenth century. While his study is also an intramural examination, McLachlan never forgot his interpretive obligations. No reader could ever confuse the category of the "academy" with that of the "prep school." (19) The institutions are in a sense what they became. Similarly, Roberta Frankfort's Collegiate Women looked for the precedents of the postbellum colleges for women, not necessarily in the antebellum seminaries, but in the broader associations of evangelical benevolence created by individuals like Elizabeth Peabody. The women's colleges became historiographical devices for reinterpreting women's "domestic" obligations. Only in the most advanced colleges like Bryn Mawr were those obligations primarily intellectual and educational. (20) Seen from the viewpoints of women themselves, women's schools changed and became more specialized in definable ways but not in ways that we would define them today. In both these cases the genre of institutional experience forced a reconceptualization of words like "college," words we use today in far different senses and for different purposes.

The problem of language in historical interpretation quickly leads to problems of policymaking in institutional analysis. Here, too, conceptualization of a pragmatic and a structural sort has played havoc with our understanding. The sheer quantity of policy discussion in Veysey's book overrides some of his specific cautions and by association suggests that policymaking in its earliest stages was a function of the institutional officers' initiatives. Now at times institutional officers simply make policy, but, as subunits of society itself, institutions experience other pressures as well. As the work of David Allmendinger, David Potts, and Colin Burke shows so well, formal policies in the nineteenth century more often represent the most tenuous evidence about the experience of education. (21) By contrast, demographic patterns of student admission, attendance, and graduation have made abundantly clear how out of step most collegiate policies were with the realities of their operation. If at times institutional leaders made policy, more often than not, in spite of the pragmatic paradigm, policy bore little direct relationship to demonstrable social needs. In both cases the articulation between policy and its environment must also remain problematic from the historian's point of view. Like the terminology of interpretation, the interaction of institutional policy and its cultural context can clarify historical change only if a historian makes the nature of the relationship a specific aim of interpretation. To leave these interpretations unstated in the name of objectivity or some other social science value opens one to the legitimate criticism of ahistorical description.

The urban decentralization crises of the sixties, as well as the broad social dislocations resulting from the Vietnam War, made many critics of the American scene channel their skepticism into productive new lines of institutional interpretation. In several important studies of our past, some historians, particularly revisionists, have produced a wholesale reexamination of institutions as bastions of ideological self-interest. Michael Katz and others have at the very least made social class considerations and shifting configurations of urban and family life integral components of institutional analysis. (22) Whether organizations have become ideological or not, the nature of an institution's place and service to particular class interests has become (or will become) a habitual facet of historical particularization. James Anderson has pressed this consideration beyond the strategic uses of institutional ideology, to argue that in some instances, ideological roots run deeper than mere

strategy.   Particularly   with   regard   to   the
educational and social history of black Americans,
he submits a distinctive category, institutional
racism. (23) Daniel Calhoun has argued that the
significance of some social ideas goes beyond the
explicit political interests they express.   The
power of such ideas lies in their service as social
metaphors, that is, as intellectual constructs like
"character"   or   "evolution"   in   the   nineteenth
century, which sustain conceptual dissonance and
contradictions in such graphic fashion that they
worked as powerful historical factors for both order
and   disorder.   Such   metaphorical   ideas   often
remained powerful and susceptible long after their
original meaning and use had disappeared. (24)
     All three viewpoints represent important sample
reformulations of the easy pragmatic assumption that
an institution is but an impersonal, neutral forum
where individuals work through their differences in
a roughly organic fashion. Any historical analysis
of institutions must necessarily account for its
degrees of irrationality and social dysfunction,
qualities that are essential to any genuine
morphology of institutions.
     In   the   future   it   will   be   difficult   to
legitimate scholarship that has treated institutions
as independent and autonomous entities as, say,
centennial histories of universities and colleges
have usually done. Indeed, the richest scholarly
advance over the past two decades has been in
studies   in   which   institutions   implicitly   or
explicitly received scrutiny as units of larger
organizational and cultural networks. (25) Among
many other citations, one might designate most
notably the work of Howard Miller, Arthur Powell,
Jay Dolan, Allan S. Horlick, Hugh Hawkins, James E.
Scanlon,   Marilyn   Tobias,   Douglas   Sloan,   Robert
Church, Ann F. Scott, and Christopher Lasch. (26)
The special advantage of the notion of network to
institutional analysis rests with its limitation
upon the necessary context for understanding any
single institution.   One need not examine all of
society to insure thoroughness or breadth of
perspective. Even the study of a single institution

often identifies the center of communal discourse. The expansion of that center through historical analysis generally reveals even local complexities or at times translocal connections, which a mere structural analysis would overlook. In these senses the institution acts as a kind of historical prism, identifying individuals, rhetorics, and groupings of a significant collective endeavor over time. (27)

It is the strength of history to study change. This strength provides the essential tool for reshaping the language and framework that we have traditionally brought to the study of institutions. The discipline of history alone ought to compel historians to think of all institutions as dependent phenomena, communities of discourse whose control operates within demarcated life spans. In depicting the changes of social institutions one of the greatest conceptual dangers is that of bipolarism, of contrasting an institution under scrutiny with another for dramatic clarity rather than illuminating the nature of the change itself. Veysey's treatment of the antebellum college, for example, made it everything the university was not. In large part, he simply took the university leadership at its word, failing to acknowledge that collegiate criticism was a political strategem for disparaging university competitors. The college never received historical treatment in its own right and became a mere foil to give the university a rhetorical power that it aspired to only in its earliest years. (28) One substitutes historical for bipolar distinctions by taking the task of analysis to be the interpretation of how similar and different institutions have actually been over time. It is essential for studies to set a range of institutional experiences in context and pursue the network over several generations. Examples of studies reflecting these assumptions include my own study, The Classless Profession: American Schoolmen in the Nineteenth Century, which benefited from the conversation and scholarship of Joseph Kett, Thomas Bender, Thomas Haskell, David Allmendinger, Peter D. Hall, William R. Johnson, among others. (29) In the work of these individuals institutional history has become the focal point for probing far broader intellectual and cultural changes.

Any morphology of institutions must recognize that the subject is only a subsection of social and cultural history. An institution is a historical and political organization whose interaction with its larger context changes over time, revealing patterns in both; it is a selective and coercive, corporate body with both rational and irrational controls at any particular moment. The delineation of those controls (or lack of them) constitutes the historian's major task. Over the past two decades the writing of such history has itself reflected some of the habits of thought in American society at large. Some of these habits have been singularly ahistorical and have ushered in extraordinarily static conceptions of institutional life. Historians of the eighties would do well to see the critique and reinterpretation of structuralist and pragmatic assumptions to be their first order of business. As the frontier of twentieth-century institutionalization beckons, we would do even better by recognizing how time bound and simplistic our basic assumptions about institutional change have been and how inept our current language is to grasp the all too familiar yet complex experience of our own institutional culture.

NOTES

1. Bernard Bailyn, Education in the Forming of American Society (Chapel Hill, N.C., 1960), p. 14.

2. For an informative discussion of the Annaliste influence on educational study, see J. Stephen Hazlett, "The New History and French Schooling," History of Education Quarterly 18 (Fall 1978): 323-39.

3. Lawrence Cremin, American Education: The Colonial Experience (New York, 1970); idem,

American Education: The National Experience (New York, 1980).

4. Patricia Graham, _Community and Class in American Education, 1865-1918_ (New York, 1974); Carl Kaestle and Maris Vinovskis, _Education and Social Change in Nineteenth Century Massachusetts_ (London and New York, 1980).

5. Bernard Bailyn, "The Challenge of Modern Historiography," _American Historical Review_ 87, no. 1 (February 1982): 1-24. For a helpful commentary on this problem, see Gordon S. Wood, "Intellectual History and the Social Sciences," in _New Directions in American Intellectual History_, ed. John Higham and Paul Conkin (Baltimore, 1979), pp. 27-41.

6. Laurence Veysey, _The Emergence of the American University_ (Chicago, 1965). For an interesting commentary on Bailyn, see Veysey's "Toward a New Direction in Educational History," _History of Education Quarterly_ 9 (Fall 1969): 343-59.

7. Paul H. Mattingly, review of Arthur Powell, _The Uncertain Profession: Harvard and the Search for Educational Authority_ (Cambridge, Mass., 1980) in _Teachers College Record_ 83, no. 3 (Spring 1982): 477-83.

8. "Symposium: Institutionalization and Education in the Nineteenth and Twentieth Centuries," _History of Education Quarterly_ 20 (Winter 1980): 449-72.

9. Ibid.

10. Paul H. Mattingly, _The Classless Profession: American Schoolmen in the Nineteenth Century_ (New York, 1975).

11. William R. Johnson, "Education and Professional Life Styles: Law and Medicine in the Nineteenth Century," _History of Education Quarterly_ 14 (Summer 1974): 185-207.

12. "Symposium: Institutionalization and Education," pp. 466-67.

13. Daniel J. Boorstin, "Universities in the Republic of Letters," _Perspectives in American History_ 1 (1967): 369-79. Also see Lawrence Stone, "Prosopography," in _The Past_

and the Present (Boston and London, 1981), chap. 2; John Gillis, "Toward a Social History of Education," History of Education Quarterly 17 (Spring 1977): 89-92.

14. Paul H. Mattingly, "Sociology and/or History: Some Private Talks on Mutual Problems," History of Education Quarterly 9 (Summer 1969: 253-59.

15. The emergence of the subsection Public History has already made some moves in this direction. The recent annual meeting (Philadelphia, April 2, 1982) of the Organization of American Historians planned seven workshops and a plenary session devoted strictly to this field and its conceptual and practical problems. In the forthcoming abstract of the convention see especially "Together (Again): Public and Academic Historians."

16. Laurence R. Veysey, The Emergence of the American University (Chicago, 1965).

17. Boorstin, "Universities in the Republic of Letters."

18. Paul H. Mattingly, "Educational Revivals in Ante-Bellum New England," History of Education Quarterly 11 (Spring 1971): 69.

19. James McLachlan, American Boarding Schools (New York, 1970).

20. Roberta Frankfort, Collegiate Women: Domesticity and Career in Turn-of-the-Century America (New York, 1977).

21. David Allmendinger, Paupers and Scholars: The Transformation of Student Life in Nineteenth Century New England (New York, 1975); David B. Potts, "American Colleges in the Nineteenth Century: From Localism to Denominationalism," History of Education Quarterly 11 (Winter 1971): 363-80; Colin B. Burke, American Collegiate Populations: A Test of the Traditional View (New York, 1982).

22. Michael B. Katz, Class Bureaucracy and Schools: The Illusion of Educational Change in America (Chicago, 1971); Michael B. Katz and Paul H. Mattingly, eds., Education and Social Change: Themes from Ontario's Past (New York, 1975). Also

see Ronald Story, <u>The Forging of an Aristocracy:</u> <u>Harvard and the Boston Upper Class, 1800-1870</u> (Middletown, Conn., 1980).

23. James D. Anderson, "Education as a Vehicle for the Manipulation of Black Workers," in <u>Work,</u> <u>Technology, and Education</u>, ed. Walter Feinberg and Henry Rosemont, Jr. (Urbana, Ill., 1975), pp. 15-40. Also see by the same author, "Northern Philanthropy and the Training of the Black Leadership: Fisk University, a Case Study," and "The Hampton Model of Normal School Industrial Education, 1868-1900," in <u>New Perspectives on Black Educational History</u>, ed. Vincent P. Franklin and James D. Anderson (Boston, 1979), pp. 97-111 and 61-96, respectively.

24. Daniel Calhoun, <u>Professional Lives in</u> <u>America: Structure and Aspiration, 1750-1850</u> (Cambridge, Mass., 1965).

25. John Talbott, "The History of Education," <u>Daedalus</u> (Winter 1971): 142-43.

26. Howard Miller, <u>The Revolutionary College:</u> <u>American Presbyterian Higher Education, 1707-1837</u> (New York, 1976); Powell, <u>Uncertain Profession</u>; Jay Dolan, <u>The Immigrant Church: New York's Irish and</u> <u>German Catholics, 1815-1865</u> (Baltimore, Md., 1975); Allan S. Horlick, <u>Country Boys and Merchant Princes:</u> <u>The Social Control of Young Men in New York</u> (Lewisburg, Pa., 1975); Hugh Hawkins, <u>Between</u> <u>Harvard and America: The Educational Leadership</u> <u>of Charles W. Eliot</u> (New York, 1972); James E. Scanlon, <u>Randolph Macon College: A Southern History</u> (Charlottesville, Va., 1982); Marilyn Tobias, <u>Old</u> <u>Dartmouth on Trial: The Transformation of the</u> <u>Academic Community in Nineteenth Century America</u> (New York, 1982); Douglas Sloan, "Science in New York City, 1867-1907," <u>Isis</u> 71 (March 1980): 35-76; Robert Church, "Economists as Experts: The Rise of the Academic Profession in America, 1870-1919," in <u>The University in Society</u>, vol. 2, ed. Lawrence Stone (New York, 1974), pp. 571-610; Ann Firor Scott, "The Ever Widening Circle: The Diffusion of Feminist Values from Troy Female Seminary, 1822-1872," <u>History of Education Quarterly</u> 19 (Spring 1979): 3-25; Christopher Lasch, "The Cultural Cold War: A Short History of the Congress for Cultural

Freedom," in Towards a New Past: Dissenting Essays in American History, ed. Barton Bernstein (New York, 1967), pp. 322-59.

27. See Thomas Bender, "The Cultures of Intellectual Life: The City and the Professions," in New Directions in American Intellectual History, ed. John Higham and Paul K. Conklin (Baltimore and London, 1979), pp. 181-95. An example of the network framework applied to institutional history can be found in Paul H. Mattingly, "Why NYU Chose Gallaudet," New York University School of Education Quarterly 13, no. 1 (Fall 1981): 9-15.

28. James Axtell, "The Death of the Liberal Arts College," History of Education Quarterly 11 (Winter 1971): 339-52. Also see James McLachlan, "The American College in the Nineteenth Century: Toward a Reappraisal," Teachers College Record 80 (December 1978): 287-306.

29. Mattingly, Classless Profession Joseph Kett, The Rites of Passage: Adolescence in America, 1790 to the Present (New York, 1977); Thomas Bender, Community and Social Change in America (New Brunswick, N. J., 1978); Thomas Haskell, The Emergence of Professional Social Science: The American Social Science Association and the Nineteenth Century Crisis of Authority (Urbana, Ill., 1977); Allmendinger, Paupers and Scholars; Peter Dobkin Hall, The Organization of American Culture, 1700-1900: Private Institutions, Elites, and the Origins of American Nationality (New York, 1982); William R.Johnson, Schooled Lawyers: A Study in the Clash of Professional Culture (New York, 1978).

3

THE LIFE STORY
BIOGRAPHIC STUDY

Geraldine Joncich Clifford
University of California, Berkeley

Biography, like other historical writing, is an "ancient but ever varying discipline." (1) Reflecting on its variations and on our requirements of knowledge of the educational past causes me to conclude that the agenda for biography in educational history could properly concentrate on two activities: (a) incorporating biographical documents and perspectives into historical synthesis, and (b) constructing life histories around the activities of educating. Before expanding upon these choices, biography in education should be placed in the context of the characteristics of the life-writing genre, which includes autobiography, the author's own life story.

Varieties of Biography
The literal meaning of biography, a written life, conceals many requirements. "Truth to the character of the human life it portrays" is the desideratum, wrote Edgar Johnson, "an absolute candor seeking neither to blacken nor to palliate." The great modern biography is controlled, sympathetic, and rendered with "discriminating

brevity." (2) Penetrating study of the events of a life, analysis of a range of possibly formative influences on that life, recreating a personality ensnared in the ambiguities and contradictions of private and public images, balancing self-knowledge and external understanding, replacing unobtainable information with plausible speculation--together all these demand creative scholarship. But biography is not a treatise on a life but the evoking of a life. Kendall defines it as the simulation of a life from all that is known of the person. It must respect available historical materials and the person both, being "facts raised to the power of revelation." (3) It is measured by standards of history and of literature.

The tradition of sympathetic fidelity meant that Samuel Johnson's biographer valued his subject's faults as well as his merits: "I will not make my tiger a cat to please anybody," Boswell insisted to Hannah More. Authors may cross cultural divides as the Puritans' biographers did in suspending their disbelief and sophisticated scorn. Thomas Carlyle once claimed for biography that we are enabled both to see into the person and "to see out of him, to view the world altogether as he views it." A century later, Theodore Parker's biographer substantially agreed: "It is Parker's life, not my own reactions to it that I have tried to tell: his interests, opinions, emotions, prejudices . . . that I have tried to interpret." (4)

Sympathy without fidelity has produced celebrational tributes, which critics call hagiography: "extended obituary notices full of extravagant praise and free from criticism." In 1901 British author Edmund Gosse satirized the commemorative urge and newspaper death notices thus:

> We regret to state that the eminent taxidermist, Viscount Beeswax, passed away after a long illness at ten o'clock last night. The funeral will take place on Friday next, and the biography will be undertaken by the Bishop of Bodkin, a life-long friend of the remains. (5)

The moral, inspirational, and didactic purposes to which various forms of literature long have been put also distorted life writing. New England's Puritans produced a flood of saintly biographies and pious autobiographies: "Flags of Mercy before a Company of Rebels to win them in." (6) More secular societies create their own "lessons on legs." In 1835 Frances Jeffrey described biography as the most instructive and interesting of writing for Victorian England,

> enabling us to look on genius in its first elementary stirrings, and in its weakness as well as its strength,--and teaching us at the same time great moral lessons, both as to the value of labour and industry, and the necessity of virtues, as well as intellectual endowments, for the attainment of lasting excellence. (7)

Hero worship contributed to biography's persisting popularity and excesses. Carlyle's statements "The History of the world is but the Biography of Great Men," and "No sadder proof can be given by a man of his own littleness than disbelief in great men," became truisms. (He also wrote, "A well-written life is almost as rare as a well-spent one.") The exploits of Napoleon and Nelson, the lionization of Byron and Scott, American statecraft, and French intellectualism all provoked monuments in stone and on paper. The "cenotaph urge" immortalized even mediocre personalities. (8)

Between 1915 and 1930 nearly 5,000 biographies were published in the United States, reflecting popular interest, apart from religion and hero worship, and historians' growing acceptance of biography. John Higham sees in biography a reaction against the depersonalization of modern society, also manifested in cravings for "human interest" news and the personality cults of the entertainment world. Some scholars, too, rejected the external approach of the various "isms" of historical and social science theory. (9) The growth of a moderately well-educated readership, attracted by good writing, freedom from jargon, and a narrative and analytical mode conceived in human terms, enlarged biography's audience. Popular historian Barbara Tuchman found its narrowed field more manageable, as well as more engrossing for showing the individual struggling, sometimes successfully, with his environment. (10)

Another stimulus came from literary and social interest in childhood and the family in the Victorian age and from the new psychology and psychiatry of the Edwardian age. Not that most biography is Freudian, but revealing personality or character, and its interactions with exploits, became expected. Commonsensical explanations of behavior and motivation shrank before unconscious psychological needs and sociological mechanisms. "Truth" became truth of fact and truth of feeling. (11) Readers wanted the intimate revelations that once were exposed only in diaries and certain autobiographies. Old assumptions that subjects for biography were admirable men receded before the cynicism in Europe left by the World War. A respect for privacy and Victorian reticence had earlier caused Carlyle to protest "how delicate, decent, is English biography, bless its mealy mouth. A Damocles' sword of Respectability hangs forever over the poor English life-writer. . . ." Nonetheless, relatives prudently burned papers--like Dr. Polidori's diary, with its account of that day in Ostend where, "as soon as he reached his room, Lord Byron fell like a thunderbolt upon the chambermaid." (12)

The respect of the new scientific history for documents furthered biography's quest for the complete portrait of personality and life. But the absence of records did not prevent surmise; omissions in the record themselves became evidence. Van Wyck Brooks's The Ordeal of Mark Twain (1920) runs on guilt. Fawn Brodie's psychobiography, Thomas Jefferson: An Intimate History (1974), deduces, on indirect or slight evidence, both that his relationships with his parents were hostile and that this shaped his position on such questions as colonial rights, linking the "inner grievances of

the man" to the "outer grievances of America."
Theories of sex, like Freud's, might be joined to
theories of political economy, like Marx's, to
establish a relationship between having a mistress
and advances in industrialization, as in
Charles Dickens: A Biographical and Critical Study
(1950). Influenced by Dostoevsky, Lytton Strachey
found those "give-away" phrases in Cardinal
Manning's letters that revealed his overweening
ambition, and the details of Florence Nightingale's
appearance that unmasked her obsessions. Strachey
left biography radically altered. (13)

Not that earlier biographers were concerned
solely with externalities and surface appearances.
Plutarch had probed for "the marks and indications
of the souls of men." Before 1700 Dryden wrote
that, unlike history, which conducted the reader
into rooms of state, biography leads "into the
private lodgings of the hero; you see him in his
undress, and are made familiar with his most private
actions and conversations." (14) Yet the earlier
biographer, unlike twentieth-century writers, saw
life as a "pilgrimage to a better world, a place of
trial and temptation, the supreme issues of which
would be determined elsewhere." (15) Nihilism set
up new measures of man. The psychological tide,
running strong by the 1920s, caused the Dutch
medievalist Huizinga to lament that "soberness,
restraint, a certain skeptical reserve in
investigating the deepest emotions of the heart--all
of which are the duty of true historical writing--do
not please the contemporary reader." (16)

The emerging history profession--given identity
by the associations, journals, and graduate seminars
that in the United States first appeared in the late
nineteenth century--came to see in biography a means
to engage that involvement thought to be necessary
even to the new "scientific history." Biographical
data were, after all, amenable to the techniques of
collection, validation, comparison, and
interpretation. (17) Confronted with computers and
"cliomentricians," a later generation of historians
could wonder about losing the "emotive qualities"
that case studies, petite histoire, bring to

professionals' debates. (18)

Despite those scholars who believe that lives, even unremarkable lives, illuminate the past, historians are typically preoccupied with the representative, exemplary, and influential. "The historical method is as harmful to biography as the method of moral edification," warned the former editor of Britain's <u>Dictionary of National Biography</u>: "history encroaches on the biographer's province to the prejudice of his art." (19) However much historians people their narratives and however much biographers take cognizance of "the times" as well as "the life," their two enterprises are not two faces of a single coin. "The historian frames a cosmos of happenings, in which men are included only as event-producers or event-sufferers," Kendall explains, but "the biographer explores the cosmos of a single being." Their work is indeed complementary but it is as probable that the one will think that the other attends too much to some matters to the grave neglect of others. (20)

The Educators

Benjamin Disraeli once urged, "Read no history: nothing but biography, for that is life without theory." (21) Critics of the historiography of education find it, however, devoid of theory also: too much unanalyzed description and fact mongering. Narrative is the dominant mode of both biography and educational history. This is to be expected. "Most men . . . speak only to narrate; not in imparting what they have thought, which indeed were often a very small matter, but in exhibiting what they have undergone or seen, which is a quite unlimited one," observed Carlyle. "Cut us off from narrative, how would the stream of conversation, even among the wisest, languish into detached handfuls . . .!" (22)

Given the previous tradition of presenting the history of American education solely as celebration of the public school and modern university, given also the primacy of ideas in its historiography, one could expect biography to have figured large in the literature. It does not. In his essay on the historiography of American education, Lawrence

Cremin commented briefly on the insufficient number and quality of detailed, critical studies of individual educators. Joe Park's standard bibliography listed (to 1965) forty published biographies for twenty-nine individuals, which included such peripheral figures as Thaddeus Stevens and De Witt Clinton, but omitted many biographies in higher education's history. (23) Unlike the larger field of life writing, biography in education had no golden age. Contemporary surveys fail to show unusual biographical activity, and references such as Biography Index demonstrate that many biographies pertinent to educational history are reprints of earlier works, reflecting new interest in the experiences of women and blacks. (24) Even this may be a reflection less of concern with individuals than with neglected social groups.

Nor should one expect an unassisted biography revival in the near future. Our times do not accept heroes, Tuchman rightly notes, and in the Berkeley Library's copy of Garraty's book on biography someone underlined his mention of Carlyle's "great man theory of history" and wrote in the margin, "totally invalid today!!" This attitude is no less true in the dispirited world of education where heroes are denied or devalued. Given the loss of consensus that once prevailed, historians now write past one another. To the earlier neglect of biography, one must add uncertainty about what biography is supposed to do in and for a disunited field. The influences of social science undermine the assumption that ideas direct historical processes; yet biography often has been the description and tracing of some man's educational ideas more than a life story or portrayal of personality.

History and biography have long had didactic and identity-conferring utility. Especially in lower education, these were underscored by a professional obligation to strengthen the sense of affiliation with other educators and to promote psychic rewards in an undervalued occupation. Reading of exemplary lives and the selfless exploits of one's predecessors was once important in teacher

education and was required in graduate programs.
This posed demands, usually unconsciously, on the
scholars. The unappreciative tone and critical
interpretations found in Merle Curti's collection of
short biographies, The Social Ideas of
American Educators (1935), is the exception that
proves the rule. More representative is the recent
volume (1974) about nine Dauntless Women in
Childhood Education, 1856-1931; albeit useful to
students of women's professions and "domestic
feminism," it fails as biography.

Life portraits in higher education are
characteristically smug, parochial, and one sided.
Often, they are commissioned works, authored by
former students or colleagues, relatives, or the
institution's registrar or alumni secretary. There
are other deficiencies of the genre. A decade ago
Mark Beach remarked that the 350-year history of
American higher education was dominated by the
perspectives of the fewer than 500 men who had been
relatively important as college or university
presidents. (25) Their papers were the chief source
for general histories of higher education; their
administrations organized institutional histories.
The most useful presidential documents, biographies
and autobiographies, typically concern the president
of a small college, not a major university, although
White of Cornell, Conant of Harvard, Jordon of
Stanford, Hall of Clark, and Gilman of Hopkins,
among others, told their own stories, usually
inadequately. After struggling with Nicholas Murray
Butler's unrewarding autobiography, Henry Seidel
Canby's Alma Mater restores faith in the unblinking
possibilities of the genre:

> I was brought up in a Philistine Community
> where education was one of the lesser
> public utilities. Teaching as a pro-
> fession was regarded by my friends and
> family as a last resort for those who
> could not do anything else. . . . It was
> always surprising to learn that a teacher
> had made money or fallen in love.
> Teachers were usually high-minded and

cultivated   people,   yet   belonged,
nevertheless, among the servile classes, a
cut above a nurse. (26)

The language of memorable biography evokes
powerful images--as of that man who "on the July
morning on the Heights of Weehawken tossed his
future in the air and shot it to pieces like a glass
pigeon, just from a whim of spite, or was it really
from a notion of honor?" (27) Most biographers in
education evidently have been too little immersed in
literature and exemplary biography, or have had
their imaginative powers blunted by a typical
professional-school curriculum. (The published
biography in education often originated as a
doctoral dissertation.) Moreover, its writers
rarely improve their advantage by undertaking a
second or third life history. (28)
     Still, apprehension of "a life time burning in
every moment" has been nearly achieved in an
occasional biography of a figure important to
education, and with it comes a new grasp on thought,
action, and institution, as well as on character and
personality. (29) Four biographies published in the
1970s merit reading by the education community,
close study by historians, and some imitating by
would-be biographers. Horace Mann (1972) by
Jonathan Messerli grows in stature as one learns
more about his context through other research on the
period. Once the excesses of current debunkery
pass, this biography of a fascinating man--neither
the plaster saint nor the faithful representative of
"his class and culture," neither the man of the myth
nor of the counter-myth--will mesh with the
dissertations on other state school leaders, the
collective biographies of the "friends of
education," the urban and rural community studies,
the monographs on Protestant culture and pluralism.
The new synthesis will probably show--as will an
adequate biography of John Dewey, if he is fortunate
enough to get one (30)--that these were not men who
"if they had not been born would have been invented"
because their times called them forth; some men and
women are more and other than their times require.

In <u>Booker T. Washington: The Making of a Black Leader</u> (1975), Louis Harlan had a legend to confront in addition to the thicket of two autobiographies, enough to deceive any biographer. Illustrating how biography, like history-writing, is partly a product of its times (the 1960s and early 1970s were years of thundering power politics and the black power movement) Harlan's Washington recognized the role of ideas in the games of power and deception in which he was a player. The sympathy and honesty of Harlan's craft makes this exemplary life writing.

Before feminists discovered his misogynism, the reputation of G. Stanley Hall had been falling steadily among psychologists and educational historians. Dorothy Ross, in <u>G. Stanley Hall: The Psychologist as Prophet</u> (1972) makes an outstanding contribution to intellectual history that furthers, not overshadows, the life story. Like Hall, Catharine Beecher had been discovered by feminist scholars and disparaged for her support of the separation of male and female roles. Unlike Hall's case, educational historians ignored Beecher because they were not taking cognizance of women even when occasionally writing about pedagogy and teachers. The scorn of the feminists and the neglect by educational historians have ended with Kathryn Kish Sklar's <u>Catharine Beecher</u> (1973).   She powerfully suggests how, by the educative example of Beecher's life and the creation of an ideology of some elasticity, Beecher furthered a movement out of domesticity whose impact on the histories of women, the family, and education have yet to be adequately addressed.

Toward Historical Synthesis

At the outset it was proposed that historians of education use biography and that they write "educational" biography. As their historiography becomes increasingly less intellectual and more social history, it is prudent to consider that

It is within the inchoate world of everyday life . . . that men and women seek to interpret reality and

> to affect it. . . . The shape of the
> objective contours of the cultural
> landscape--its structures, productive
> modes, and hierarchies of power--diminish
> in importance. The subjective dimensions
> of human experience take precedence. (31)

Should historians not go this far it must still be
admitted that the "subjective dimensions" add
proportion to history's tale. Biographical data
assist in getting inside the skins of the
participants, to know how an era was experienced
and, specifically, how people conceived of their
education and what educated them.

Heretofore, for example, educational historians
have attended to the Civil War chiefly for causing
Northerners to go South to educate the Freedmen and
for forcing the establishment of its public school
systems. Biography assists outsiders to grasp the
omnipresent importance of the Civil War in educating
the collective consciousness of whites growing up in
the region, both in the chaotic War and
Reconstruction years evoked in Mary
Chestnut's Civil War and for later generations.
Elsie Dunn, born into comfort in Tennessee in 1893,
having fled to South America with a married man and
later publishing novels under the name of Evelyn
Scott, was clearly atypical: "I wanted to get out,
and be able to arrive somewhere else--on the other
side of the strange taboos and inscrutable
injunctions which hedged and hemmed me in." When
placed alongside other sources, however, her
reminiscences describe more general experience, with
verisimilitude and power:

> "The war," I was taught to call it; there
> in the South, where we were all brought up
> to regard ourselves as little princesses
> defrauded of their heritage. . . . I
> think no one not reared below Louisville
> can ever grasp how the phrase "before the
> war" ran through a southern childhood,
> re-echoing and reiterating, a nostalgia
> for ineffable things. Until it had become

a poem not alone of what had been lost
through war, but of what had never
existed! (32)

Life-history data and individual and collective
biography offer corroborative or corrective detail,
especially in the realms of behaviors, outcomes, and
unintended consequences. This is essential given
academic historians' emphasis on ideas and words, or
social scientists' assumptions about the potency of
fundamental categories like economic class, social
origins, nationality, gender, and age. Like other
kinds of evidence, biographies "test" theories.
Historians will, therefore, be most interested in
biography--or autobiographies like Hamlin Garland's
A Son of the Middle Border (1917)--if they think the
data concern individuals who shaped events, who
exemplify general trends or representative
conditions, or who bring neglected groups forward.
Individual lives make "historical sense" if they
particularize, make concrete, or prove something
about aggregable experiences, as might be deduced
from census data, governmental reports, economic
surveys, institutional records, and other sources.
Consider Daniel Boorstin's The Americans: The
Democratic Experience (1973), using biographies of
inventors and business leaders to vivify the impact
of technology on modern life. Or Susan Conrad,
combining literary, historical, and biographical
materials in Perish The Thought (1976) to explain
intellectual women's appearance in mid-nineteenth-
century America. Or consider how recent
historiography and biography on the Quakers can
combine with standard works to create a new
synthesis on the Quakers as educators, from Anthony
Benezet to the Peace Corps.
     As historical writing becomes more
comprehensive and eclectic--concerned with the
individual and the group, the public and the
private, the conscious and the unconscious, with
change and continuity--selectivity becomes
essential, along with what Cockshut calls an
"informing principle." For educators writing life
histories, that informing principle should, with

whatever else it may do, produce educational biography; the convention of writing life histories of educators, educational theorists, and system builders is too limiting. By emphasizing personality and how it developed, modern interpretive biography points the way. Educational historians presumably bring the additional resources of professional knowledge of the complexities of educational institutions and of the family, church, and peer group as educators, as well as an understanding of schoolbooks, juvenile literature, youth culture, theories of learning and socialization, and change over the life cycle.

Two readily apparent difficulties of educational biography are (a) defining what is "education" and determining how to document its operations and effects, and (b) gathering and recreating sufficient reliable information on childhood and youth, when education probably establishes constructs important for later educability.

A broad definition of education appears more workable and satisfying for writing biography than for writing history, but exposure to school and college no longer suffices in either case as parameter and proof of education. Lawrence Cremin reconstructs seven nineteenth-century educational minibiographies to illustrate the common in educational experience as well as variations among individuals in the configurations of institutions and experiences that educated them and the differences in outcomes resulting from human variability. (33) An extended effort to try out a definition of education for biographical purposes is Ellen Lagemann's unique collective educational biography, A Generation of Women: Education in the Lives of Progressive Reformers. (34)

How is education other than socialization? How much is education the learner's struggle to distinguish the "me" from the "not me," to adjust, to overcome--the individual's agenda? How much is it socially defined by various would-be "teachers"? Different source materials will skew the answer. Edmund Gosse's candid autobiography, Father and Son

(1907), places education in the context of a struggle between a prayerful father and an increasingly skeptical son; in some sense the conflict itself becomes educative. Other modern biographies and autobiographies are, even more, written as life-as-education. The most familiar example Kendall calls that "bleak quest," The Education of Henry Adams (1918). John Stuart Mill's Autobiography (1873) was written to record an unusual, life-long education. John Ruskin's Praetorita (1885-89) is protest against his miseducation by spiritual repression. Agnes Meyer is self-consciously introspective about her educative experiences in Out of These Roots (1953). There are numerous briefer critiques of schools and universities: Emily Dickinson's wry protest against the suffocating protectiveness of Mount Holyoke Female Seminary ("Please tell me who the candidate for President is!. . . Is any nation about to besiege South Hadley?") and S. S. McClure's disappointment at finding himself at his college graduation, contrary to eight years' expectation, "no taller, no wiser, and with no plans at all." (35)

There is no lack of rich life documents from which to build. Subjects for individual and collective biography abound: in local elites who supported school builders, influential figures in public higher education, activists in teachers' organizations, clerical and lay leaders in parochial school systems, public school students and faculty, founders of early female seminaries, "administrative progressives," even unremarkable people. What is lacking are clearer ideas of the values and limitations of biography, sufficient creative exploitations of biography in historical synthesis, and a disciplined examination of teaching and learning in actual lives. We need biography that satisfies the researcher's demand for information and the artist's demand for illumination.

NOTES

1. Fritz Stern, ed., The Varieties of History, from Voltaire to the Present (New York, 1956), p. 11.

2. Edgar Johnson, One Mighty Torrent: The Drama of Biography (New York, 1937), p. 39; Sidney Lee, Principles of Biography (Cambridge, 1911), p. 42; Albert Britt, The Great Biographers (New York, 1936), p. 221.

3. Paul Murray Kendall, The Art of Biography (New York, 1965), p. 15; A. O. J. Cockshut, Truth to Life: The Art of Biography in the Nineteenth Century (London, 1974), pp. 11-15. A recent model of the biographer's art is Jean Strouse, Alice James: A Biography (Boston, 1980).

4. William Roberts, Memoirs of the Life and Correspondence of Mrs. Hannah More, 2d ed. (London, 1834) 1: 403; Richard Schlatter, "The Puritan Strain," The Reconstruction of American History, ed. John Higham (New York, 1962), pp. 33-35; Thomas Carlyle, "Biography" (1832), reprinted in Critical and Miscellaneous Essays (New York, 1900), vol. 3, p. 44; Henry Steele Commager, Theodore Parker (Boston, 1936), p. vii.

5. Marietta A. Hyde, ed., Modern Biography, 2d ed. rev. (New York, 1934), p. xvi; Edmund Gosse, "The Custom of Biography," Anglo-Saxon Review 8 (1901): 195.

6. Protestant emphasis on the individual and Puritan curiosity about personal salvation and spiritual experience produced so much life writing that hundreds of diaries have survived fires, housecleanings, and movings. Kenneth B. Murdock, Literature and Theology in Colonial New England (Cambridge, Mass., 1949), pp. 100, 116.

7. The phrase "lessons on legs" is from Dwight Durling and William Watt, eds., Biography: Varieties and Parallels (New York, 1941), p. 3. Frances Jeffrey, Edinburgh Review, 62 (1835), p. 209. Quoted in Richard D. Altick, Lives and Letters: A History of Literary Biography in England and America (New York, 1965), p. 87.

8. The term is Harold Nicolson's, quoted in

Altic, Lives and Letters, p. 49. Carlyle's lectures
on hero worship and biography are reproduced, in
part, in Stern, Varieties of History, pp. 101-7.
    9. John   Higham,   History: Professional
Scholarship in America (New York, 1973), pp. 75, 79,
205. The peak year for biography publication was
1929, when 667 new works appeared (Kendall, Art of
Biography, p. 115). Another indication of demand
for biography was the appearance of extended series
of reference works. The first volume of England's
Dictionary of National Biography appeared in January
1885 and a volume was issued every three months
until July 1900 (Altick, Lives and Letters, p. 78n).
In the United States, The National Cyclopedia of
American Biography has been in continuous
publication since 1892. Appleton's Cyclopedia of
American Biography was published from 1888-1922.
The Dictionary of American Biography was issued in
twenty volumes from 1928-1937, with supplementary
volumes appearing irregularly since then. Notable
American Women has been issued in four volumes since
1971. For a comparative study see Donald C. Yelton,
Brief American Lives: Four Studies in Collective
Biography (Metuchen, N.J., 1978).
    10. Barbara W. Tuchman, Practicing History:
Selected Essays (New York, 1981), pp. 54, 81.
    11. Roy   Pascal,   Design and Truth in
Autobiography (Cambridge, Mass., 1960).
    12. Thomas Carlyle on Lockhart's Scott,
Westminister Review 28 (1838): 299. Quoted in
James Anthony Froude, Thomas Carlyle, The History
of the First Forty Years of His Life, 1795-1835,
(New York, 1882, 1906), 1: xi; Altick, Lives and
Letters, p. 162.
    13. Tuchman, Practicing History, p. 47. See
also Altick, Lives and Letters, pp. 281-300, 334;
Wallace Notestein, "History and the Biographer,"
Yale Review, 22 (March 1933), 555-56; William Roscoe
Thayer, The Art of Biography (New York, 1920), pp.
34, 84; Claude M. Fuess, "Debunkery and Biography,"
Atlantic 151 (March 1933), 347-56; Catherine Drinker
Bowen, Biography: The Craft and the Calling
(Boston, 1968), pp. 40-47; John A. Garraty, The
Nature of Biography (New York, 1957), pp. 121-51.

14. John Dryden is thought to have coined the term biography around 1680. Quoted in Dana K. Merrill, American Biography: Its Theory and Practice, (Portland, Me., 1957), p. 30.

15. Britt, Great Biographers, p. 185.

16. Johan Huizinga, Men and Ideas: History, the Middle Ages, the Renaissance, trans. James S. Holmes and Hans van Marle (New York, 1959), p. 48. One biographer and critic contends that Freud's greatest contribution was encouraging the biographer to examine his own motives while writing. Robert Gittings, The Nature of Biography (Seattle, 1978), p. 42.

17. On the subtle but persisting interest in the moral and didactic uses of history and biography, see Deborah L. Haines, "Scientific History as a Teaching Method: The Formative Years," The Journal of American History 63 (March 1977), 905-6.

18. Frank Manuel, in "Daedalus Dialogues: New Trends in History," Daedalus 98 (Fall 1969): 947.

19. Lee, Principles of Biography, p. 26.

20. Kendall, Art of Biography, p. 4. If it exists, a fundamental difference in perspective might account for the way that Michael B. Katz "misunderstands" Jonathan Messerli's biography of Horace Mann; see Reviews in American History 1 (June 1973): 218-23.

21. Benjamin Disraeli, Contarini Fleming (London, Peter Davies, 1927), p. 110. (Originally published in 1832.)

22. Thomas Carlyle, "On History" (1830). Reprinted in Critical and Miscellaneous Essays, (New York, 1900), 2: 84. There is a discussion of the relative merits of narrative and analytical approaches in James A. Henretta, "Social History as Lived and Written," American Historical Review 84 (December 1979): 1318-22.

23. Lawrence A. Cremin, The Wonderful World of Ellwood Patterson Cubberley (New York, 1965), p. 79; Joe Park, ed., The Rise of American Education: An Annotated Bibliography (Evanston, Ill., 1965); Jurgen Herbst, comp., The History of American Education (Northbrook, Ill., 1973); William

Brickman, Guide to Research in Educational History
(New York, 1949); Francesco Cordasco and William
Brickman, A Bibliography of American Educational
History (New York, AMS, 1975), esp. pp. 228-48.
    24. Douglas Sloan, "Historiography and the
History of Education," Review of Research in
Education, vol. 1, ed. Fred N. Kerlinger (Itasca,
Ill., 1973); Geraldine J. Clifford, "Education: Its
History and Historiography," Review of Research in
Education, vol. 4, ed. Lee S. Shulman (Itasca, Ill.,
1977). Also see Biographical Books, 1950-1980 (New
York, 1980) and Biography Index (New York,
quarterly).
    25. Mark Beach, "Presidents'-Eye-View of the
History of Higher Education," History of Education
Quarterly 12 (Winter 1972): 575, 584.
    26. Henry Seidel Canby, Alma Mater: The
Gothic Age of the American College (New York, 1936),
pp. 101-2.
    27. Gamaliel Bradford, "Aaron Burr," Damaged
Souls (Boston, 1923), p. 102. There is so much that
could be quoted from Bradford's biographical
writing, which is marvelously evocative prose.
    28. The only author of multiple, full-scale
biographies in education who comes to mind is Robert
Downs. He has written lives of Horace Mann, Henry
Barnard, Fredrich Froebel, and Heinrich Pestalozzi.
Hugh Hawkins has written about aspects of the life
and work of Booker T. Washington, Daniel Coit
Gilman, and Charles W. Eliot.
    29. The phrase is T. S. Eliot's, quoted in
Cockshut, Truth to Life, p. 13.
    30. See Alan Lawson, "John Dewey: Growth for
More Growth," The Review of Education 2 (September-
October 1976): 499-507.
    31. Henretta, "Social History," p. 1309.
    32. Evelyn Scott (Elsie Dunn), Background in
Tennessee (New York, 1937; Knoxville 1980), pp.
119-22.
    33. Lawrence A. Cremin, American Education:
The National Experience, 1783-1896 (New York, 1980),
p. 471.
    34. Ellen Lagemann, A Generation of Women:
Education in the Lives of Progressive Reformers

(Cambridge, Mass., 1979). See her extended "Note on Method and Sources," pp. 167-80. Kendall gives an example of how the biographer may plausibly fill in even enormous gaps in the record, as he did for the boyhood of Richard III (Art of Biography, pp. 19-20).

35. Martha Dickinson Bianchi, The Life and Letters of Emily Dickinson (Boston, 1924), p. 26; Samuel S. McClure, My Autobiography (New York, 1963), p. 140.

4

THE EMPIRICAL MODE
QUANTITATIVE HISTORY

David L. Angus
University of Michigan

Recent assessments of the state of the art in quantitative educational history have struck an optimistic note. (1) There has been a remarkable increase in both the quality and amount of research in the field. The oft-noted isolation of educational historians has melted away as scholars from other disciplines have contributed to educational studies and as those trained in the field have reached out to connect their work to broader social and economic theory. The application of quantitative methods in educational history has not produced the acrimonious debate that divided other subdisciplines a decade ago. (2) There is a spirit of excitement in the field as questions thought to be long settled are reexamined and as entirely new interpretations of our educational past are explored.

But there is another side to this coin. The actual number of educational historians who employ quantitative methods in their research remains small, and many of those who do look outside the field to receive the informed critical comment that their work deserves. Quantitative studies that are flawed often exert more influence within the profession than do more carefully executed studies, largely because of their contributions to ideological debates within the field. (3) The ready acceptance of quantitative methods may better be understood as signaling acquiescence, or even intimidation, on the part of those untrained in them.

There are several characteristics of that portion of the profession working in schools of education that mitigate any rapid improvement. Members of "social foundations" departments often hold a self-image as defenders of a beleaguered humanism in a computer-dominated world. Many historians remain content to focus their attention on what Americans have said about their educational institutions rather than on how those institutions have actually functioned in the social order. Teachers of educational history are expected to cover the whole sweep of the American experience in a two- or three-hour course. This encourages the use of such grand, conceptual platitudes as urbanization, industrialization, Progressivism, and more recently, social control, and we find it faintly disturbing when these grow shaky under the rigorous empiricism of the new methods. Finally, even though young scholars are more likely to be trained in quantitative methods, the tight job market forces many out of the field and into other jobs, leaving an aging profession with few such skills.

The burden, then, falls on those already established in the profession to overcome their reluctance and to retrain themselves to add quantitative techniques to their array of methods and to become more critical consumers of quantitative research. For this reason, this essay is directed toward those in the field who have not used quantitative methods in the hope that discussion of potentially fruitful research questions and underutilized data sources will tempt more scholars to take up this work. The ambiguous term "quantitative methods" carries a spectrum of meanings ranging from the simple idea that historians of all persuasions ought to be more precise and explicit in their use of comparative statements to the notion of a totally different way of organizing historical inquiry, a notion more fully conveyed by the term "social scientific history." Since this latter meaning is discussed elsewhere in this volume, I have confined my role to highlighting some research questions that clearly seem to require or to suggest the systematic collection and analysis of readily quantifiable information using appropriate statistical techniques. (4) My discussion is intended to be illustrative, not exhaustive, and I have chosen to focus on two sets of questions concerning the history of schooling, because however broadly the field is defined, the development of mass schooling remains its central concern.

Politics of Education

Educational historians have long been interested in the political aspects of educational reform. In recent years, quantitative techniques "borrowed" from the new political history have sharpened and intensified a debate about the sources of support for the extension and reform of schooling, a debate which has tended to focus on two periods, the era of common school reform and the Progressive era. Following Charles Bidwell and Michael B. Katz (5), a number of scholars have examined episodes of educational reform during the second quarter of the nineteenth century. (6) Going beyond the analysis of reform rhetoric, these studies attempt to identify the very nature of the social divisions that provided the dynamics of antebellum political conflict, be they those of social class, religion, ethnicity, political ideology, or whatever. While political historians have begun to favor an ethnoreligious interpretation of the period, educational historians mainly stress a social class interpretation in which wealthy elites are seen to impose schooling on a reluctant working class. This debate is far from settled.

Similar questions have been raised about the politics of Progressive reform. Reacting against an

older image of enlightened Progressives doing battle
against corrupt business and political leaders to
achieve democratic reforms in the name of the
people, a large group of scholars has attempted to
penetrate the humanitarian aura of reformers by
establishing their social locations and interests
and by more closely identifying the sources of
resistance to reform. (7) This work has been more
consistent in its results than the work on the
antebellum period, and the elite status of
Progressive reform leaders seems beyond doubt. What
remains to be understood is under what conditions
labor unions and other working-class groups
supported or opposed Progressive reforms, the extent
to which ethnoreligious identifications, as
contrasted to occupational identifications,
continued to divide the electorate in the
Progressive era, and how a business and professional
elite could be so successful at the ballot box.

Not all the studies cited have used
quantitative methods. Those that have usually draw
on one or more of three techniques now common in
political history: collective biography, the
analysis of voter behavior, and role-call analysis.
The first of these is usually, though it need not
be, applied to elites. It consists of collecting a
set of common facts about a group of actors and
analyzing which fact or combination of facts best
accounts for their membership in the group or in a
subdivision of the group. It is a way of lending
some precision to the loose generalizations that
historians are wont to make about social groups. In
an analysis of voter behavior, the results of a
particular election becomes the dependent variable,
and social characteristics of the electorate are
studied as predictors. The level of analysis is the
smallest group for whom election returns are
available, the precinct, the ward, the county. In
extremely rare circumstances, the performance of
individual voters is known. (8) Role-call analysis
is a variant of collective biography in which the
group to be analyzed is a legislative body, where
the dependent variable in the analysis is the way

each member voted on an issue or issues of interest, and in which facts about the home district of each member can be included as predictor variables.

The statistical procedures required by these methods are relatively easy to understand and to use appropriately. It is now agreed that where the number of cases being analyzed permits, some form of multivariate analysis should be used, depending on the nature of and the interrelationships between the variables. (9) Much of the information to be coded will be found in sources already familiar to most historians, that is, biographies, census abstracts, church rolls, and the like. Political analysis of this sort would seem to be a good place for the novice quantifier to begin. (10) Yet, there are a number of conceptual pitfalls that await the researcher who fails to study the related literature in political history. It is important to construct a data set with which several hypothetical interpretations can be tested. Obviously, if all the predictors are economic, we are more than likely to sustain an economic interpretation. In collective biography, the need to establish control groups is increasingly recognized. In roll call analysis, the mixing of individual-level and district-level predictors poses difficult interpretation problems. In election analysis, it is important to be thoroughly familiar with such concepts as the "ecological fallacy" and "neighborhood effects."

Where can future research on the politics of education be most fruitfully directed? First, considerably more work needs to be done on the "common school movement." If, as Robert Church suggests, the common school movement was really a loosely connected series of state and local reform movements (11), we will need many more case studies before we can safely generalize beyond Massachusetts and New York. State referenda on the common schools in such places as Indiana and Kentucky could be analyzed to test the view of an earlier generation of historians that common schools were supported most strongly in those areas settled by northeasterners. The exercise of local taxation options in some states, Ohio and Indiana for example, provides an opportunity to compare communities of varying size and type. The passage of special acts by state legislatures to create common school systems in urban areas could be studied through roll-call analysis.

Beyond the antebellum period, the possibilities are almost limitless. I have already suggested some priorities for the Progressive era. Some periods have been neglected totally. There has yet to be produced a single quantitative study of the "politics of retrenchment" during the Great Depression. Many of the post-Civil War reforms adopted by state legislatures, such as compulsory attendance and child-labor laws, laws to authorize kindergartens or to make certain curricular matters mandatory, laws to require or prohibit Bible reading, have not been examined as political events. The list could go on. We should not forget that the Progressive campaign to rid the schools of politics was itself a political campaign. A large share of the history of education in this country is political history, and we have much to learn by employing the techniques basic to the "new" political history.

School Attendance

Another major application of quantitative methods in recent years has been the study of school attendance. Rejecting the Progressive historians' assumption of unremitting linear growth, scholars have begun to explore in detail the patterns of nineteenth-century school attendance. Two different, but related, concerns have emerged. Some studies have focused on the institutional growth of schooling, using school attendance rates and other measures to link schooling with other social and economic changes. (12) Others examine the "social distribution" of schooling.

Albert Fishlow's classic study in 1966 opened the debate on the growth of school attendance by suggesting that the common school movement neither responded to declines in school attendance in the Northeast nor resulted in increases. (13) Since then, researchers have probed this issue with surprising results. It now appears that (a) the growth of public school attendance in the Northeast during the second quarter of the nineteenth century occurred at the expense of private school enrollments and did not represent a major shift in gross attendance rates; (b) school attendance rates were already quite high during the early national period in that region; (c) the school attendance rates of young children actually declined after 1840; (d) the apparent growth of aggregate school attendance after the Civil War masks actual declines in the Northeast and North Central states, particularly among young children and teenagers; and (e) attendance rates throughout most of the nineteenth century were higher in rural areas than in cities and towns. (14)

As Harvey Graff has rightly observed, "trends in school attendance form the very center of the history of education." (15) It is hard to imagine that too much attention could be given to the study of school attendance. We need to produce, over the next few years, a complete and accurate portrait of school attendance across the whole sweep of educational history. To do this, we must probe behind the aggregate data provided in the Reports of the U.S. Commissioner of Education and the Census Bureau to explore the variations that existed between regions, between states, between rural and urban areas, between communities of different size and type, and between children of different ages. To do this, we must make better use of individual-level census data, particularly in our choices of areas to be studied, but we must also utilize a seldom-used source, the annual reports of state and local school superintendents. Each source has advantages and limitations. Census manuscripts permit us to calculate age-specific rates of attendance and to link school attendance to a host of other social and demographic variables. They reveal nothing about what level of school, or grade, a child attended or whether they were in a private or public school. State and local superintendents' reports provide only aggregate data, but this is often available by county, village, town, or city, by school level, and by public versus private. The two sources should be seen and used as complementary.

It should not be assumed that this task is purely descriptive. Carl Kaestle and Maris Vinovskis have shown how school attendance rates can be treated as dependent variables in multivariate analyses that are structured to test hypotheses about the "causes" of the growth of schooling. (16) Using county-level data from New York, 1845, they were able to show that, in the static situation, school attendance rates were not powerfully related to their urbanization and industrialization indices, but were most strongly related to the percentage of the population born in New England, thus lending support to an interpretation more closely associated with "Cubberley-style" historians than with modern revisionists. Clearly, there is need for much more analysis along these lines.

While most recent interest has focused on the assumption that mass schooling arose as a response to the social dislocations associated with early industrialization, other hypotheses should be tested. In 1973, Charles Tilly set forth a particularly intriguing suggestion that a rise in school attendance might be associated with a constellation of largely demographic factors, a falling mortality rate, declining fertility, declining family size, a growing potential for social mobility, and the loosening of community cohesion. (17) Aside from the difficulty of obtaining suitable measures of these concepts at a community level, the testing of this demographic model depends on the relative timing of these changes and requires that we go beyond the kind of cross-sectional analysis exemplified by the Kaestle and Vinovskis study and begin to work with time-series analysis, a technique common to modern economic history. (18) In a time-series data set, the cases represent a standard time interval and the variable values are quantities measured at those intervals. Analysis is aimed at establishing general trends over time, the nature and extent of deviations from trends, and the interrelationships between different factors measured over the same intervals. Time-series analysis will allow investigation not only of complex hypotheses of the sort suggested by Tilly, but will permit a thorough study of the notion of schooling as an investment by communities in economic development.

Several studies have explored the social distribution of schooling. (19) Relying mainly on individual-level data from census manuscripts, these analyze the extent to which such factors as father's occupation and wealth, ethnic background, family size and composition, and birth position helped to determine which children attended school in the nineteenth century. The findings from these studies have been somewhat mixed. While most research has shown a relation between school attendance and parental occupation, there is considerable disagreement about the importance of ethnicity, family size, and other variables. (20) Except in the rare instance where direct measures of family income were available, attempts to link school attendance to some socioeconomic measure other than the father's occupation have not been successful. (21)

As helpful as these studies have been in clarifying the relations between school and society in the nineteenth century, they illustrate both the need for more such research and the limitations inherent in the use of census manuscripts as the data source. First, only rarely do studies based on census manuscripts range beyond a local community--a city or a county. (22) Great care must be exercised in constructing community studies so that comparison, the essence of generalization, is possible. (23) With respect to the selection of communities to be studied, we need to give less attention to large cities and more to smaller communities and rural areas, less attention to the Northeast region and more to the Midwest, South, and West. Second, as fruitless as it is to hope that this will be done, we need to adopt a more consistent approach to the coding and analysis of census data. The coding of occupations takes on a

heightened importance since this is the primary
indicator, if not determinant, of social class. To
date, investigators have used various classification
schemes, making comparison between studies
difficult. (24) Quantitative historians now seem to
agree that some type of multivariate analysis must
be used if we are to construct predictive models of
school attendance. (25) Cross-tabulation does not
provide a clear sense of the relative importance of
predictors.

Beyond the need for a broader and more
carefully chosen purview and the need to adopt
consistent methods, we must face up to the inherent
limitations of census manuscripts. Increasingly,
political and social historians are recognizing the
vitality of religious sectarian differences in
structuring social conflict throughout the
nineteenth century; yet studies of individual-level
school attendance have not taken this factor into
account since religious preference is not available
from the census manuscript. This illustrates the
need to utilize multiple data sources and to link
data from several sources at the individual and
family level. Another and perhaps more serious
problem is the fact that the census provides only
the grossest possible measure of school attendance,
the presence of a child in a school sometime during
the census year. There is no way to determine from
the census alone how much schooling children
received or what grade levels they attained at given
ages, how well they performed in school, or whether
they attended a public or private school. No
serious attention can be given to the question of
the consequences or outcomes of schooling until
scholars begin to link information from student
records to the full range of data available from
other sources. Record linkage, which still must be
accomplished largely by hand, is time consuming,
tedious, and seldom fulfilling work; yet, several
scholars have begun to use student records and their
work is promising. (26)

While educational historians have shown a
lively interest in the social distribution of
schooling, they have shown little interest in its

spatial distribution or in how these two patterns might be related. (27) In the context of the politics of education, a recent finding is that "distance from school" might be a more important predictor of how voters reacted to school proposals than are social indicators. (28) My own exploratory work on the establishment of public high schools in the Midwest throughout the nineteenth century suggests that differences in population density between governmental units constituted the greatest impediment to developing workable statewide plans. No one has yet explored the demographic aspects of the failure of the district system, what Katz has called "democratic localism," to function effectively in cities and towns in the 1830s and 1840s. The graphic and mapping capabilities of the computer have been expanded enormously in recent years, yet social historians have barely begun to exploit these capabilities. (29) There would seem to be great potential in developing a new area that might be called the "Historical Geography of Education."

In summary, though considerable attention has been devoted recently to the study of school attendance, the subject holds an enormous potential for further work. An understanding of the causes of the emergence of mass schooling depends on the study of changes in school attendance rates in a wide variety of carefully chosen communities, particularly in areas outside the Northeast. The rise of mass secondary education has scarcely been studied at all and needs to be approached in much the same way, though this presents special problems. We are far from agreement on the answer to the question "Who went to school?" and are just beginning to recognize the need to supplement the census manuscripts with data from other sources. The equally important questions, how much and what kind of schooling did children receive, and how did this affect their life chances, only now are receiving some attention. Questions of the spatial distribution of schooling and of the economic benefit of schooling as a community investment have yet to be explored.

Conclusions
    These examples of the type of questions that
should be more vigorously explored with quantitative
methods do not encompass the full range of interests
of quantitative educational historians. Kenneth
Lockridge, Harvey Graff, and several other
researchers have been focusing on literacy, not only
detailing the extent and distribution of literacy in
the past, but, in the case of Graff's work,
attempting to assess the value and utility of
literacy to individuals. (30) The social origins of
teachers has begun to receive some attention, though
the scope of studies in this area has been rather
narrow. (31) The technique of collective biography,
discussed earlier, would enable researchers to
expand the range of their investigations. A few
scholars have begun to exploit the fact that
education-related problems in the past were often
addressed with statistical studies, studies which
generated data that can be reanalyzed and
reinterpreted in light of contemporary
interests. (32)
    It is hoped that this brief discussion of
quantitative research possibilities has demonstrated
both the magnitude and the relative importance of
the work that remains to be done. My purpose has
been to encourage many more educational historians
to become familiar with quantitative techniques and
to begin to utilize them. Many of the works cited
here can serve as entree points to what seems to
many an arcane and mystifying realm. In a field
that has long claimed eclecticism in method,
quantitative methods cannot be neglected.

NOTES

    1. Harvey J. Graff, "'The New Math':
Quantification, the 'New' History, and the History
of Education," Urban Education 11, 4 (January 1977):
403-40; Maris A. Vinovskis, "Quantification and the
History of Education: Observations on Ante-Bellum
Educational Expansion, School Attendance, and

Educational Reform" (Unpublished paper delivered at U.S.-U.S.S.R. Colloquium on Quantitative Research in History, Tallin, Estonia, May/June, 1981).

2. William O. Aydelotte, Quantification in History (Reading, Mass., 1971).

3. The best example is Michael B. Katz, The Irony of Early School Reform (Boston, 1970). For a reexamination of Katz's data, see Maris Vinovskis, "The Politics of Educational Reform in Nineteenth Century Massachusetts: The Controversy over the Beverly High School in 1860. Final Report" (ERIC Document Reproduction Service No. ED 200495, August 15, 1980).

4. Though a number of works have appeared that attempt to introduce quantitative methods to historians, only a few seem useful as "handbooks" for the novice. Perhaps the best is Edward Shorter, The Historian and the Computer: A Practical Guide (New York, 1975). Also useful are Roderick Floud, An Introduction to Quantitative Methods for Historians (Princeton, N.J., 1973); Charles Dollar and Richard Jensen, Guide to Statistics: Quantitative Analysis and Historical Research (Huntingdon, N.Y., 1974).

5. Charles Bidwell, "The Moral Significance of the Common School," History of Education Quarterly 6, no. 3 (Fall 1966): 59-91; Katz, Irony.

6. Alexander James Field, "Educational Development and Manufacturing Development in Mid-Nineteenth Century Massachusetts" (Ph.D. diss., University of California, Berkeley, 1974); idem, "Educational Expansion in Mid-Nineteenth Century Massachusetts: Human-Capital Formation or Structural Reinforcement?," Harvard Education Review 46, no. 4, (November 1976): 521-52; idem, "Industrialization and Skill Intensity: The Case of Massachusetts," Journal of Human Resources 15, no. 2 (1980): 149-75; Carl F. Kaestle and Maris A. Vinovskis, Education and Social Change in Nineteenth Century Massachusetts (Cambridge, 1980); Samuel Bowles and Herbert Gintis, Schooling in Capitalist America: Educational Reform and the Contradictions of Economic Life (New York, 1976); Carl F. Kaestle, The Evolution of an Urban School System: New York

City, 1750-1850 (Cambridge, Mass., 1973); Diane Ravitch, The Great School Wars: New York City, 1805-1973 (New York, 1974); David L. Angus, "Detroit's First 'Great School War': The Politics of the Common Schools in a Frontier City, 1836-1842," Journal of the Midwest History of Education Society 8 (1980): 161-88; idem, "Detroit's 'Great School Wars': Religion and Politics in a Frontier City, 1842-1853," Michigan Academician 12, no. 3 (Winter 1980): 261-80; Jeffrey Mirel, "The Matter of Means: The Campaign and Election for the New York Free Academy, 1846-1847," Journal of the Midwest History of Education Society 8 (1981): 134-57.

7. Bowles and Gintis, Schooling in Capitalist America; Ravitch, Great School Wars; Sol Cohen, Progressives and Urban School Reform (New York, 1964); David Tyack, The One Best System (Cambridge, Mass., 1974); David L. Angus, "The Politics of Progressive School Reform: Grand Rapids, 1900-1910," Michigan Academician 14, no. 3 (Winter 1982): 239-58; Edward W. Stevens, Jr., "School Personnel and Political Socialization: Rochester, New York, 1900-1917," Urban Education 6, no. 2 (July 1971): 197-213; Diana M. Wood, "A Case Study in Local Control of Schools: Pittsburgh, 1900-1906," Urban Education 10, no. 1 (April 1975): 7-26; Victor L. Schrader, "Ethnicity, Religion, and Class: Progressive School Reform in San Francisco," History of Education Quarterly 20, no. 4 (Winter 1980): 385-402; William J. Reese, "Trade Unions and School Reform, 1890-1920: Comparison of Four American Cities," (Unpublished paper presented to the Social Science Historical Association, Rochester, New York, Fall 1980).

8. This was the discovery that prompted Katz's study of Beverly. Katz, Irony.

9. The use of multivariate analysis has been debated in the pages of the History of Education Quarterly. See Frank T. Denton and Peter J. George, "Socio-Economic Influences on School Attendance: A Study of a Canadian County in 1871," 14, no. 2 (Summer 1974): 223-32; Michael B. Katz, "Reply," ibid.: 233-34; Denton and George, "Socio-Economic

Influences on School Attendance: A Response to
Professor Katz," 14, no. 3 (Fall 1974): 367-69;
Daniel Calhoun, "Letter to the Editor," 14, no. 4
(Winter 1974): 545-46. Subsequent to this debate,
Katz began to use multivariate analysis. The
question of what type of analysis to use requires
careful judgment. The assumptions of the standard
multiple regression analysis often cannot be met
with historical data. For a useful discussion of
this, see Carl S. Kaestle and Maris A. Vinovskis,
"Quantification, Urbanization, and the History of
Education: An Analysis of the Determinants of
School Attendance in New York State in 1845,"
Historical Methods Newsletter 8, no. 1 (December
1974): 1-9. Probably the most useful program for
social and educational historians using cross-
sectional data is Multiple Classification Analysis.
See Frank N. Andrews et al., Multiple Classification
Analysis, 2nd ed. (Ann Arbor, Mich., 1973).

     10. See Dollar and Jensen, Guide to
Statistics; Richard E. Beringer, Historical
Analysis: Contemporary Approaches to Clio's Craft
(New York, 1978).

     11. Robert L. Church, Education in the United
States (New York, 1976), p. 55.

     12. Field, "Educational Development"; Kaestle
and Vinovskis, Education and Social Change; idem,
"Quantification, Urbanization"; Kaestle, "Common
Schools Before the 'Common School Revival': New
York Schooling in the 1790s," History of Education
Quarterly 12, no. 4 (Winter 1972): 465-500;
Vinovskis, "Trends in Massachusetts Education:
1826-1860," Ibid.: 501-30; Haley P. Bamman,
"Patterns of School Attendance in Toronto, 1844-
1878: Some Spatial Considerations," History of
Education Quarterly 12, no. 3 (Fall 1972): 381-410;
Jon Teaford, "The Transformation of Massachusetts
Education, 1670-1780," ibid., 10, no. 3 (Fall 1970):
287-307; A. R. Williams, "The Impediments to Popular
Education," History of Education Bulletin no. 13
(Spring 1974): 46-52.

     13. Albert Fishlow, "The American Common
School Revival: Fact or Fancy," in
Industrialization in Two Systems: Essays in Honor

of Alexander Gerschenkron, ed. Henry Rokovsky (New York, 1966), pp. 40-67.

14. See primarily Kaestle and Vinovskis, Education and Social Change.

15. Graff, "'The New Math,'" p. 427.

16. Kaestle and Vinovskis, "Quantification, Urbanization."

17. Charles Tilly, "Population and Pedagogy in France," History of Education Quarterly 13, no. 2 (Summer 1973): 113-28.

18. Floud, An Introduction, contains a useful chapter on time-series analysis. Also see Jerome M. Clubb and Erwin K. Scheuch, eds., Historical Social Research: The Use of Historical and Process-Produced Data (Stuttgart, Germany, 1980), chap. 5; Thomas H. Wonnacott and Ronald L. Wonnacott, Introductory Statistics for Business and Economics, 2nd ed. (New York, 1977), Part 5.

19. Katz, Irony; Kaestle and Vinovskis, Education and Social Change; Kaestle, Evolution of an Urban School System; Denton and George, "Socio-Economic Influences"; Michael B. Katz, The People of Hamilton, Canada West: Family and Class in a Mid-Nineteenth Century City (Cambridge, Mass., 1975); idem, "Who Went to School?," History of Education Quarterly 12, no. 3 (Fall 1972): 432-54; Michael B. Katz and Ian Davey, "School Attendance and Early Industrialization in a Canadian City: A Multivariate Analysis," ibid., 18, no. 3 (Fall 1978): 271-94; Selwyn K. Troen, "Popular Education in 19th Century St. Louis," Ibid., 13, no. 1 (Spring 1973): 23-40; David Hogan, "Education and the Making of the Chicago Working Class, 1880-1930," Ibid., 18, no. 3 (Fall 1978): 227-70; Ronald Story, "Harvard Students, the Boston Elite, and the New England Preparatory System, 1800-1876," Ibid., 15, no. 3 (Fall 1975): 281-91; David L. Angus, Barbara A. Hilbert, and Jeffrey E. Mirel, "The Social and Economic Correlates of School Attendance among the Children of Textile Workers, 1890," Journal of the Midwest History of Education Society 10 (1982): 1-42; Lee Soltow and Edward Stevens, The Rise of Literacy and the Common School in the United States: A Socioeconomic Analysis to 1870 (Chicago, 1981).

20. Katz, Denton and George, Angus, and Hilbert and Mirel found ethnicity to be relatively unimportant, while Kaestle and Vinovskis found it to be significant. Family factors were significant in the studies by Troen, by Angus, and by Hilbert and Mirel, while they were not significant in those by Katz and by Kaestle and Vinovskis.

21. Only Angus and Hilbert and Mirel used direct measures of family income. Kaestle and Vinovskis developed a work/consumption ratio, which expressed the number of income-producing family members in relation to the number and ages of those consuming. This measure was also used by Katz and Davey. See Kaestle and Vinovskis, Education and Social Change.

22. For a full discussion of the use of census data, see Maris A. Vinovskis, "Problems and Opportunities in the Use of Individual and Aggregate Level Census Data," in Historical Social Research, pp. 53-70.

23. For a discussion of the research design problems in community studies, see Maris A. Vinovskis, "Community Studies in Urban Educational History: Some Methodological and Conceptual Observations," in Community Studies in Urban Educational History, ed. Diane Ravitch and Ronald Goodenow (forthcoming).

24. See, e.g., Michael Katz, "Occupational Classification in History," Journal of Interdisciplinary History 3 (1972): 63-88; Clyde Griffin, "Occupational Mobility in Nineteenth Century America: Problems and Possibilities," Journal of Social History 2 (1972): 310-30; Margo Anderson Conk, "Occupational Classification in the United States Census, 1870-1940," Journal of Interdisciplinary History 9, no. 1 (Summer 1978): 111-30.

25. See note 9 above.

26. For a discussion of the use of student records, see Joel A. Perlman, "The Use of Student Records for the Study of American Educational History," Historical Methods 12, no. 2 (Spring 1979): 66-75; David L. Angus, "Vocationalism and the Blueing of the High School: Grand Rapids,

Michigan, 1900-1920" (Unpublished paper delivered at the History of Education Society, Pittsburgh, October 1981); Paul Joseph Ringel, "The Introduction and Development of Manual Training and Industrial Education in the Public Schools of Fitchburg, Massachusetts, 1893-1928" (Ed.D. dissertation, Teachers College, Columbia University, 1980); Carolyn Schumacher, "Who Was Moving Up: High School Students in Nineteenth Century Pittsburgh" (Paper delivered at the History of Education Society, Pittsburgh, October 4-6, 1981).

27. Nothing published in this country compares to the work of W. E. Marsden in England. See "Education and the Social Geography of Nineteenth-Century Towns and Cities," in Urban Education in the Nineteenth Century, ed. David Reeder (London, 1977). Also see Bamman, "Patterns of School Attendance."

28. See Vinovskis, "The Politics of Educational Reform," pp. 45-55.

29. A computer program was developed recently at The University of Michigan capable of linking census data to tiny geographical samples of a city. See Olivier Zunz, "Detroit En 1880: Essai D'Histoire Urbaine," 2 vols., Working Paper of the Center for Research on Social Organization of The University of Michigan, Ann Arbor, January 1977.

30. Kenneth Lockridge, Literacy in Colonial New England (New York, 1974); Harvey J. Graff, The Literacy Myth: Literacy and Social Structure in the Nineteenth Century City (New York, 1979); Harvey J. Graff, "'Pauperism, Misery and Vice': Illiteracy and Criminality in the Nineteenth Century," Journal of Social History 2 (1978): 245-68; idem, "Towards a Meaning of Literacy: Literacy and Social Structure in Hamilton, Ontario, 1861," History of Education Quarterly 12, no. 3 (Fall 1972): 411-31; Solton and Stevens, Rise of Literacy; Lawrence Stone, "Literacy and Education in England, 1640-1900," Past and Present 42 (February 1969): 69-193; Michael Sanderson, "Literacy and Social Mobility in the Industrial Revolution in England," ibid., 56 (1972): 75-104.

31. George E. Bates, Jr., "Minnesota Normal School Students, 1860-1900" (Paper delivered at the

History of Education Society, Chicago, October 27-29, 1978); Joseph W. Newman, "The Social Origins of Atlanta's Teachers, 1881, 1896, 1922," Urban Education 11, no. 1 (April 1976): 115-22; A. C. O. Ellis, "The Training and Supply of Teachers in the Victorian Period," History of Education Bulletin, no. 24 (Autumn 1979): 22-37; Michael Heaford, "Women Entrants to a Teacher's Training College, 1852-1860," Ibid., no. 23 (Spring 1979): 14-20; Marjorie Murphy, "Public Elementary School Teachers: The Origin of the Species" (Paper delivered at the Conference on Community Studies in Education, Teachers College, New York, December 1979).

     32. Michael R. Olneck and Marvin Lazerson, "The School Achievement of Immigrant Children: 1900-1930," History of Education Quarterly 14, no. 4 (Winter 1974): 453-82; David L. Angus, "A Note on the Occupational Background of Public High School Students Prior to 1940," Journal of the Midwest History of Education Society 9 (1981): 158-83; Angus, Hilbert, and Mirel, "Social and Economic Correlates."

5

ASKING FOR ANSWERS
ORAL HISTORY

William W. Cutler, III
Temple University

A decade ago historians and librarians were buying tape recorders, interviewing their elders, and establishing oral history collections at an astonishing rate. In 1973 the Oral History Research Office at Columbia University counted 316 oral history centers in the United States, almost five times as many as there had been ten years before. Since then, the pace of institutional expansion has slackened, but public awareness and enthusiasm have not. Such popular publications as Alex Haley's book, Roots, and the Foxfire series, edited by B. Eliot Wigginton, have made many Americans conscious of the historical resources embedded in people's minds. (1)

During the 1970s oral historians devoted considerable time and energy to refining their craft. They debated the definition of oral history, the best procedures for its conduct, and the topics most likely to yield significant results. They concluded that it could be used both as a research tool and as a teaching technique in such fields as history, sociology, and social studies. Such progress notwithstanding, oral history as a method for studying the past is, and always will be, limited by the extent of human memory. In those cultures with an oral tradition, handed down from generation to generation, the oral historian may reach beyond the personal experience of the living. But even there the historical interviewer must rely on the power of recollection. (2)

Critics have faulted oral history for depending on the human memory, an often fickle and unreliable source of information. Historians--no matter how they gather their data--should, of course, be familiar with the written record, but, as any social science researcher knows, it is never complete. Memories must be tapped to supplement existing documents or even to substitute for them where the written record is especially sparse. Oral history can be used to preserve feelings and attitudes, shedding light on the emotional atmosphere in which decisions were made or actions taken. Talking to people, asking them about their lives, listening to what they have to say--these steps can expose the richness and fullness of human experience, challenging researchers to confront their biases and accept the diversity in society. But oral historians must do more than document the past. If the meaning of their findings is to be conveyed to others, they must help bring order out of diversity. Both the careful selection of respondents and their in-depth investigation are essential if oral history is to contribute to our understanding of the past. (3)

Oral History and the History of Education

In American Education: The Colonial Experience, 1607-1783 Lawrence A. Cremin defined education as "the deliberate, systematic, and sustained effort to transmit or evoke knowledge, attitudes, values, skills, and sensibilities." This broad characterization, which Cremin has reiterated and refined, challenges the historian of education to transcend the school and include other learning institutions and experiences in historical research. (4) The oral historian of education must do the same. In fact, in the study of education it may be especially important for the oral historian to take a wide perspective. Institutions like the family, the community, and the peer group which, by Cremin's definition, are educational, cannot always be researched through written records. Despite the lack of documentation, the often private process by which children have learned from their parents must be examined. This is not to say, of course, that the school should be neglected; rather, in addition to schooling, the oral historian must explore other educational institutions and not be blind to the many ways in which learning has occurred and continues to occur in childhood, adolescence, and adulthood. (5)

Schooling and Other Kinds of Formal Education

Oral historians interested in schools can move in many different directions. Like other educational historians, they can investigate the development of particular schools or colleges. They can address specific topics relevant to schooling such as educational politics, student life, and desegregation. They can even ask leading educators to explain the evolution of their professional attitudes and beliefs. At one time or another in the last fifteen years all these topics, and many more besides, have been the subject of oral history interviews. (6)

But if oral historians are to make the most of what they can contribute to the history of schooling, they must go beyond those topics for which substantial documentation already exists. They must open the classroom door and examine schooling from the perspective of its principal participants--teachers and students. The success or failure of the school is theirs to determine, but classroom activities and feelings are often preserved only in the minds of those who were there. It is important to save knowledge about the relationship between teachers and children in America's past. It is important to save knowledge about the interactions among students as well as their memories of their teachers, their schools, and their reasons for being there.

Since the beginning of the twentieth century, a few participants in American school life have documented their experiences. In the 1960s, for example, teachers like James Herndon, Jonathan Kozol, and Herbert Kohl wrote books about their work in the public schools of urban America. In 36 Children Kohl even shared some of the writings of his pupils, revealing much about their attitudes toward schooling. (7) While significant, the reports of these men were not unbiased and certainly did not exhaust the field. In a more detached fashion the oral historian of education should explore the same territory. Some indication of the information and insights to be discovered may be had from reading what little there is in print by former students interviewed about their life in school.

In First Generation: In the Words of Twentieth Century American Immigrants, June Namias has preserved bits and pieces of reality in the schooling of new Americans. One Cuban refugee recalled "going to school and being kind of odd. I was much bigger and older. . . . My soul felt stale through those years," he recalled, and "through many years afterwards." A child in California before World War II, Kyoko Takayangi felt ashamed to be Japanese. Although friendly with her American schoolmates, her "social life was separate." One perceptive child of a Soviet expatriate understood the intricacy of these peer relationships. In school "it's not just [that] everybody is friendly with everybody. There are levels. It's very clear in the lunchroom. On the left there are black kids and on the right there are Jewish kids and somewhere else there are kids from Israel and . . . Spanish kids and . . . the . . . intellectual elite." (8)

Children in school often work under pressure, some of which is imposed at home. Working-class parents have often encouraged their children to drop out of school. "In high school I quit," said one Italian immigrant when interviewed about his childhood. "Since my family could use the money, I went back to work, which was a mistake I made; I should have gone back to school." An Estonian youth who came to the United States with his parents in

1949 experienced a different kind of pressure. "My parents were very eager for me to succeed. . . . I was supposed to be number one in what I chose to do." Being valedictorian in high school and college "was the way I made my identity." (9)

Success or failure in school may shape a life; it depends on the nature of the school experience as well as one's beliefs about the value of schooling in creating opportunities or demonstrating personal worth. The oral historian can document all these aspects of childhood education and perhaps even explore the relationship between them and the events of a respondent's adult life. One black youth, interviewed by child psychiatrist Robert Coles, attributed his "big ideas" to his having been bused to a white school across town. "It all started with the bus," he told Coles. "We'd be sitting on the bus and we'd say: look at this, look at that, look at everything." (10) However, as interviewers for the American Youth Commission discovered in 1936, such high hopes can lead to frustration in adolescence or young adulthood. "My brother went [to college]," reported one black high school graduate. "He and his friends are Summa Cum Laude A.B.'s--but [they] can get no work. They are less happy than I am." (11)

The scope of oral history in the study of schooling may extend beyond the public or private school. Children receive formal instruction in many settings, including the church, the youth organization, and the workplace. What has occurred in these settings, not to mention their impact on children and adolescents, is largely undocumented, and oral historians should not overlook them. They cannot hope to be comprehensive--what historians can? But they can preserve and learn much about what it was like to be a Boy or Girl Scout or to attend Hebrew school. They can phrase their questions to shed some light on the relationship between these experiences and those of the school or home. They can help us understand the full extent of formal education.

Experience
     To understand education, John Dewey believed,
one must examine the learner's experience. Oral
historians of education should not expect to do
less. In fact, they can investigate the role of
experience better than historians wedded to
traditional documentation. According to one
psychologist, interviews can reveal much about how a
child "conceptualizes his life experiences." (12)
They can tell us something about how a child
acquires both facts and values and how the cultural
environment in particular contributes to the
learning process. In his work, for example, Robert
Coles discovered much about how children adjust to
racial diversity. In the South the desegregation of
public schools forced many children, white and
black, to come to terms with a variety of others.
"I like some of the colored kids, and some I don't
like," said Laura, a white child in an integrated
school. "They are like us; they look different, but
after a while I forget that they're colored." (13)
     The oral historian of education should be
equally interested in how adults learn from
experience. Indeed, no educational historian should
overlook the importance of adult education. What
gaps there are in the written record of childhood
education exist for adults to a much greater degree.
Most adults, after all, do not go to school; they
are thought to have finished their educations. But
no one, of course, ever stops learning, and oral
historians should never forget this fact.
Meanwhile, they also must confront some fundamental
questions about the nature of their work. When does
the interviewer become an oral historian? Must the
subject matter be many years in the past? Can
children or adults be interviewed about their recent
experience? There is no definitive answer to the
question, "When does the past begin?" Accordingly,
oral historians should not confine themselves to
interviewing the elderly, just as in education they
should not limit themselves to researching schools.
Because of the many variables that impinge on the
learning process, Lawrence Cremin has argued that
"it is as necessary to examine the lives of those

undergoing education as it is to examine the efforts
of the educators." The oral historian of education
should be a biographer of all the living, young and
old alike, and, as Michael Frisch has said, expose
"patterns and choices that, taken together, begin to
define the reinforcing and screening apparatus of
the general culture, and the ways in which it
encourages us to digest experience." (14)

Family
       For   as   long   as   there   have   been   social
scientists,   families   have   been   studied.
Anthropologists,   psychologists,   and   sociologists
together with counselors and social workers have
scrutinized the family, searching for theory as well
as clinical understanding. (15) But only in the
last twenty years have historians discovered the
family and begun to unravel its past. Well aware of
its educational significance, educational historians
like   Bernard   Bailyn   and   Lawrence   Cremin   have
challenged   their   colleagues   to   determine   how
families perpetuate culture. Families, of course,
have never lived in a social vacuum. Husbands and
wives   have   always   taught   each   other   about,   and
introduced their children to, the prevailing complex
of social realities and ideals.   At the same time,
every   family   has   its   own   traditions   and
understandings to preserve among its adult members
and communicate to the young. The concerns of the
family researcher, including the historian, are by
no means simple.
       What can the oral historian contribute to the
study   of   the   family   and   education?   Such   a
researcher must begin with the idea of the family as
a cultural storehouse, a repository of the memories
and values shared by those in society as well as the
beliefs   and   traditions   specific   to   a   particular
blood line and conjugal group. Through interviews
with each of its members, the oral historian must
explore   this   storehouse,   examining   its   cultural
contents and the ways in which those contents are
arrayed and displayed. The researcher should also
be sensitive to the differences between families,
because depending on such variables as class, race,

and location, each will participate differently in
the culture as a whole.

If possible, the oral historian of education
should conduct a longitudinal study of a
representative sample of families, returning to each
periodically to look for continuity and change in
their cultural display. At the very least, such a
researcher should interview members of the same
family from at least three generations, searching
for similarities and differences in the values and
beliefs they hold and retain. The cultural
kaleidoscope of grandparents and grandchildren will
differ, especially if the young grew up in a nation
or city unlike the childhood home of their elders.
More than a few social scientists have observed that
the children of immigrants to American cities
adapted to urban life faster and better than their
parents or grandparents. In assessing any family's
complex of values and beliefs, the oral historian of
education should document intergenerational
differences as well as the full range of social and
familial elements preserved.

But the family is more than a cultural
storehouse. It is a teacher of the young--the first
and perhaps most important source of knowledge,
skills, and values in life. The oral historian of
education must examine how families educate their
young. Given the privacy in which this training
usually occurs, it may well be that only the oral
historian can gain access to information about the
ways that families have socialized their children in
the past. In this work, the historical researcher
will have to rely on the human memory more than
anything else and be aware of ways to maximize its
reliability. Psychologists have discovered that
among adults the best recollections of the
growing-up years tend to come from early childhood
and late adolescence and to cluster around the
significant events or crises in young lives. (16)
But regardless of the mind's idiosyncrasies and
limitations, the oral historian of education must
explore certain key issues and elements in family
life.

In researching the family the oral historian of

education must examine the cognitive and affective relationship between parents and children. The researcher must investigate the extent to which they interacted and the ways in which this interaction occurred. Did parents associate closely with their children or leave them largely on their own? Did they read to them and answer their questions? Were the children included in family discussions? How was the mother's role in the socialization process different from that of the father? One study, conducted in 1978, found that among a sample of 85 Americans born between 1890 and 1910 it was recalled that mothers, more frequently than fathers, disciplined the children. (17) In different ethnic groups the respective contributions of mothers and fathers have not always been the same, but some sexual division of labor has been a part of American family life for more than 200 years. (18) In general, newcomers have not diminished this distinction. Among Armenians, said one immigrant who came to the United States in 1934, "the man has always been the head of the family. The mother has . . . been there for the children; to educate them, to clothe them." Her care was crucial, for "family education is . . . what the children take with them all their lives." In his research Robert Coles learned from one black man about the role of the father. "He's out in the world," said this respondent, "and he finds out what is happening, and he can go back and make sure the wife and kids get to know." (19)

In studying the child-rearing practices of Americans, historians have had to rely mainly on the prescriptive literature prepared for parents by popular writers, social scientists, and medical experts. Unfortunately, such work reveals much more about the dominant ideals in society on the subject of parenting than actual practice. The oral historian, on the other hand, can delve into what people remember about child rearing in the real world. There are dangers, of course, in relying exclusively on interviews; when discussing a topic as subjective as parenting, a respondent may say what he or she thinks the interviewer wants to hear.

If children are supposed to obey at all times, the interviewer may learn about disciplined children whether or not they ever existed. Direct observation of family behavior can help the researcher discover such distortions, but in historical investigation such personal involvement is not possible. Instead the oral historian must take pains to obtain several angles of vision by interviewing as many family members as possible. (20).

The oral historian gathering data on child rearing can pursue many lines of inquiry. The ways in which parents taught children about God and country, work and play, or brotherhood and prejudice can be examined. Religious worship in the home can leave a lasting impression on the young. Recalling his childhood, one Irishman said that there never was "a night when the rosary wasn't said in our house." (21) The lesson of ethnic or racial prejudice may be taught in a more subtle way. The son of a New Orleans businessman learned from his parents that "the rednecks hate the colored, and the colored hate the rednecks." My mother, this child said, would "rather be with the rednecks, but my father says he trusts the colored more." (22)

Teaching children about sex can be one of the most difficult responsibilities of parenthood. Too often the subject breeds more embarrassment than enlightenment. Researchers may be able to rely on written sources to learn about the school curriculum in human reproduction, but even today most children learn much of what they know about sex by word of mouth. The record of that learning process exists only in the mind. In 1936 interviewers for the American Youth Commission discovered that peers were the most important source of information about sex for most teenagers. "I got an earful here and an earful there," said one respondent. "My mother would never tell me anything," said another, but a third reported that when she was thirteen, her mother told her everything. (23)

Clearly, in this significant aspect of child rearing the oral historian of education has a unique opportunity and an important role to play. Aside from establishing whether or not children were taught about sex in the home, the historical interviewer can explore many related issues. Was the child's sex or age an important factor in his or her parents' decision to raise the subject of sex? Did mothers and fathers assume different responsibilities in the sex education of their daughters and sons? Eliciting candor on this delicate topic will never be easy, but only by asking will social scientists, including historians, be able to develop adequate information and understanding about the role of the family in sex education.

Methodological Model: Robert Coles
     Historians of education have begun only recently to look carefully at childhood, adolescence, and the family. In the study of these subjects and their relationship to education, oral history can be useful, but oral historians of education must look outside their field to find researchers to emulate. One scholarly model is Robert Coles, author of Children of Crisis, a five-volume study of childhood, race, and social class in America. In preparing this series Coles talked with hundreds of children and adults, becoming a highly skilled interviewer and observer of American life. His work has made him a firm believer in the value of acquiring in-depth familiarity with a few key respondents.
     Compared with quantitative research, oral history can never offer the same opportunity to generalize. But if Coles is correct, the reality of a child's or adult's experience cannot be understood in statistical terms alone. "This work," Coles said, "does not depend on questionnaires, but on long acquaintance, never less than a year in duration, and upon occasion up to five years." An admirer of the work of Anna Freud, he believes in "direct observation," the "intensive study of a relatively small number of individuals" which, he thinks, "can shed some light, a little light, on matters that many of us are concerned with in one way or another: the emotions and purposes that make

us human beings." (24) Of course, the oral
historian of education should not pretend to be a
psychologist, psychiatrist, or social worker; nor
can he practice direct observation when his subject
matter is in the past. But, like Coles, the
historical interviewer can work intensively with
selected respondents, developing a thorough
knowledge of their education, including a full range
of their feelings and experiences in learning to
cope with the world.

Perhaps more than any other theme, the
diversity and complexity of human experience
dominates Coles's work. He is committed to the view
that human diversity and dignity go hand in hand.
To overlook the former diminishes the latter. In
his respect for every style of life, Coles shares
more with the historian than with the psychologist
or psychiatrist. More than any other students of
human activity, historians are aware of the degree
to which human affairs defy generalization. Like
Coles, they understand the dangers of categorization
and are ready to accept the element of
surprise. (25) To oral historians of education this
appreciation of the diversity of human experience
should be a reminder of both the nature and the
value of their work. In exploring the ways in which
people learned in the past they cannot fail to see
how multifaceted the educational process has been.
They should not shy away from the documentation and
analysis of this variety.

Conclusion
Oral history is a methodological resource for
the study of the history of education. It bears no
ideological bias; its use implies no theoretical
orientation. It has been employed to document the
inner thoughts and memories of leaders in education
as well as in other fields. But it can be used just
as well to capture the educational experiences of
ordinary Americans. In fact, it is especially well
suited to research on the lives of those whose
personal histories often disappear when they do. If
we are ever to identify, let alone understand, the
many factors contributing to one person's education,

we must look beyond the school to the private lives of learners. In the home, church, club, and community children and adults acquire important skills, knowledge, and values every day. How that learning occurs and how the learner perceives it can be fully appreciated only through intensive and individualized research. Social scientists, including historians, must ask to learn. Beginning with yesterday's experiences, they must rely in part on the oral historian to provide them with the data necessary to understand education in every respect.

NOTES

1. "Oral History," Encyclopedia of Library and Information Science, ed. Allen Kent and Harold Lancour (1977), 20: 449-51.

2. See, e.g., John A. Neuenschwander, "Remembrance of Things Past: Oral Historians and Long-Term Memory," The Oral History Review 1978 (Burlington, Vt., 1978), pp. 45-53; Oral History Evaluation Guidelines (1980).

3. William W. Cutler, III, "Oral History--Its Nature and Uses for Educational History," History of Education Quarterly 11 (Summer 1971): 186; R. L. Schnell, "Contributions to Psychohistory: IV. Individual Experience in Historiography and Psychoanalysis: Significance of Erik Erikson and Robert Coles," Psychological Reports 46 (1980): 591-97.

4. Lawrence A. Cremin, American Education: The Colonial Exoerience, 1607-1783 (New York, 1970), p. xiii; idem, Traditons of American Education (New York, 1976), p. viii; idem, American Education: The National Experience 1783-1876 (New York, 1980), pp. ix-x.

5. See Cutler, "Oral History," pp. 184-94.

6. The Oral History Collection of Columbia University (New York, 1964), pp. 138-39; Bulletin of Cornell Program in the Oral History: Cornell University Libraries, (July 1967), 1:2-3; Reel to

Real: The   College of St. Catherine Oral   History
Collection (St. Paul, Minn., 1981), p. 6; Mary Jo
Deering, "Oral History and School Integration
Research: A Case History," The Oral History Review
1979 (Burlington, Vt, 1979), pp. 27-41.

7. James Herndon, The Way It Spozed To Be (New
York, 1965); Jonathan Kozol, Death at an Early Age:
The Destruction of the Hearts and Minds of Negro
Children   in   the Boston Public Schools (Boston,
1967); Herbert Kohl, 36 Children (New York, 1967).

8. June Namias, First Generation: In the
Words of Twentieth Century American Immigrants
(Boston, 1978), pp. 129, 160, 215. Italics hers.

9. Ibid., pp. 34, 144.

10. Robert Coles, The South Goes North.
Volume III of Children of Crisis (Boston, 1967), pp.
90, 93.

11. Howard M. Bell, Youth Tell Their Story:
A Story of the Conditions and Attitudes of Young
People in Maryland Between the Ages of 16 and 24
(Washington, D. C., 1938), p. 123.

12. Leon Yarrow, "Interviewing Children,"
Handbook of Research Methods in Child Development,
ed. Paul H. Mussen (New York, 1960), p. 561.

13. Coles, The South Goes North, p. 301.

14. Lawrence A. Cremin, "The Family as
Educator: Some Comments on the Recent
Historiography," Teachers College Record 76
(December 1974): 260; Michael Frisch, "Oral History
and Hard Times, A Review Essay," Red Buffalo: Oral
History (Buffalo, n.d.): p. 228.

15. Ronald L. Howard, A Social History of
American Family Sociology, 1865-1940, ed. John Mogey
(Westport, Conn., 1981); Christopher Lasch, Haven in
a Heartless World: The Family Besieged (New York,
1977).

16. Klaus F. Riegel, "The Recall of Historical
Events," Behavioral Science 18 (1973): 356, 362.

17. D. Keith Osborn and Janie D. Osborn,
"Childhood at the Turn of the Century," Family
Coordinator 27 (January 1978): 29.

18. Carl N. Degler, At Odds: Women and the
Family in America from the Revolution to the Present
(New York, 1980).

19. Namias, First Generation, p. 97; Coles, The South Goes North, p. 159.

20. Joan McCord and William McCord, "Cultural Stereotypes and the Validity of Interviews for Research in Child Development," Child Development 32 (1961): 178-83; Leonard Weller and Elmer Luchterhand, "Comparing Interviews and Observations on Family Functioning," Journal of Marriage and the Family 31 (February 1969): 115; Betty J. Ruano, James D. Bruce, and Margaret M. McDermott, "Pilgrim's Progress II: Recent Trends and Prospects in Family Research," Journal of Marriage and the Family 31 (November 1969): 698.

21. Namias, First Generation, pp. 19-20.

22. Robert Coles, Privileged Ones: The Well-Off and the Rich in America. Volume V of Children of Crisis (Boston, 1977), p. 103.

23. Bell, Youth Tell Their Story, p. 42.

24. Coles, The South Goes North, p. 36; Privileged Ones, p. 51.

25. Schnell, "Contributions to Psychohistory: IV," pp. 609, 611.

6

THE SCHOOL AND PERSONALITY DEVELOPMENT INTELLECTUAL HISTORY

Sol Cohen
University of California, Los Angeles

Education has been . . . too much confined to teaching, it needs to be developed as a scheme for assisting and guiding the developing personality.

William Alanson White,
"Childhood: The Golden Period
For Mental Hygiene," Mental
Hygiene 4 (1920): 262.

The schools . . . must assume the primary responsibility for the healthy development of the whole personality of each child.

Edward A. Richards, ed.,
Proceedings of the Mid-Century White House
Conference on Children and Youth
(Raleigh, N.C., 1950), p. 175.

The National Academy of Education in 1969 issued a call for studies in the history of ideas (1), studies that would deepen our understanding of the development of the "key

notions" of American education. (2) But despite the
Academy's urging, study in the history of ideas has
largely fallen into disfavor with historians of
education in recent years. (3) In fact, there has
been a tendency to downgrade intellectual history, a
tendency to assume that ideas are a meaningless
superstructure, and to subordinate ideas to
interpretations of class struggle, intellectual
history to social history. (4) Consequently,
studies in the history of ideas that could deepen
our understanding of the development of "key
notions" of modern American education have been much
neglected.

One of these "key notions" of modern American
education and one in need of exploration has been
the idea that the school should be responsible for
the personality development of children. Indeed,
concern for personality may be as central a concept
of twentieth-century American education as it is of
twentieth-century American culture in general. (5)
By the 1940s the idea of the school's responsibility
for children's personality development was firmly
entrenched in the literature of powerful
professional educational organizations like the
National Education Association, the American Council
on Education, and the Educational Policies
Commission. The historic 1950 Mid-Century White
House Conference on Children and Youth took as its
motto, "For Every Child A Healthy Personality," and
ratified the idea that the school is an institution
to develop children's personality.

That the school should be responsible for the
development of children's personality has had deep
and lasting, if today unrecognized, effects on the
way we educate children. The idea of the school's
responsibility for "personality development" is a
kind of ideogram which serves as shorthand for a
systematically related cluster of attitudes,
assumptions, and practices with profound
implications for curriculum, grading and promotion
practices, methods of instruction, notions of
achievement, authority, and discipline, and which
also includes a tacit assumption by the schools of a
broad parent-surrogate function. What is ultimately

involved in this doctrine is a reconceptualization of American education. At its base is a paradigm shift from a rationalistic-moral model of schooling whose major objective was to "develop the mind and will," transmit the "wisdom of the race," and give every child command of the "tools of thought," to a therapeutic model of schooling whose guiding principle is the development of personality. (6) Moreover, the idea of the school's responsibility for the development of personality includes the essential corollary that the teacher and the school must counterbalance or, if need be, replace the parents and the family so far as possible in the molding of the child's personality.

The modern idea of personality development has its roots not in philosophical tradition or educational theorizing, but in turn-of-the-century psychiatry. (7) The inspiration and driving force behind its dissemination was the mental hygiene movement, the "social arm of psychiatry." The mental hygiene movement has aroused considerable interest among historians in recent years. (8) Its impact on American education is just now beginning to receive the scholarly attention it deserves. This paper, in fact, is part of a larger work in which I am engaged, an exploration of the impact of the mental hygiene movement on American education from preschool through the university for the years approximately 1895 to the present.

This essay will present an overview of the origin, development, and dissemination of the idea of the school's responsibility for the development of personality. It is intended as an illustrative and suggestive sketch rather than a finished study. It calls attention to certain indispensable sources for a history of American education in this century that do not yet figure in historical accounts of the period. In addition, its subject matter intersects with current analyses by Rieff and others of the "triumph of the therapeutic," the infiltration of psychiatric categories of authority, discourse, and value into all aspects of American life and thought in the past fifty years. (9) Finally, this paper may have some practical usefulness for current

educational concerns, if not for action, then for
debate, the necessary propaedeutic to effective
action.

I

        Turn-of-the-century modernizing America and the
Progressive Movement, that broad, many faceted
response to the problems of life in urban,
industrial, multicultural society, constitutes the
general matrix within which the mental hygiene
movement originates. The National Committee for
Mental Hygiene (NCMH), the organizational spearpoint
of the mental hygiene movement, was organized in
1909 by a small group of reform-minded academicians,
social workers, physicians, and psychiatrists.
Prominent among the lay persons who took part in the
birth or early years of the NCMH were such notables
as William James, Julia Lathrop, and Charles W.
Eliot. The founder of the movement was Clifford
Beers, author of the inspirational and path-breaking
memoir, A Mind that Found Itself. A cadre of
"psychiatric progressives," including August Hoch,
Stewart Paton, William F. Russell, Llewellys F.
Barker, and William Alanson White, among others, and
led by Adolf Meyer, the country's foremost
psychiatrist, provided the movement's early medical
leadership. (10)
        Inspired by developments in the field of public
health, especially the campaign against
tuberculosis, hygienists were eager to launch an
aggressive campaign for the prevention of mental
illness. Still, through its first decade NCMH
activities were modest. Funds were hard to come by,
and the general therapeutic pessimism regarding the
mentally ill, characteristic of late
nineteenth-century American psychiatry and medicine,
was hard to combat. The earliest concerns of the
NCMH were limited to investigating and publicizing
the extent of the problem of the mentally ill and to
improving the treatment and alleviating the
condition of the institutionalized mentally ill. By
the 1920s, however, the scope of the NCMH had become
grandiose--broadening from an essentially
meliorative objective into a crusade for the

prevention of mental illness, expanding from a concern with insanity to mental deficiency, then juvenile delinquency, to include finally, "all forms of social maladjustment and even unhappiness," and extending far beyond the confines of the hospital and the mental asylum to all agencies having to do with individual and social welfare.

The theoretical basis for the optimism and crusading zeal that characterized the mental hygiene movement in the 1920s was largely formulated in the pre-World War I period. It was constructed out of such diverse sources as the new dynamic psychiatry, preeminently Meyer's "psychobiology" or eclectic psychiatry of "the whole person," combined with the behavioristic psychology of John B. Watson, to which was added psychoanalytic concepts extrapolated from Freud (as well as, in lesser degree, from Jung and Adler). Psychoanalysis was the catalyst, an attenuated and diluted psychoanalysis, to be sure. To go beyond this generalization to generalizations about mental hygiene doctrine, one must proceed with greater caution. The mental hygiene movement sought to appeal to as many groups and interests as possible, many of them with conflicting motives and ends. The movement included, said Meyer, "tendencies of almost kaleidoscopic variety." The movement, as Burnham puts it, "had something for everybody." (11) It had room for psychiatrists who were convinced that mental illness was due mainly to psychological causes, as well as for psychiatrists who were convinced that mental illness was due to organic brain disease or heredity. But the mainstream or dominant camp was determinedly psychological, environmentalist, and optimistic. Its hopes rested on a new conception of mental illness, which placed the emphasis on "personality," and which for all practical purposes chose to ignore or disregard organic damage or heredity. The central assumptions of the dominant camp of the mental hygiene movement follow.

Mental illness was not a "disease" of the brain or the nervous system, but a personality disorder. (12) This was crucial. Mental illness refers to disorders of the personality confronting the stresses of life. Disorders of personality were not only responsible for individual suffering, but social problems like delinquency, crime, dependency, and industrial unrest. The cause of mental illness and social problems of all sorts lay within the personality. But personality was no longer a mystery or a fate to be passively accepted; its secrets were known. The emotions were fundamental, the "essential core" of personality, "the most determining aspect of mental life." Childhood was "the conditioning period of personality." (13) And, this was critical--the fundamental working assumption of the mental hygiene movement-- personality was basically malleable. (14) Belief in the malleability of personality inclined the hygienists to optimism regarding treatment and cure, inspired their belief in prevention, and finally led them to the schools.

Mental disorder and social maladjustment of all sorts were due to faulty personality development; consequently they could be prevented by the wholesome development of personality, or the proper "adjustment" of personality. Childhood was the critical period. "Childhood," in William Alanson White's notable phrase, was the "golden period for mental hygiene." (15) On this all hygienists, Freudians, Behaviorists, and Meyerians agreed. The implications were clear. Why leave personality development to chance or fate or the vagaries of experience, when the means were at hand to shape or guide the personality in the making? The strategic institutions for a mental hygiene of childhood were obvious: the family and the school. Even before World War I, hygienists were excited by the school's potential as an untapped resource in the war against mental illness. (16) "Psychiatrists . . . must be permitted to enter the schools," declared NCMH Medical Director Thomas W. Salmon in 1917. (17) The hygienists' therapeutic imperialism, cautious at first, gradually grew stronger. Hygienist experience during World War I was pivotal. Their success in treating so-called "shell-shock," the war neuroses, confirmed the hygienists' belief in the essentially psychological nature of mental illness.

The psychological basis of the war neuroses, like
that of neuroses in civil life, Salmon explained,
refers to the sufferer's own incapacity for making
adjustments; the fault was in his personality
make-up. (18)   Obviously, maladjustments could
arise from precipitating events in adult life and
could be ameliorated or even cured then.   But
psychotherapy with adults was a slow, difficult, and
inefficient use of the psychiatrist's time.   The
lesson driven home for the hygienists was that
prevention was the only feasible approach to the
problem of mental illness.   The hygienists'
well-publicized "cures" of shell shock created an
atmosphere in the 1920s in which the mental hygiene
movement thrived.

II

In the post-War period many hygienists
envisioned a kind of psychiatric end-of-days:
mental illness extirpated, the asylums and hospitals
emptied, even unhappiness abolished.   It seemed
feasible.   The knowledge was available.   The means
were at hand.   The pieces fit.   Convinced that its
view of mental illness rested on secure scientific
foundations, equally convinced of the urgency of its
cause, the NCMH confidently sought to recruit allies
among laymen and the helping professions, especially
social work, and to extend their influence as widely
as possible into all areas of American life.
Salmon's ambition for years had been to steer the
NCMH into a mission of mental hygiene maximally
conceived, with the focus on children and the
schools.   On leave during the War, when he resumed
his post as Medical Director in 1920, Salmon pushed
the NCMH forward.   Before he resigned in 1922,
Salmon planned the momentous Commonwealth Fund
"Program for the Prevention of Delinquency," which
launched the child guidance movement and greatly
stimulated the visiting teacher movement, the
development of psychiatric social work and, finally,
the dissemination among teachers, parents, and the
community at large of the "mental hygiene point of
view" of the school. (19)
The hygienists were confident that the whole

problem of prevention stood or fell on the handling
of children. The hygienists' goal was to surround
the child with what a French historian calls a
"tutelary complex," an "infrastructure of
prevention," comprising the child guidance clinic,
the visiting teacher, the family, and the
schools. (20) The visiting teacher (for the early
identification of children with minor personality
problems) and the child guidance clinic (with its
child psychiatrists and psychiatric social workers
for the treatment of "problem" children) were
important components of the network. In the
interests of prevention, however, it was critical to
reach children before they became "problems."
Hygienist literature is suffused with this salient
conviction--parents were the weakest link in the
preventive network. Hygienists made a direct causal
connection between the parents' treatment of
children and later personality maladjustment. The
chief pathogenic factor was the parents' treatment
of children. In hygienist writings of the 1920s,
there is an almost endless reiteration of
parent-blaming. (21) Parents were not so much
deliberately bad as they were misguided, or ignorant
and untrained for their highly demanding
responsibilities. Parents were especially ignorant
of the significance of children's personality. (22)
One solution was parent education, an important
strategy of the NCMH in the twenties. (23) But
parent education had one major drawback--parents
could not be required to take courses or to obtain a
degree in mental hygiene before having children. To
the hygienists, the problem of reaching the parents
was perplexing if not intractable. The NCMH left
parent-education to allied organizations; it
concentrated on the school.
     The hygienists posed the alternatives starkly:
not the parents and the school, but the parents or
the school. Dr. Ralph Truitt, head of the NCMH
division on child guidance clinics, spoke for the
hygienists when he declared that the child guidance
clinic was too late and the parents too difficult to
reach. "If we are going to prevent delinquency,
insanity, and general inadequacy, the school should

be the focus of our attack." (24) A handful of psychologists, early converts to the mental hygiene movement, agreed. (25) Social worker allies, the chief intermediaries between the psychiatrists and the schools in the twenties and thirties were even more emphatic. They dismissed parents as hidebound and inaccessible. "The only practical and effective way to increase the mental health of the nation is through its schools," psychiatric social worker and social work educator Jessie Taft declared. "Homes are too inaccessible. The school has the time of the child and the power to do the job." Why spend one's life trying to make over a bad job, she continued, "when children are at hand to be guided into the kingdom of good adjustment." (26) The schools were the key strategic agency in the fight against mental illness. All children were compelled to attend school. One didn't have to wait for them to come to the child guidance clinic; there was no need for social workers to go to their homes to deal with recalcitrant parents; "school was the golden period for mental hygiene." (27) Given the schools' potential for reaching the greater part of the juvenile population, thanks to compulsory education, little wonder that leaders of the mental hygiene movement were dazzled by the prospect.

For the public schools to contribute to the prevention of mental illness and social maladjustment required not merely some slight changes but a sweeping alteration of the whole system of education. A hygienist consensus began to emerge. The consensus was defined in two ways: negatively, hygienists rejected the intellectualistic-moral emphasis of American education; positively, hygienists argued that development of personality had to become the focus of education. "Education," in White's prophetic words, "has been . . . too much confined to teaching; it needs to be developed as a scheme for assisting and guiding the development of personality." (28) This was fundamental, the central tenet of the hygienist consensus on education.

If development of personality were to become

the guiding principle of American education, then everything depended on how "personality" was perceived. The hygienists had a certain orientation to personality, a model of the wholesome personality from which their school reform program was ultimately derived and which it was intended to foster. Here, Adolf Meyer in the pre-World War I period laid out the orientation to personality that hygienists were to follow in the twenties. The ideal was the assertive, active, social, outgoing personality--the extrovert. Deviations from the model, especially shyness, daydreaming, passivity--introversion--were psychiatric danger signals. A frequently reiterated theme in the mental hygiene literature of the twenties was that the teacher's responsibility was the early identification of the child "out of adjustment." There were two groups of children whose personalities were "out of adjustment"; a category which did not include children unable to learn, but encompassed only the aggressive and the inhibited or repressed. The hygienists stressed that the quiet, timid, or shy child, the "so-called 'good' child," was the more serious problem than the child who overtly misbehaved, because the child typically was overlooked. (29) But the interests of prevention of mental illness required the creation of a school environment that would foster the healthy personality development of all children, what a leading hygienist called "presumptive prevention." (30)

What emerges from hygienist writings in the 1920s is a cohesive educational reform program. Hygienists assumed that there was a direct relationship between tension and stress and personality problems; personality buckled under stress. Hygienists identified three sources of stress in the school that needed to be rectified: (a) failure and nonpromotion, (b) the subject-matter-centered curriculum, and (c) the traditional methods of discipline. Hygienists were convinced that school failure and nonpromotion were psychologically damaging to the child. Failure led to "feelings of inferiority," withdrawal, or the

development of an "unsocial attitude, the shut-in
personality." On the other hand, success bred
confidence and a positive management of reality.
Failure, "regardless of whether 'deserved' in the
older moralistic sense," would have to be eliminated
or minimized, and replaced by success. The school's
responsibility, declared Clark University's William
Burnham, an influential hygienist and popularizer of
mental hygiene, "is to see to it that every child at
some time, in some way, in some subject, achieves a
marked success." (31) The hygienists left it up to
the educationists to work out the concrete
applications of this doctrine. The demands of the
set subject-matter-centered curriculum were another
ubiquitous source of stress. Hygienists made few
concrete suggestions as to curricula reforms. They
were content to leave curricula matters to the
professionals in education. Hygienists simply urged
that subject matter be deemphasized. Teachers must
pay less attention to content and subject matter and
more attention to the child, that is, the child's
personality development, as opposed to the child's
intellectual development. (32)

Disciplinary procedures were another cardinal
offense against wholesome personality development.
Hygienists would invariably depict teachers as
rigid, moralistic, punitive, authoritarian. And
such teachers forced children to hide their
emotions, thus contributing to the faulty
personality development started in the home. One of
the key planks of the hygienist consensus was to
persuade teachers to view children's misbehavior
with "objectivity of attitude" or "scientifically"
instead of moralistically, that is, to view
children's misbehavior not in terms of "bad," to be
punished, but as a "symptom" of warped or stunted
personality, to be "adjusted." The teacher had to
pay less attention to the child's overt behavior and
more attention to understanding the motives,
frequently "unconscious," underlying behavior. The
interests of "understanding" the child's personality
make-up required the establishment of a
nonauthoritarian classroom environment. Hygienists
called upon the teacher to "ruthlessly sacrifice her

sense of authority," and to provide the sort of classroom climate that would encourage the child to "show himself for what he is" and not "deceive," that is, inhibit or repress feelings or behavior for the sake of good discipline. (33)   Finally, hygienists agreed that the success or failure of mental hygiene in the classroom ultimately depended on the teacher's own personality, which they believed to be more important than the method of teaching or the curriculum.   All attempts to make the school an institution for children's personality development fail if the teacher is emotionally immature, takes out personal problems on children, is ignorant of how his or her personality powerfully affects children. (34)   Hygienists called for a completely new kind of teacher-training, one which emphasized not only the personality development of children but also that of teachers.   What emerged by 1930 was a therapeutic model of the school: the school as clinic, the child as patient or "problem," the teacher as therapist, the ideal teacher-student relation that of therapist-patient, the general ambience of the class period that of a therapeutic session, and the goal--the adjustment of personality. (35)

III

In spite of a large and rich outpouring of books and articles on reform movements in education in the past twenty years, historians of education have rarely concerned themselves with the problem of the dissemination of ideas, of how educational innovation or change occurs. (36)   Study of the mental hygiene movement in education may shed some light on this subject.   The goal of the mental hygiene movement was to disseminate through the entire field of education a knowledge of the mental hygiene point of view and its application to schooling.   The hygienists' goal was not to tell teachers concretely what or how to teach but to change their idea of education, their attitude, or, as Jackson and Kieslar put it in their discussion of educational innovation generally, "to alter the practitioner's view of reality." (37)   To succeed, the hygienists had to disseminate a mental hygiene consciousness to a broader public of parents and professionals which would facilitate the schools' acceptance of the mental hygiene point of view. Here the role of the middlemen, the disseminators, is crucial. The main disseminator of mental hygiene influence on American education through the 1920s and into the 1930s was the Commonwealth Fund's "Program for the Prevention of Delinquency," the spearpoint of mental hygiene penetration in the schools.

The Program employed several dissemination strategies. In the first place, the visiting teacher served indirectly as a "change agent" in the schools. (38) Then, in the late twenties, the Program launched a promotional plan directly among teachers and teachers-in-training via summer session courses at a score of carefully selected sites. (39) Ultimately the Program put its faith in education, in, to use Herbert Croly's phrase, "education or the Subsidized Word," or in what Janowitz calls "innovation by enlightenment." (40) The Program operated a vast educational extension service: a publishing house, a monthly newsletter, free reprints of articles and addresses, a reference and bibliographic service for inquirers, and a speakers' bureau. The Commonwealth Fund's promotional activities on behalf of the mental hygiene movement were extraordinary in the scope and vigor with which they were conducted. (41) This was a deliberate and systematic effort to reach a carefully classified list of elite opinion, including "leaders in education, teachers and professors in schools, colleges, and universities, physicians, social workers, judges, probation officers, writers, editors," as well as leaders of public opinion in the fields of public health and child welfare. Here is where the Fund made its real contribution to the mental hygiene movement in education. By 1933, when the Commonwealth Fund finally terminated the Program, the mental hygiene movement in education had almost taken on a life of its own; there was little left for the NCMH to do.

In the 1920s, the NCMH was for the most part

content to disseminate the mental hygiene point of view among social workers, psychologists, and the helping professions in general, as well as important groups involved in parent education and child welfare, and to let that point of view trickle down to teachers. (42) By the late 1920s, the idea of the school's responsibility for the personality development of children finally began to filter into books for teachers or teachers-in-training. (43) The idea steadily gained force, and in the thirties and forties it was becoming firmly entrenched in the literature and activities of the Progressive Education Association (PEA). (44) In the late 1930s and through the 1940s, publications of the National Education Association, the American Council on Education, and the Educational Policies Commission were permeated by the idea of personality development and the mental hygiene point of view. (45) The climax of the NCMH's efforts to make personality development the guiding principle of American education was reached in 1950, at the Mid-Century White House Conference on Children and Youth, one of the key historical events both in education and mental hygiene. (46) The conference took as its slogan "A Healthy Personality for Every Child" and ratified the hygienists' decades-long contention that the school is basically an institution to develop children's personality and that personality development of children should take priority over any other school objective. (47)

IV

By the early 1950s the doctrine of personality development was firmly entrenched in the schools. Concern for personality development had become a central concern of American education, if not its central concern. (48) But what does it all amount to? What conclusions can we draw today? What was the appeal of the idea of the school's responsibility for personality development to the mental hygiene movement? To the education profession?

The recent revisionist historical interpretations of progressivism and of reform movements in general have been deeply suspicious of "doing good." Revisionist historians have seen doing good as a mask for privilege and "social control." (49) In the meantime, the entire field of psychiatry has received its share of critical attention. Foucault, Laing, Goffman, and Szasz, among others, argue that psychiatry can be best understood if treated not as a medical or scientific discipline but as "political ideology" or "moral tactic." Study of the mental hygiene movement in education would seem to provide strong evidence for a skeptical view of do-gooders, reformers, and the helping professions. A reminder of the historical context is appropriate here.

The 1920s was a period of deep divisiveness in American life, a time of xenophobia and nativism, of a ferocious "assault on Victorianism." (50) In the interests of social control, some Americans turned to violence or to the passage of repressive laws, rules, and regulations. Leaders of the mental hygiene movement were also concerned with the problem of social control. But eschewing the increasing reliance on prohibitive laws and restrictions, they turned to the more benign techniques of psychology for a scientific regulation and control of behavior. (51) Their new understanding of personality opened up exhilirating possibilities for the control of behavior, and the hygienists turned to the schools as the strategic agency for social control. There was no more benign or more certain way to control social life than through the shaping of children's personalities. The idea of the school's responsibility for personality development thus reflects an ambition to absorb the sphere of personality in order to ensure a correct psychological disposition; the ideal of personality "adjustment" bespeaks the essential concern of the hygienists. The well-adjusted personality was happy, efficient, productive, and above all, "social." It served a self-evident need in the twenties. (52) In addition, to expand the school's role to include "personality" involves the matter of professionalization. It was in the interests of the emerging "psy" professions--

psychiatry, clinical psychology, and psychiatric social work--to expand their province to include the schools.

It would not be fair, however, to ignore the altruism of the hygienists, their humanitarian zeal, their generous impulses, their intention to "do good." Maladjustment seemed to be ubiquitous, afflicting the nation like a modern plague, an individual tragedy and a social problem of vast if unspecified dimensions. The hygienists hoped to save children from later personality breakdown. The hygienists saw themselves as socially progressive and democratic. They rejected eugenics and all hereditarian assumptions. The path to mental health was not through "breeding a better race," but through molding the personality. (53) The school would counterbalance unhealthy personality traits acquired at home, while fortifying the personality of all children. The hygienists sought to make the school a haven for children, a place where all children would experience success, build confidence or self-esteem, and develop wholesome personalities immunized against mental illness. But hygienists' hopes were not simply meliorist but utopian. As Jessie Taft put it in that insistent note of Protestant moralism in which many hygienists phrased their hopes for the future, the school's mission was to usher in "the kingdom of good adjustment." Convictions like these help explain the enthusiasm and energy with which hygienists sought to transform American education.

What did the idea of personality development have to offer to the education profession? What was its appeal? Briefly, two factors made educators receptive to the mental hygiene point of view: the impact of immigration and the imperatives of compulsory education. In the pre-World War I period, as immigrant children flocked into the schools, educators were forced to broaden their concept of schooling to encompass a concern for the "whole child," to encompass legatee functions. (54) To add a concern for "personality development" was a natural progression in the education of the "whole child" and may be seen as an extension of the school's Americanizing function.

Perhaps the most decisive factor that made educators receptive to the mental hygiene point of view were the imperatives of compulsory education and the concommitant phenomenon of school failure. Educators awakened to the magnitude of school failure in the pre-World War I period. (55) The connection between failure and nonpromotion and "early" school-leaving, and the latter with the twin evils of waste and inefficiency, forced educators to seek alternatives to the traditional subject-matter-centered education. When the mental hygiene movement appeared on the scene, educators were in need of a new paradigm. The vocational education movement and the Gary School Plan provided popular alternatives for a time, but the mental hygiene movement ultimately provided educators with the most appealing alternative. The idea of personality development pointed to the solution of the dilemma of what sort of education was appropriate under conditions of universal education. In the background, one suspects, is a conviction that the majority of children in the schools would be unable to cope with the demands of an academically oriented program, a conviction which the intelligence test movement, with its well-publicized findings about how scarce a resource intelligence seemed to be in the general population, helped to foster. In this light the traditional academic fare seemed irrelevant, even undemocratic. The idea of personality development provided the ideological legitimization educators needed to deemphasize academic education. The appeal of becoming shapers of healthy personalities was hard to resist. With personality development as the fundamental test of the educational program, schoolmen were able to unite science with efficiency and democracy to promise a happier and more productive life for all children. (56)

Acceptance of the idea of the school's responsibility for personality development helped solve some problems, but created others. The kingdom of good adjustment soon began to display some deficiencies. To make the teachers and the schools responsible for the development of children's personality contributed to the teachers' bewilderment. Older ideas and traditions about curriculum and discipline have a dogged persistence which cannot simply be forgotten or exorcised. Teachers who could not ignore the fact that they were still supposed to achieve certain academic objectives and to maintain discipline, were confused and overburdened with conflicting messages. By 1932 even Adolf Meyer was having second thoughts about the incursion of mental hygiene into the school. "We must," he said, "look to the school to attend to things that it can do." Then, "I am very skeptical about the wisdom of introducing too much pathology into the school. . . . We have to cultivate in the school interest in the things which are of the school and for the school." (57) Few were willing to listen to Meyer's warnings then. Personality development became a firmly rooted educational priority.

Finally, this study may offer some practical insights for today's schools. A major problem of American education currently is that of declining academic skills and achievement. (58) One current popular remedy is to take a tough line, as exemplified by the calls for "back to the basics," accountability, and minimum competency testing, backed up by sanctions like failure, nonpromotion, and nongraduation. Another remedy is to call on parents to reassert their educational responsibility and for the school to divest itself of parental functions, especially in the area of psychological development. (59) But such remedies may be ineffective. The school today has its legacy of strong commitment to personality development. It may not be possible to turn the clock back. There are many facets to the current predicament of the public school. But no remedy for its problems will get very far that neglects the body of ideas bequeathed by the mental hygiene movement and now part of our "common sense." No remedy for the predicament of the school can advance unless it takes into account the deeply held, if today rarely articulated, concern for the development of personality, a legacy of the mental hygiene movement, with which any proposed new hard line may ultimately be incompatible. The idea of the school's responsibility for personality development, however, generally remains an unexamined assumption underlying educational discourse. If the idea of "personality development" is moved into the forefront and made an explicit object of scrutiny, at least it would be possible to open for public debate the whole question of the relative responsibilities of parents and schools in the development of children's personality.

NOTES

1. Two recent discussions of intellectual history have particularly influenced this work: Paul H. Conkin, "Intellectual History," in The Re-Interpretation of American History and Culture, ed. William H. Cartright and Richard L. Watson, Jr. (Washington, D.C., 1973), p. 227, 243; Robert Darnton, "Intellectual and Cultural History," in The Past Before Us: Contemporary Historical Writing in the United States, ed. Michael Kammen (Ithaca, N.Y., 1980), p. 337.

2. Lee J. Cronbach and Patrick Suppes, eds., Research for Tomorrow's Schools: Disciplined Inquiry for Education, Report of the Committee on Educational Research of the National Academy of Education (London, 1969), p. 259.

3. Lawrence A. Cremin is the notable exception. Cremin accords priority to intellectual history in both volumes of his American Education. To Cremin, ideas are not "disembodied notions" or "mere rationalizations of existential reality, but . . . moving forces that compete for attention and that profoundly influence what people believe is possible and desirable in the realm of education." American Education: The National Experience, 1787-1876 (New York, 1980), p. x; American Education: The Colonial Experience, 1607-1783 (New

York, 1970).

4. There is a helpful discussion of some of the issues in intellectual history that are especially pressing for historians of education in Douglas Sloan, "Historiography and the History of Education," in Review of Research in Education, ed. Fred N. Kerlinger (Itasca, Ill., 1973), 1: 241-43.

5. Warren I. Susman, "Personality and the Making of Twentieth Century Culture," in New Directions in American Intellectual History, ed. John Higham and Paul H. Conkin (Baltimore, Md., 1979), pp. 212-26.

6. The difficulty in discussing the late nineteenth-century educational paradigm is that our knowledge about it is tacit. A useful beginning in explicating the paradigm has recently been made, however, in Herbert M. Kliebard, "Education at the Turn of the Century: A Crucible for Curriculum Change," Educational Researcher 11 (January 1982): 16-23. Also see Jerome Kagan, "The Moral Function of the School," Daedalus 110 (Summer 1981): esp. 152-53. The older Walter B. Kolesnick, Mental Discipline in Modern Education (Madison, 1962) is still helpful. In the meantime as historian J. G. A. Pockock remarks about historical study of paradigms in general, by virtue of the rhetoric of the exercise, it is necessary to start with a straw man. In Politics, Language and Time (New York, 1971), p. 4.

7. The idea of "personality" is protean, dating back to the ancient Greeks. The modern idea of personality emerged in the early twentieth century and comes into its own only in the post World War I period. By 1930 interest in personality had reached "astonishing proportions." Gordon W. Allport and Philip E. Vernon review the literature in "The Field of Personality," The Psychological Bulletin 27 (1930): 677-730. The authors point out that many psychologists declare that the concept of personality is indefinable. Still they list 327 items in their bibliography. Edward Sapir gives five understandings of the term "personality": philosophical, physiological, psychological-physical, sociological, and psychiatric. He adds

that "it is the peculiarly psychiatric conception of personality . . . which it is most difficult to assimilate but important to stress." Encyclopedia of the Social Sciences (New York, 1934), 12: 85-87. It is the psychiatric conception of personality with which we are concerned here.

8. Roy Lubove, The Professional Altruist: The Emergence of Social Work As a Career (Cambridge, Mass., 1965); John C. Burnham, "The New Psychology: From Narcissism to Social Control," in Change and Continuity in Twentieth Century America, ed. John Braeman et al. (Columbus, Ohio, 1968), pp. 396-98; Fred Matthews, "In Defense of Common Sense: Mental Hygiene as Ideology and Mentality in Twentieth-Century America," Prospects 2 (Winter 1979): 459-516. And, in general, see Norman Dain, Clifford W. Beers, Advocate for the Insane (Pittsburgh, Pa., 1980).

9. In general, see Philip Rieff, The Triumph of the Therapeutic: Uses of Faith After Freud (New York, 1968), chap. 8; Philip Rieff, Freud: The Mind of the Moralist (New York, 1959), chap. 10; Christopher Lasch, The Culture of Narcissism: American Life in an Age of Diminishing Expectations (New York, 1979); passim; Thomas C. Cochran, "The Inner Revolution," in his Social Change in Industrial Society (London, 1972), chap. 2.

10. For the beginning and early years of the movement, see Dain, Clifford W. Beers; Barbara Sicherman, The Quest for Mental Health in America, 1880-1917 (Ann Arbor, Mich., 1967), chaps. 5, 6.

11. Adolf Meyer, "Organization of Community Facilities for Prevention, Care, and Treatment of Nervous and Mental Diseases," in Proceedings of the First International Congress on Mental Hygiene, 2 vols., ed. Frankwood E. Williams (New York, 1932), 1: 238; Burnham, "New Psychology," p. 364.

12. See especially C. Macfie Campbell, A Present-Day Conception of Mental Disorders (Cambridge, Mass., 1924), as well as his Destiny and Disease in Mental Disorder (London, 1935). Also see William Alanson White, Twentieth Century Psychiatry (New York, 1936); idem, Medical Psychology: The Mental Factor in Disease (New York, 1931); Adolf

Meyer's "Modern Conceptions of Mental Disease," in _Suggestions of Modern Science Concerning Education_, ed. Herbert S. Jennings et al. (New York, 1917).

13. Three popular and popularized summaries of mental hygiene principles are George K. Pratt, _Your Mind and You: Mental Health_ (New York, 1924); William H. Burnham, _The Normal Mind_ (New York, 1924); Ernest R. Groves and Phyllis Blanchard, _Introduction to Mental Hygiene_ (New York, 1930).

14. "Mental Hygiene and Social Progress," _Mental Hygiene_ 13 (April 1929): 249.

15. "Childhood: The Golden Period for Mental Hygiene," _Mental Hygiene_ 4 (April 1920): 256-67; C. Macfie Campbell, "Education and Mental Hygiene," _Mental Hygiene_ 3 (1919): 399-401.

16. See especially Meyers, "What Do Histories of Cases of Insanity Teach Us Concerning Preventive Mental Hygiene During the Years of School Life?" _Psychological Clinic_ 2 (June 15, 1908): 89-101; and his "Mental and Moral Health in a Constructive School Program," in Jennings, _Suggestions of Modern Science Concerning Education_. Also see C. Macfie Campbell, "Educational Methods and the Fundamental Causes of Dependency," _Mental Hygiene_ 1 (1917): 235-37.

17. Quoted in Sicherman, _Quest for Mental Health_, p. 180.

18. Thomas W. Salmon, "War Neuroses and Their Lesson," _New York Medical Journal_ 109 (1919): 933-96; idem, "Notes and Comments," _Mental Hygiene_ 2 (1918): 480-81; Groves and Blanchard, _Introduction to Mental Hygiene_, pp. 40-43; Henry N. May, _Mental Diseases: A Public Health Problem_ (Boston, 1922), pp. 192-93.

19. Sol Cohen, "The Mental Hygiene Movement, The Commonwealth Fund, and Public Elementary and Secondary Education, 1921-1933," in _Private Philanthropy and Public Elementary and Secondary Education: Proceedings of the Rockefeller Archive Center Conference_, June 8, 1979, ed. Gerald Benjamin, pp. 33-46. Responsibility for the Program was distributed among three agencies. The visiting teacher demonstration went to the Public Education Association of New York City. Responsibility for

the recruitment and training of psychiatric social workers and child psychiatrists went to the New York School of Social Work. The nationwide organization and demonstration of child guidance clinics, the largest phase of the Program, went to the NCMH. The CF's New York office coordinated and administered the entire project.

20. Jacques Donzelot, The Policing of Families, trans. Robert Hurley (New York, 1979), pp. 96ff.

21. I discuss this phenomenon at length in "The Mental Hygiene Movement, Parent-Blaming, and the Schools," (Unpublished paper prepared for Pacific Coast History of Education Society, University of California, Berkeley, May 7, 1982).

22. Frankwood E. Williams, "Finding a Way in Mental Hygiene," Mental Hygiene 14 (1930): 246-47; idem, "Everychild: How He Keeps His Mental Health," the Annals of the American Academy of Political and Social Science, 121 (1925): 181ff. Also see Miriam Van Waters, Parents on Probation (New York, 1928), passim.

23. Through the CF Program, the hygienists advocated and demonstrated parent education, issued a large literature aimed at parents, and made liaisons with the major parent-oriented interest groups.

24. Ralph P. Truitt, "Mental Hygiene and the Public School," Mental Hygiene 11 (1927): 270.

25. For example, Arnold Gesell, "Mental Hygiene and the Public School," Mental Hygiene 3 (1919): 59-64; Walter Dearborn, "Facts of Mental Hygiene for Teachers," ibid., 11-15; Lewis M. Terman, The Hygiene of the School Child (Boston, 1914), from chaps. 16-18; J. E. Wallace Wallin, The Mental Hygiene of the School Child (Boston, 1914).

26. Quoted in Virginia P. Robinson, Jessie Taft, Therapist and Social Work Educator (Philadelphia, 1962), p. 63. Also see Jessie Taft, "Mental Hygiene and Social Work," in Social Aspects of Mental Hygiene, ed. Frankwood E. Williams (New Haven, 1925); Jane Culbert, "The Public School as a Factor in the Training of the Socially Handicapped

Child," Proceedings, National Conference of Social Work (1923), p. 93; M. Edith Campbell, "The Strategic Position of the School in Programs of Social Work," ibid., pp. 362ff; Elizabeth Woods, "The School and Delinquency: Every School A Clinic," ibid. (1929), pp. 213-21.

27. Esther Loring Richards, "What Has Mental Hygiene to Offer Childhood at the End of 1926," Mental Hygiene 11 (1927): 8.

28. White, "Childhood: The Golden Period," pp. 262-63; Burnham, The Normal Mind, pp. 18-19.

29. Ralph P. Truitt, "Community Child Guidance Clinics," in The Child Guidance Clinic and the Community, ed. Ralph P. Truitt; M. E. Haggerty, "The Incidence of Undesirable Behavior in Public School Children," Journal of Educational Research 12 (September 1925): 102-22; Groves and Blanchard, Introduction to Mental Hygiene, pp. 98-99, 187-93.

30. "Presumptive," because of the absence of research. In the meantime, it is "doing the best possible." George S. Stevenson, "The Prevention of Personality Disorders," in Personality and Behavior Disorders, ed. J. McVickers Hunt, 2 vols. (New York, 1944), 2: 1165.

31. "Success and Failure as Conditions of Mental Health," Mental Hygiene 3 (1919): 387-97.

32. The "primary question is not 'What does the child learn in school.' But rather 'How does the child feel because of school.'" William Healy and Augusta Bronner, "How Does the School Produce or Prevent Juvenile Delinquency," Journal of Educational Sociology 6 (April 1933): p. 470.

33. Here especially one sees the direct influence of psychoanalysis. The teacher's personality is critical because of the Freudian mechanisms of "transference" and "identification." Bernard Glueck, "Some Extra-Curricular Problems of the Classroom," School and Society 19 (February 9, 1924): 143-149; Ralph P. Truitt, "Barriers to Mental Hygiene--Teachers," Proceedings, National Conference of Social Work, 1925, pp. 426-30; Clara Bassett, The School and Mental Health (New York, 1931): pp. 14-21.

34. "What the Teacher Can Do," Southern

California Society for Mental Hygiene, Bulletin, III
(April 1927), 5; Bassett, op. cit., pp. 45-61.
        35. I discuss this at length in "The Mental
Hygiene Movement, The Development of Personality and
the School: The Medicalization of American
Education," in a forthcoming issue of the History of
Education Quarterly.
        36. This point is also made in Wayne J. Urban,
"Some Historiographical Issues in Revisionist
Educational History," American Educational Research
Journal 12 (1975): 348-49. Urban calls for studies
in the "institutionalization" of ideas.
        37. Philip Jackson and Sara B. Kieslar,
"Fundamental Research and Education," Educational
Researcher 6 (September 1977): 14.
        38. Lois Meredith French, Psychiatric Social
Work (New York, 1956), pp. 63-66.
        39. Commonwealth Fund, Annual Report, 1928, p.
58; W. Carson Ryan, "The Preparation of Teachers for
Dealing with Behavior Problem Children," School and
Society 28 (August 18, 1928): 208-15.
        40. Programs of innovation may succeed in
fostering change indirectly and over time, says
Janowitz, by the provision of an intellectual
framework of conceptions, propositions,
orientations, vocabulary, nomenclature. Ultimately
our way of comprehending "reality" is changed.
Morris Janowitz, Political Conflict: Essays in
Political Sociology (New York, 1970), pp. 243ff.
        41. Commonwealth Fund, Annual Reports,
1926-1928.
        42. Persuasive evidence of how successful the
NCMH was in the 1920s in infiltrating the mental
hygiene point of view into all groups concerned with
child welfare can be found in White House Conference
on Child Health and Protection, White House
Conference, 1930, Addresses and Abstracts of
Committee Reports, pp. 170-74, 189-90; idem, Report
of the Committee on the Socially Handicapped--
Delinquency, The Delinquent Child (New York, 1932),
pp. 38-41; and "The Child and the School," pp.
99-133; idem, Parent Education: Types, Content,
Method (New York, 1932), passim.
        43. Examples of the literature are William

Burnham, The Wholesome Personality (New York, 1932); Mandel Sherman, Mental Hygiene and Education (New York, 1934); Percival M. Symonds, Mental Hygiene of the School Child (New York, 1934); W. Carson Ryan, Mental Health Through Education (New York, 1938); Harry N. Rivlin, Educating for Adjustment (New York, 1936); Lawrence A. Averill, Mental Hygiene for the Classroom Teacher (New York, 1939); C. R. Myers, Toward Mental Hygiene in School (New York, 1939); Norman Fenton, Mental Hygiene in School Practice (Stanford, Calif., 1943); E. W. Tiegs and B. Katz, Mental Hygiene in Education (New York, 1941); H. W. Bernard, Mental Hygiene for Classroom Teachers (New York, 1952).

44. The idea of the schools' responsibility for the development of personality suffuses the PEA's activities having to do with the reconstruction of the high school in the 1930s, e.g., "The . . . mental-hygiene point of view--its recognition of the complex wholeness of personality at all times . . . must come to pervade every department, activity, relationship of the school . . . From the point of view of this book, the distinctions commonly drawn between education . . . and guidance and therapy . . . are not so fundamental as they seem." In V. T. Thayer, Caroline B. Zachry, and Ruth Kotinsky, Re-Organizing Secondary Education (New York, 1939), pp. 364-65. Also see Lois Hayden Meek, The Personal-Social Development of Boys and Girls (New York, 1940); Caroline B. Zachry, Emotion and Conduct in Adolescence (New York, 1940).

45. For example, National Education Association, Department of Elementary School Principals, Fifteenth Yearbook, Personality Adjustment of the Elementary School Child (Washington, D.C., 1936); National Education Association, Mental Health in the Classroom, 13th Yearbook (Washington, D.C., 1940); Association for Supervision and Curriculum Development, Fostering Mental Hygiene in Our Schools, 1950 Yearbook; American Association of School Administrators, Health in the Schools, 20th Yearbook, 1951. For the American Council on Education, see Daniel A.

Prescott, <u>Emotion and the Educative Process</u>
(Washington, D.C., 1938). In the meantime, concern
for personality and the mental hygiene point of view
had begun to appear prominently in the literature of
that vast and amorphous enterprise known as
educational "guidance" or "counseling," e.g., Ruth
Strang, "Guidance in Personality Development,"
National Society for the Study of Education, 37th
Yearbook, <u>Guidance in Educational Institutions</u>, ed.
Guy M. Whipple (Bloomington, Ill., 1938). School
psychology was also profoundly influenced by the
mental hygiene movement. At mid-century, the school
psychologist defined herself as a "mental hygiene
specialist." Norma E. Cutts, ed., <u>School
Psychologists at Mid-Century</u> (Washington, D.C.,
1955), pp. 52-53, and passim.

46. Wesley Allinsmith and George W. Goethals,
in <u>The Role of the Schools in Mental Health</u> (New
York, 1962) make the interesting claim that Isaac
Kandel considered the life adjustment education
movement of the late forties as marking the alliance
between vocational education and mental hygiene,
pp. 33, 308.

47. Edward A. Richards, ed., <u>Proceedings of
the Mid-Century White House Conference on Children
and Youth</u> (Raleigh, N.C., 1950), pp. 175, 176. Also
see Helen Leland Witmer and Ruth Kotinsky, eds.,
<u>Personality in the Making: The Fact-Finding Report
of the Mid-Century White House Conference on
Children and Youth</u> (New York, 1952), esp. chaps. 1,
4, 11.

48. R. Freeman Butts and Lawrence A. Cremin,
<u>A History of Education in American Culture</u> (New
York, 1953), pp. 541, 589; Paul R. Mort and William
S. Vincent, <u>Introduction to American Education</u> (New
York, 1954), pp. 137-39; Geraldine Joncich Clifford,
<u>The Shape of American Education</u> (Englewood Cliffs,
N.J., 1975), p. 144.

49. For example, David J. Rothman, <u>Conscience
and Convenience: The Asylum and Its Alternatives in
Progressive America</u> (Boston, 1980); idem, "The State
as Parent: Social Policy in the Progressive Era,"
in <u>Doing Good: The Limits of Benevolence</u>, ed.
Willard Gaylin et al. (New York, 1978).

50. Stanley Coben, "The Assault on Victorianism in the Twentieth Century," _American Quarterly_ 27 (December 1975): 604-25.

51. Stewart Paton, _Signs of Sanity and Principles of Mental Hygiene_ (New York, 1922), p. 133; idem, _Education in War and Peace_ (New York, 1921), p. 16.

52. The ideal of mental health, declared Dr. William Alanson White, is "the all-round, through and through personality, and that personality is the social personality." "Mental Hygiene," _Proceedings of the National Conference on Social Work, 1922_, p. 48. William H. Burnham voices the same idea in up-to-date hygienist nomenclature: "The school's essential task . . . is the integration of personality that makes right adjustment possible." _The Normal Mind_, pp. 18-19.

53. For the general background, see Hamilton Cravens, _American Scientists and the Heredity-Environment Controversy, 1900-1941_ (Philadelphia, 1978); Mark H. Haller, _Hereditarian Attitudes in American Thought_ (Philadelphia, 1963).

54. Lawrence A. Cremin, _The Transformation of the School: Progressivism and American Education, 1876-1957_ (New York, 1961), pp. 66-75.

55. The seminal work is Leonard P. Ayres, _Laggards in Our Schools_ (New York, 1909).

56. For the utility of the idea of "progressive education" to school administrators, but with broad relevance to this discussion, see David W. Swift, _Ideology and Change in the Public Schools: Latent Functions of Progressive Education_ (Columbus, Ohio, 1971), passim.

57. _American Journal of Orthopsychiatry_ 2 (1932): 228-29.

58. Report of the Commission on the Humanities, _The Humanities in American Life_ (Berkeley, Calif., 1980), p. 4, and chap. 2, passim.

59. For example, the Carnegie Council on Children asserts:

The school should not assume non-educational, essentially family functions. Schools . . . should not play amateur psychologist in treating or even diagnosing children as normal, disturbed, emotionally unstable, or the like. Only if the child's educational achievement is suffering or if his or her behavior in school is markedly disruptive should the school involve itself with the child's psychological development. And, any action in such situations . . . should be initiated or approved by parents.

Kenneth Keniston et al., All Our Children: The American Family Under Pressure (New York, 1977), p. 205.

7

THE COURSE OF THE COURSE OF STUDY
HISTORY OF CURRICULUM

Herbert M. Kliebard
University of Wisconsin, Madison

Barry M. Franklin
Augsburg College

In his essay on British education in The Long Revolution, Raymond Williams noted that it was a mistake to consider education simply as "a settled body of teaching and learning" presenting us only with the problem of distribution. (1) Beyond the question of access to education, what we mean by education is itself in a constant process of evolution, and the most concrete expression of what we mean by education in any period is embodied in the curriculum. Curriculum history is the scholarly attempt to chronicle, interpret, and ultimately understand the processes whereby social groups over time select, organize, and distribute knowledge and belief through educational institutions. It includes consideration not only of the impetus for the emergence in schools of certain forms of knowledge, but the effect of their incorporation into the course of study. Like any other area of specific historical inquiry, such as the history of science or urban history, curriculum history cannot be isolated absolutely from significant events and ideas that, strictly speaking, are not part of its central concern; but it derives its principal impetus and direction from its focus on the question of what gets taught in schools, as well as (or perhaps especially) the ways in which "a settled body" of knowledge, the curriculum, undergoes or fails to undergo change. The reasons why the knowledge that gets embodied in the curriculum of schools changes or, conversely, is resistant to change cover so wide an area as to defy enumeration. They include, of course, social change, potent elites, the legal structure, the weight of tradition, economic considerations, the organizational structure of schools, changes in the size and nature of the school population, the energy and dedication of individuals and interest groups, intellectual movements, general demographic factors, political upheaval, significant changes in certain social institutions, and even, here and there, a powerful idea.

In one sense, curriculum history is intimately bound up with traditional questions of the sociology of knowledge. The knowledge issue for the curriculum historian is not so much what is ultimately true or rultimately right, but what counts as knowledge in a given time and place and, more particularly, why knowledge that is taken to be important or even unimportant makes its way into the curriculum. But importance here should not be construed, as is commonly the case, to be simply what is immediately useful or practical. Much knowledge of high survival value never makes its way into the curriculum (2), and this in itself presents an interesting theoretical issue. Some knowledge may derive its importance and therefore its entree into the curriculum because of its symbolic value, its status as a rite of passage, its association with dominant social class considerations, or its relationship to religious, national, regional, or ethnic concerns. Sometimes, knowledge regarded as important for whatever reason does not make its way into the curriculum of schools because another institution, say the family, reestablishes its claim to that area of knowledge.

In practice at least, from about the mid-1960s on, curriculum history has taken at least three major forms. The predominant one considers the curriculum as a whole and attempts to interpret why certain curriculum ideas or ways of thinking about the curriculum arise and take hold. Under consideration are attempts to transform the curriculum in some fundamental way. The main focus here is usually on a major curriculum movement or on a group of like-minded individuals such as the so-called scientific curriculum-makers or the social reconstructionists who were seeking to build a curriculum on a new set of principles. Almost inevitably, an attempt is made to account for their successes and failures and, occasionally, an appraisal of the merits of their ideas. The second basic form focuses on the way in which a particular area of curriculum came into being and met with success (or failure) in its attempt to gain a foothold in the curriculum. This would include studies of manual training, special education, sex education, driver education, and vocational education. Conceivably, the opposite phenomenon, the demise of a given subject, such as the virtual disappearance of Greek from the American curriculum or the sharp decline in the teaching of Latin, could also be the object of such a study. Finally, there are studies that take as their principal concern the internal changes that may have occurred in a given time within a particular subject. The evolution of history as a school subject from the way it was taught in nineteenth-century schools to current practices in the teaching of social studies would be one such example. Likewise, English as a school subject has undergone much in the way of internal transformation. The curriculum when seen only as the enumeration of subjects has changed only modestly since the latter part of the nineteenth century; but when it is seen in the context of what is actually being taught under the various subject labels, a quite different picture may emerge.

General Interpretations

The development of curriculum history reflects in at least one respect the development of both American educational history and American historiography in general. As a subject for study and research, curriculum history attracted some interest among American educators during the first three decades of this century. (3) These early historical treatments of curriculum issues approached their subject much as did their early twentieth-century counterparts in educational history generally and as did those German-trained scholars who had in the previous century set the tone for history as a professional area of study and research in the emerging American university. (4) They tended to depict the development of the school curriculum, just as other historians had characterized the development of schooling and the nation itself, as the continuing triumph of the forces of progress and democracy over a benighted and aristocratic past. (5) While certain vestiges of this view of history remain, it has also been seriously challenged. During the 1960s that tradition fell into disrepute among educational historians under the influence of two revisionist movements. One was a movement of educational scholars of a politically liberal viewpoint who were allied at least in spirit with the consensus school of American historiography of the 1950s. The other represented an effort of educational historians of a politically radical bent who eschewed the idea of consensus in favor of an emphasis on conflict. (6)

That latter effort, however, has been less successful than that of its counterpart in general educational history. Despite the low esteem that many educational historians accord the notion that the development of the American public school represents an embodiment of the forces of progress and democracy, this viewpoint continues to exert a reasonably strong influence among those closely identified with the curriculum field. It is in fact the controversy between curriculum historians who adhere to a basic optimism and a sense of progress with respect to the role of education in American society and those who favor the more critical interpretation that has shaped a large portion of the contemporary field of curriculum history. At one pole, some historians interpret the course of curriculum change, particularly in the twentieth century, as an attempt to make the curriculum relevant to a broader constituency; at the other pole, some historians see the curriculum as evolving into an ever more direct and potent instrument for preserving the status quo and maintaining social stability; and there are, of course, many gradations between these poles.

This debate can be illustrated by examining how curriculum historians allied to these different schools of thought interpret one of the most important periods in curriculum history, the so-called "scientific" reform movement of the 1920s. Those who subscribe to a "progress" position argue that, in the wake of increased emigration from eastern and southern Europe and sharply rising enrollments in public schools, particularly secondary schools, the American school population was becoming more diverse as to ability, social class, and ethnic background. The founders of the curriculum field, they suggest, sought to reconstruct a college-oriented curriculum, grounded on what they believed were the outmoded views of the Committee of Ten (1893) in order to provide this new student population with an education that would offer them opportunity for social and economic mobility in what was already an urban, industrial society.

Curriculum historians who see the course of twentieth-century education as basically salutory interpret that movement as establishing a more comprehensive and functionally oriented curriculum thereby contributing to an egalitarian system of education. Curriculum differentiation, for example, was one attempt to adapt the curriculum to the growing school population. Although they may, here and there, criticize some practices of these first curriculum workers, such as their overly mechanistic and behavioristic view of curriculum making, generally, they argue that such undesirable features of curriculum work were soon to disappear in the years after 1930 as the curriculum field came under the influence and leadership of a new generation of curriculum leaders and continued to progress. (7)

On the other hand, the critics see the scientific curriculum movement as consisting of efficiency-minded curriculum makers who viewed the increasingly diverse school population of their day, particularly the children of eastern and southern European immigrants and children of the urban poor, as potential threats to social order and stability. Curriculum changes were impelled primarily by the belief that these children had neither the intelligence nor the moral capacity to assume the responsibilities of democratic citizenship without specific and direct training. The net effect, according to this interpretation, was a curriculum that served, at least in part, to channel the children of the immigrants, the minorities, and the poor into subordinate economic and political roles. The extent to which these misguided policies were prompted by genuine humanitarian impulses or by conscious class domination, however, remains in dispute. Nevertheless, these historians suggest that such practices as curriculum differentiation, consciously or unconsciously, became potent instruments of social control and stultified rather than enhanced social mobility. Curriculum differentiation, in other words, did not so much serve the needs of a diverse student population as it determined their social and occupational destinies. They go on to argue that the curriculum field has never divested itself of this legacy of social control. Those who have come to lead the field after 1930 are, they maintain, the largely unconscious intellectual heirs of these efficiency-dominated curriculum workers. According to this interpretation, curriculum thought and practice today are similarly oriented, either unintentionally or by design, to using the curriculum as a mechanism for preserving existing patterns of power and privilege in American society. (8)

Special Subject Areas
The division between those who favor a fundamentally sanguine interpretation of recent curriculum history and those who assume a fundamentally critical one has had some impact on

those curriculum historians who have examined the development of such specialized subject areas as vocational education and special education. They have for the most part embraced one or the other of these interpretive frameworks. As such, they are usually divided about whether the development of the subject under consideration represents a drive for progressive reform or an effort to use the curriculum to control segments of the population who were thought to threaten order and stability. (9)

Others who have examined the history of the subjects of art, reading, English, and mathematics have found diverse patterns of development. These curriculum historians have been less inclined to identify the development of these subjects with any clear and consistent political purpose. Art, according to curriculum historians who have charted its development, first appeared in the public school curriculum in the mid-nineteenth century in the form of industrial drawing. During the next seventy years, this functional orientation gradually disappeared as art came under the influence of such child-centered educators as Froebel, Parker, and Dewey, an influence that has not waned throughout this century. They appear to be suggesting that art has remained virtually untouched either by the mental discipline movement of the nineteenth century or by the efficiency-minded curriculum reforms of the early twentieth century. (10)

Reading, one of its historians has argued, evolved out of a series of intense and still unresolved struggles beginning in the mid-nineteenth century and continuing to the present day between one group of educators who favored a whole word or "look see" method of teaching reading and another group who advocated phonic and similar synthetic methods of teaching the subject. (11) The controversy that this historian describes between the adherents of these two methods of teaching reading is quite similar to the controversy that has divided so-called child-centered educators from their efficiency-minded antagonists throughout this century.

Those who have investigated the development of

the English and mathematics curricula find neither
the dominance of one school of thought nor a
conflict between competing schools of thought.
Instead, they see it as an interplay ending in a
quid pro quo between contradictory forces. One
historian of English as a school subject has argued
that during the first three decades of this century,
English was for the most part transformed from a
subject defended on mental disciplinary grounds to a
subject justified by its functional outcomes. It
was, for example, during this period that business
English emerged as a part of the high-school
curriculum and that English educators began to
advocate the ideas of scientific curriculum-making
and curriculum differentiation. (12) During these
same years, however, the literature curriculum
remained virtually unchanged. The efficiency-
oriented 1917 report on the Reorganization of
English in the Secondary Schools recommended the
same reading list of essentially classical works for
high school literature study as did the mental
discipline-minded National Conference on Uniform
Entrance Requirements in English in 1899. (13) The
creative writing curriculum, according to another
historian of English education, was only marginally
influenced by efficiency ideas. More important to
its development, she argues, was the influence of
progressive ideas that viewed creative writing as a
means of encouraging artistic expression and
personality development. (14)

Similar contradictions can be found in the
development of the mathematics curriculum. The
Committee of Ten, for example, recommended that all
subjects be "taught in the same way" to all
students. (15) Despite that recommendation, two
historians of mathematics education have noted that
the Committee's Conference on Mathematics suggested
that students planning a business career should,
unlike their college-bound counterparts, devote some
part of the algebra course to the study of
commercial arithmetic. (16) These historians also
point out that different areas of the mathematics
curriculum were subject to conflicting influences.
During the early years of this century, they argue,

mathematics educators tended to justify the place of arithmetic and algebra in the curriculum by appealing to the practical value of these subjects in preparing children for life in modern society. At the same time, however, they note that these same educators defended geometry's place in the curriculum on the basis of its alleged disciplinary value. (17)

One historian who traced the development of the biology curriculum, however, raised what may prove to be an interesting issue for those who wish to examine the history of the school curriculum in general. The best picture we have of the evolution of biology, he argues, is of a subject introduced around the turn of the century as a functionally oriented alternative to existing individual courses in botany, physiology, and zoology. (18) The growth of the biology curriculum from this viewpoint appears to parallel the demise around the turn of the century of the mental discipline movement and the emergence in its place of efforts at efficiency-oriented curriculum reform. This historian, however, makes the important point that this interpretation is based primarily on the study of the recommendations of national and regional committees charged with the reform of the natural science curriculum. It is not really, he emphasizes, a history of the development and implementation of the biology curriculum in the schools, a process which did not necessarily mirror these recommendations. (19)

Virtually all the research considered thus far has been based primarily on the study of committee reports or the proposals of university professors and other leaders in education. These recommendations are certainly appropriate as a major source for reaching conclusions about curriculum thought and, in a more limited way, curriculum practice. The work of prominent figures in the curriculum world, for example, may be seen not so much as influencing the actual curriculum in schools as they are barometers of the direction the school curriculum was taking anyway. The work of such curriculum leaders as Franklin Bobbitt and David

Snedden, in other words, may be reasonably accurate indicators of the ways in which the school curriculum was changing. In and of itself, however, this approach probably does not address adequately the issue of the curriculum as it actually became incorporated in schools.

A Research Agenda

There are at least two distinct issues that require further examination by curriculum historians. First, curriculum historians are obviously divided in their interpretation of the development of American curriculum thought. That crucial division needs further exploration. Is the controversy between the optimistic, favorable interpretation and the critical alternative the result of the kind of interpretive difference that enlivens and enriches historical inquiry? Is one interpretation clearly more sound and persuasive than the other? Or, finally, are both positions fundamentally deficient, and should curriculum historians seek new and better explanations of the development of curriculum thought? The clarification and interpretation of curriculum ideas, apart from the question of their incorporation into school practice, is itself a worthwhile endeavor.

But, there appears little to be gained in our understanding of the history of curriculum thought simply by arguing the correctness of either the "progress" interpretation or its critical alternative. Both viewpoints represent more or less single-factor explanations that by their very nature tend to focus on a restricted segment of curriculum history, whether it be its progressive thrust or its inherent conservatism, at the expense of other possibly important factors. There is a certain presentism in the way they perceive historical events that may serve to distort or even ignore what was significant in the past. To be sure, these models may have been useful at certain times. The conventional viewpoint did provide early curriculum workers with a rationale for molding a field of study and the sense of professional identity and ideological drive to accomplish that difficult task. Its politically radical alternative, emerging most vigorously in the 1960s, seems to have injected a needed sense of critical reflection and self-awareness in a field preoccupied by an ameliorative mission. Despite the utility these interpretations may once have had, their focus on limited aspects of our historical experience tends to flatten our understanding of that experience and leads us ultimately to miss its complexity and ambiguity. Rather than a monolithic thrust engineered by one political wing or another, the American curriculum is more likely a product of an unexpressed and uneven compromise among several conflicting forces, some no doubt progressive and others clearly conservative, with much that is in between or simply different. What curriculum history needs are not heightened political antagonisms but what Carl Kaestle has called "elegant" explanations that will explore the various dimensions and ramifications of that compromise. (20)

Second, as already suggested, curriculum historians have not satisfactorily examined the arena of the school curriculum itself. Studies of committee recommendations and the proposals of leaders in education are unquestionably helpful in gaining a perspective on the development of curriculum thought, but they are less helpful in understanding the intricacies of curriculum practice. Curriculum historians need to engage in studies that will explore the curriculum as it actually was incorporated into school settings. Apart from matters of broad interpretation, our knowledge of curriculum practice in the schools themselves is woefully sketchy. Curriculum historians are just beginning to address this problem, especially through the use of case studies of curriculum practice in individual schools and school systems. Some investigations have looked broadly at curriculum change and stability in several school systems including those in Minneapolis, Gary, Denver, and Atlanta. (21) Others have focused on more limited issues, such as the development of the junior high school in Berkeley,

California, and Richmond, Indiana, the Dalton Plan
in Scarsdale, New York, industrial education in
Fitchburg, Massachusetts, and the role of the
Victory Corps during World War II in
Indianapolis. (22)

Case studies of curriculum change offer a
potentially fruitful approach to curriculum history
research. What seems to emerge from these studies
is the view that the relationship between curriculum
thought and curriculum practice is far more subtle
and complex than is commonly assumed. These studies
taken together suggest that important mediating
factors such as local political pressure, legal
restraints, ideology, financial resources, and even
powerful and energetic individuals typically impinge
on the ability or willingness of school systems to
implement curriculum ideas in anything but a limited
or superficial manner. There are also significant
regional differences like the rate of growth of
urban centers in certain periods and demographic
factors such as the entry of women into certain
segments of the work force that may have had a
profound effect not only on who went to schools but
what they studied. (23) Case studies also pose
considerable difficulties for the curriculum
historian. The most important sources for these
kinds of studies are not always preserved, and if
they are, they are often incomplete and
uncatalogued. They include the correspondence of
middle-level administrators within school systems,
minutes of the meetings of teachers and principals,
courses of study, and staff bulletins. They are
more often to be found in the back files of school
systems rather than in the archives of libraries.
Using these data clearly presents problems of time,
expense and, of course, patience for the curriculum
historian. Yet, it is this kind of data that is
needed to advance our understanding of what a
curriculum was like in actual school settings.

Why Curriculum History?

Why then is this research agenda important?
What contribution to our understanding of American
intellectual life and thought might we reasonably

expect from this specialized subarea within the field of educational history? Given the fact that history of education is, in most people's minds, already a subspecialty within the arena of social and intellectual history, one might reasonably raise the question as to whether a further subspecialty within history of education serves any useful purpose.

First, it can be argued that those who are identified with the specialized area of history of curriculum bring with them a special sensitivity to certain issues that the general historian or even the educational historian may tend to overlook. Historian Richard Hofstadter, for example, in aligning twentieth-century educational reform with a pervasive spirit of anti-intellectualism in American life, has argued that Dewey's "vocabulary and ideas, which were clearly evident in the Cardinal Principles of 1918, seem to appear in every subsequent document of the new education." (24) To most curriculum historians, however, it is probable that the educational ideas of John Dewey and the basically social-efficiency ideas that Clarence Kingsley incorporated in the Cardinal Principles Report would be patently incompatible. To be sure, neither Dewey nor Kingsley was happy with the traditional education he had inherited, but each brought to that dissatisfaction a totally different agenda for reform. The chasm between the two is illustrated to some extent by the bitter clash between Dewey and David Snedden, Kingsley's long-term colleague and mentor, a controversy over vocational education ably interpreted by Arthur Wirth. (25) Moreover, to associate Dewey's ideas with "every subsequent document of the new education" is, from a curriculum perspective, not only to misread Dewey but to misinterpret in fundamental ways the direction that the "new education" did in fact take. To be sure, there are "unresolved problems of interpretation" in Dewey's work, as Hofstadter claims, but these problems need not lead to associating Dewey's work with that of those educational leaders of his time who represented almost diametrically opposing positions

on critical matters of curriculum doctrine. (26)
Much of the so-called "new education" bore no
resemblance whatever to what Dewey stood for, and to
stir all those disparate ingredients together in one
pot just spoils the soup. It is not a case of where
the general historian is always wrong in these
matters and the curriculum historian is always
right; it is simply that the curriculum historian is
obliged to bring a different, perhaps more
discriminating, perspective to bear on matters
pertaining to curriculum, and this may, under
certain circumstances, enrich our understanding of
the issues involved. The danger for the curriculum
historian is that he or she may allow that sense of
discrimination to degenerate into splitting hairs.

Second, it is safe to say that every
occupational or professional group, whether teamster
or psychiatrist, has a history, and in one sense
curriculum history is a history of those people who
identified themselves with the curriculum field,
addressed themselves to curriculum issues, and whose
ideas gave shape and direction to a professional
area of study. As Thomas Kuhn once argued,
professionals in general "live and work both within
a larger culture and within a quasi-independent
disciplinary tradition of their own. Both
environments shape their creative projects, but the
historian all too often considers only the
first." (27) One function that curriculum history
as a special entity serves, therefore, is to bring
to light that special "disciplinary tradition,"
which complements the larger culture in which the
curriculum exists. It seems likely that an
interpretation of the course of curriculum change,
for example, would be incomplete if tied only to
broad social and intellectual movements. Moreover,
the ideas of Franklin Bobbitt, W. W. Charters, David
Snedden, and other shapers of the curriculum field,
have, consciously or (more likely) unconsciously,
become incorporated into the way new professionals
are socialized into the curriculum field.
Curriculum history is one way to bring to bear a
critical self-examination on that professional
socialization.

Third, a curriculum is itself an important element in social history. To the extent that we can uncover and bring to light the curriculum of a particular time and place, we have unearthed a highly significant artifact of our culture. The curriculum, as the historian Frederick Rudolph has noted, is "one of the places where we have told ourselves who we are." (28) From that fragment of the culture we call the curriculum, we may be able to reconstruct some of the ideas that define and give meaning to our social life. After all, what any society chooses deliberately to pass on to its young in systematic ways is a statement of what that society prizes and wishes to preserve. What makes the interpretation of curriculum at any given time and place so difficult, however, is that what the curriculum represents does not reflect any kind of unanimity of judgment about what should be taught. Rather, at least in modern times, it is much more likely to be an unacknowledged detente among competing groups within the society. Williams, for example, has argued that British education following the industrial revolution evolved from the efforts of three groups within British society: the public educators, the industrial trainers, and the old humanists. "The curriculum which the nineteenth century evolved," he says, "can be seen as a compromise between all three groups, but with the industrial trainers predominant." (29) The curriculum in this sense becomes an important cross-section of a society's values, values that are tied to particular social groups within the society. A consciousness of those elements that comprise the curriculum in relation to the social groups that supported them is, in turn, a vital factor in broadening our sense of the options available to us in seeking to address the question of what gets taught.

Finally, one caveat about curriculum history must be mentioned. Curriculum development in schools is a supremely practical activity and, given the pressures of making immediate decisions of consequence, it is probably more tempting here than in the case of general history or history of

education to look for handy solutions to those
problems in historical studies. While important
values may be legitimately associated with
historical inquiry into the curriculum, as with any
historical inquiry, special care must be taken to
avoid the notion that there are particular "lessons"
to be learned from curriculum history or that
immediate solutions to practical problems may be
found in this way. While such an attitude may be
understandable within a field like curriculum, such
presentism can only serve to narrow and corrupt the
perspective from which curriculum history must be
approached. In the long run, it may be that the
most enduring value that can be derived from
curriculum history is, rather, the very distance it
creates from the problems at hand. By making the
familiar strange, curriculum history may serve to
heighten our critical sensibilities and thereby help
us reformulate our problems in fresh and
constructive ways.

NOTES

1. Raymond Williams, The Long Revolution
(London, 1961), p. 215.
2. J. M. Stephens, The Process of Schooling:
A Psychological Examination (New York, 1967).
3. Research and writing on the history of the
curriculum clearly predates the twentieth century.
One can identify what we would call curriculum
history in Plato's discussion of the development of
Greek education in Book 7 of the Laws. See Plato,
Laws, vol. 7, of the Great Books of the Western
World, 54 vols., ed. Robert Maynard Hutchins
(Chicago, 1952), pp. 713-31. Closer to our own time
and place is the discussion of the development of
curriculum in a number of American school systems
during the first half of the nineteenth century in
Henry Barnard, American Journal of Education. See
American Journal of Education 19 (1869): 417-576.
4. For a discussion of the parallels between
the development of the study of American educational

history and American historiographical research in general, see Sol Cohen, "The History of the History of American Education, 1900-1976: The Uses of the Past," Harvard Educational Review 46 (August 1976): 303-8.

5. Franklin Spencer Edmonds, "The Central High School of Philadelphia, 1838-1902," The School Review 11 (March 1903): 211-26; Frank Fitzpatrick, "The Development of the Course of Study in American Schools," Educational Review 49 (June 1915): 1-19; Emit Ducan Grizzell, Origin and Development of the High School in New England Before 1865 (New York, 1923); Alexander Inglis, The Rise of the High School in Massachusetts (New York, 1911), chaps. 5-6; Harold Rugg, "A Century of Curriculum Construction in American Schools," in Curriculum-Making Past and Present. Twenty-Sixth Yearbook of the National Society for the Study of Education, Part 1, ed. Harold Rugg (Bloomington, Ind., 1926), sec. 1; John Elbert Stout, The Development of High School Curriculum in the North Central States from 1860 to 1918 (Chicago, 1921); Willis Uhl, Secondary School Curriculum (New York, 1927), pt. 1.

6. Carl F. Kaestle, "Conflict and Consensus Revisited: Notes toward a Reinterpretation of American Educational History," Harvard Educational Review 46 (April 1976): 390-91.

7. John McNeil, Curriculum: A Comprehensive Introduction, 2nd ed. (Boston, 1981), chap. 14; David Pratt, Curriculum Design and Development (New York, 1980), pp. 26-28, 38-39; Mary Louise Seguel, The Curriculum Field: Its Formative Years (New York, 1966); Daniel Tanner and Laurel Tanner, Curriculum Development: Theory into Practice, 2nd ed. (New York, 1980), chaps. 3, 7-10; Robert Zais, Curriculum Principles and Foundations (New York, 1976), pp. 49, 54-73.

8. Michael W. Apple and Barry M. Franklin, "Curriculum History and Social Control," in Ideology and Curriculum, ed. Michael Apple (London, 1979), chap. 4; Herbert M. Kliebard, "Bureaucracy and Curriculum Theory," in Freedom, Bureaucracy, and Schooling, ed. Vernon F. Haubrich (Washington, D.C., 1971), pp. 74-93; Herbert M. Kliebard, "The Drive

for Curriculum Change in the United States, 1890-
1958. I--The Ideological Roots of Curriculum as a
Field of Specialization," Journal of Curriculum
Studies 11 (July-September 1979): 191-96; Edward A.
Krug, The Shaping of the American High School, 1880-
1920 (Madison, 1969), pp. 87-92, 249-55; Steven
Selden, "Conservative Ideology and Curriculum,"
Educational Theory 27 (Summer 1977): 205-22.

9. For favorable interpretations of the
history of vocational education and special
education see Grant Venn, Man, Education, and Work:
Postsecondary Vocational and Technical Education
(Washington, D.C., 1964), chap. 2; Leo Kanner,
A History of the Care and Treatment of the Mentally
Retarded (Springfield, Ill., 1964). For critical
interpretations of the history of these same
subjects see Walter Drost, David Snedden and
Education for Social Efficiency (Madison, 1967);
Seymour B. Sarason and John Doris, Educational
Handicap, Public Policy, and Social History: A
Broadened Perspective on Mental Retardation (New
York, 1979), chaps. 8-15.

10. Elliot Eisner, "American Education and the
Future of Art Education," Art Education, Sixty-
Fourth Yearbook of the National Society for the
Study of Education, Part 2, ed. W. Reid Hastie
(Chicago, 1965), chap. 13; Frederick Logan, Growth
of Art in American Schools (New York, 1955).

11. Mitford M. Mathews, Teaching to Read
Historically Considered (Chicago, 1966).

12. Arthur N. Applebee, Tradition and Reform
in the Teaching of English: A History (Urbana,
Ill., 1974), pp. 59-60, 66, 85, 91-92.

13. Ibid., pp. 66-67.

14. Alice Glarden Brand, "Creative Writing in
English Education: An Historical Perspective,"
Journal of Education 162 (Fall 1980): 63-78.

15. National Education Association of the
United States, Report of the Committee of Ten on
Secondary School Studies (Washington, D.C., 1893),
p. 17.

16. Alan R. Osborn and F. Joe Crosswhite,
"Forces and Issues Related to Curriculum and
Instruction, 7-12," A History of Mathematics

Education in the United States and Canada,   Thirty-
Second Yearbook of the National Council of Teachers
of Mathematics (Washington, D.C., 1970), pp. 164-65.
      17.   Ibid., pp. 218-25.
      18.   Paul DeHart Hurd, *Biological Education in
American Secondary Schools, 1890-1960*   (Washington,
D.C., 1961), pt. 1.
      19.   Ibid., p. 72.
      20.   Kaestle,   "Conflict   and   Consensus,"   pp.
394-396.
      21.   Barry M. Franklin, "The Social Efficiency
Movement   Reconsidered: Curriculum   Change   in
Minneapolis,   1917-1950,"   *Curriculum Inquiry*   12
(Spring 1982):   9-33; W. Lynn McKinney and Ian
Westbury, "Stability and Change: The Public Schools
of Gary,   Indiana,   1940-70," in *Case Studies in
Curriculum Change*, ed. William Reid and Decker
Walker (London, 1975), chap. 1; Gary L. Peltier,
"Teacher Participation in Curriculum Revision: An
Historical   Case   Study,"   *History of Education
Quarterly* 7 (Summer 1967):   209-19; Wayne J. Urban,
"Educational Reform in a New South City: Atlanta,
1890-1925,"   in   *Education and the Rise of the New
South*, ed. Ronald Goodenow and Arthur O. White
(Boston, 1981), chap. 6.
      22.   Murry R. Nelson and H. Wells Singleton,
"Richmond and Berkeley: Paradigms for Curriculum
Innovation at the Turn of the Century," *Papers of
the Society for the Study of Curriculum History* 1
(Spring 1981):   60-67; Carol A. O'Connor, "Setting a
Standard for Suburbia: Innovation in the Scarsdale
Schools, 1920-1930," *History of Education Quarterly*
20   (Fall   1980):   295-311;   Paul   J.   Ringel,
"Cooperative Industrial Education: The Fitchburg
Plan" (Paper delivered at the Annual Meeting of the
American Educational Research Association, Los
Angeles, April 15, 1981).
      23.   John Leslie Rury, "Women, Cities, and
Schools: Education and the Development of an Urban
Female Labor Force, 1890-1930" (Ph.D. diss.,
University of Wisconsin-Madison, 1982).
      24.   Richard Hofstadter, *Anti-Intellectualism
in American Life* (New York, 1962), p. 361.
      25.   Arthur G. Wirth,   *Education in the*

Technological   Society: The   Vocational-Liberal
Studies Controversy in the Early Twentieth Century
(Scranton,   Pa.,   Intext   Educational   Publishers,
1972).
     26. Hofstadter, Anti-Intellectualism, p. 361.
     27. Thomas S. Kuhn, "The Relations between
History and History of Science," in Historical
Studies Today, ed. Felix Gilbert and Stephen R.
Graubard (New York, 1972), p. 180.
     28. Frederick Rudolph, Curriculum: A History
of the American Undergraduate Course of Study Since
1936 (San Francisco, 1977), p. 1.
     29. Williams, The Long Revolution, p. 142.

8

THE FEDERAL INTEREST
POLITICS AND POLICY STUDY

Donald Warren
University of Maryland

Historical policy analysis in education blends strengths from two research areas. Education policy analysis probes for structural elements that shape and explain relevant arrangements and practices. Like policy analysis in general, including program evaluation, it tends to be guided by conceptualizations derived inductively rather than by abstract definitions of policy. (1) This lack of theoretical prescription guards against the premature exclusion of data and the fallacy of self-fulfilling prophecy, an error that erases utility and rationale from policy research. History enlarges the scope of possible explanations in education policy analysis. It permits access to any enduring relations among the varieties of power that act on education. Although history alone cannot explain change and repetition in educational arrangements, without history no aspect of the education policy cycle, from intention to results to reformulated goals, can be reliably tested for durability.

Historical policy analysts draw resources from the humanities and the social and behavioral

sciences, combining narrative and quantitative
methods in eclectic search for power variables. (2)
With interests that are more expansive and complex
than the history of policies, they test the
assumption that any political arena is isolated or
self-contained. They inquire into the origins and
effects of power and the multiple ways power is
organized and reflected. They examine educational
phenomena as dependent on power variables and the
extent to which education represents the
accumulation of political, economic, cultural, and
symbolic power. They look beyond prevalent modes of
education for features that are persistent, stable,
transitory, or dynamic. They try not to discount or
simplify conflict over education. Rather than
describe or analyze merely the effects of schooling
and programs, they intend to identify and assess the
developing influences at work on educational
institutions and processes through an evolving
network of policy, in short, to discover the
structure of effective policy.

Interest in that objective arises from
contemporary preoccupations with state and federal
education policy in the 1980s. It also accompanies
a growing recognition that such policy areas have
been subjected to relatively little historical
political scrutiny. Valuable work has been
completed on the history of federal involvement in
education, although it tends to be segmented
topically and focused on the years after 1933. (3)
The absence of a comprehensive history of federal
education policy in the United States reflects a
belief that there is no policy to investigate, at
least not before the Depression and perhaps not
afterward either. (4) Accepting that assumption
leaves unexplained the various educational
activities undertaken or subsidized by the federal
government during its formative years in the
nineteenth century.

Nor has much research has been done on the
political history of state education policy. While
state school agencies have been generally dismissed
as unimportant relative to local education policy
and practice prior to the twentieth century, large

gaps appear in the political history of state governments, particularly legislatures. (5) Without this research base, historians and political scientists lack the necessary context for examining the development of state education policy or making reliable judgments about state school agencies. The history of state school finance legislation, school tax structures, and education articles in state constitutions represents another major research need. Comparative histories of state education policy would provide valuable resources for understanding the history of federal educational activities.

The following discussion focuses selectively on federal involvement in education during the early nineteenth century. It suggests lines of inquiry rather than conclusions. One intent is to lay to rest the fiction that federal educational activity represents a twentieth-century development. Another is to illustrate the junctures and interdependence of state and federal involvement in education. Finally, the discussion indicates policy research that historians and political scientists might pursue collaboratively.

Throughout the first half of the nineteenth century, Congress repeatedly affirmed its belief that education fell within the purview of the states. It denied motions to establish standing committees on education, ignored Congressman William Cost Johnson's effort in 1837 to earmark federal lands and funds specifically for public education, rejected every proposal for using the Smithson bequest to support schooling, and refused to consider plans for a national bureau of education. President Buchanan listed state prerogatives over education as a major reason for vetoing the land grant college bill in 1859. Debate over Justin Morrill's bill revealed how sharply drawn the issue over federal involvement in education had become. Senator James M. Mason of Virginia insisted:

> If you have the right to use the public property or the public money either, to establish agricultural colleges, cannot

> you establish a school system in each
> state. . . ? Would it not be in the power
> of a majority in Congress to fasten upon
> the southern States that peculiar system
> of free schools in the New England States
> which I believe would tend . . . to
> destroy that peculiar character which
> [happily] . . . belongs to the great mass
> of the southern people[?] (6)

To which Iowa's Senator James Harlan retorted:

> It may be that it is a blessing to
> Virginia that she is now more largely
> represented by adult white people who
> are unable to read and write, in
> proportion to her population, than
> any other State of the Union; it is a
> blessing, however, that the people of
> my state do not covet. (7)

Here was the clash of ideas: federalism viewed as
enabling centralization of power, on one hand, and
diffusion of opportunity, on the other. The
conflict reflected suspicion on both sides that the
extent and quality of opportunity depended on the
locus of control over education.

Despite congressional protestations that
education belonged to the states, federal roles in
education began to take shape early in the century.
Several types of activity can be detected: indirect
support for general schooling, direct support for
specialized schooling, institution-building, and
knowledge-building. As an illustration of
antebellum federal involvement in education, the
first type is outlined here in greater detail than
the others.

Efforts grouped in this category of indirect
support for general schooling took the form of
federal incentives to municipalities and states to
establish and sustain formal educational activities.
The federal lands reserved for schools in the new
public land states constituted the most striking and
familiar example of indirect federal support. The

policy followed the practice originated by several colonial governments, Georgia for one, of setting aside land for educational purposes. Most states admitted between 1800 and 1860 also received two or more townships of land to endow a university. During this period additional grants of land totaling almost 52,000 acres went to support specific schools, academies, and universities in various states and territories. Finally, grants of proceeds from land sales could be applied by states toward internal improvements, including education. Despite the fact that some of the school lands proved to be valueless, nineteenth-century school leaders viewed the various grants as evidence of federal interest in education. (8) Later scholars saw them as strategies to achieve stable governments and populations in public land states. (9) No federal control of schooling was involved, but as Henry Barnard learned in 1860, even in new southern states, the incentives enriched permanent school funds that in turn supported emerging networks, if not systems, of public schools. (10)

On the other hand, the grants were not gifts. The lands could be used only to support public education. In the early public land states, local governments administered the grants; later, the states received them. To political scientist Daniel Elazar, the grants-in-land indicated that "the problem of education was simultaneously of both local and nationwide concern and, consequently, was attacked by all planes of government." (11) Listing them as one illustration of nineteenth-century cooperative federalism, he would probably disagree that they represented only a form of indirect support for schooling. "The grants directly stimulated, financed, or helped to finance" public education in most states admitted after 1800. (12)

In addition, by changing the level of government receiving the lands, Congress involved the grants in one of the earliest efforts to equalize local ability to finance schools, a clear intrusion on local and state education policy. In Indiana, where the school lands were ceded to local jurisdictions, citizens learned that the grants varied in value, thus giving some districts greater resources to support schools. When the legislature attempted to collect the income from the lands to form a state school fund that would be distributed to districts on the basis of school age population, the effort failed to survive a court test. (13) Congress had explicitly placed the lands under local authority. After a prolonged legislative struggle, a similar effort in California succeeded because Congress had given the school lands to the state. (14) For both states the grants-in-land served to alert citizens to the problem of education inequity posed by variations in local wealth. In California and elsewhere, they also offered states a modest fund from which to subsidize schools in low-wealth counties and districts.

Additional indirect aid arrived as loans to the states distributed by the Surplus Revenue Act of 1836. The Act permitted states to use interest on the monies, which totaled over $28 million, to support education. Most did, although in varied ways. (15) Georgia, for example, received over $1 million, and in 1840 was able to apply almost $60,000 in accumulated interest to its school fund. Until after the Civil War, the Georgia school fund was restricted to support the "education of the poor." The $285,000 received by Delaware was applied to the support of schools for white children exclusively. Between 1838 and 1860, the loan to Illinois added on the average $20,000 annually in interest to the permanent school fund. In all, the twenty-six states admitted prior to 1837 benefited from the surplus revenue distribution. In 1876, after surveying the extent to which states voluntarily employed interest on the loans to support schools, U.S. Commissioner of Education John Eaton concluded that only one barrier had blocked the adoption of "some general, comprehensive, and equitable plan for the aid of education" prior to the War. (16) Most states admitted the need for assistance, even if some equated public education with philanthropy. The cotton-raising states stopped the effort, not because of constitutional scruples but because "universal education would

imperil" slavery. (17)   Eaton's postwar rhetoric
aside, the Treasury surplus enabled a clear, if
circuitous distribution of federal funds to support
schools. Elazar noted another effect. Unlike the
grants-in-land for educational purposes, the surplus
distribution monies went to all states on the basis
of their representation in Congress. (18)   The
amounts accruing to eastern states tended to balance
the federal grant-in-land assistance to western
states.

Elazar detected a tacit commitment in Congress
throughout the nineteenth century to use federal
resources to stimulate educational development.
Although strict constructionists prevented "formal
earmarking," unspoken agreements resulted in federal
support for schools through not only the surplus
revenue distribution but also reimbursements to
states for war debts. (19)   During a period
stretching from the Revolutionary War to the
Spanish-American War, Congress repaid states for war
expenditures with the understanding that the funds
would be used to support public schools.

Direct federal support of specialized schooling
during the first half of the nineteenth century can
be illustrated in two cases. In both it resulted in
control, not merely diffusion, of resources for
education. In neither instance was schooling the
single objective. Congress established military
training academies and appropriated funds for Indian
schools in large measure to promote effective war
policies. Support for the service academies began
in the first decade of the nineteenth century. (20)
Annual appropriations for Indian education became
available through the Civilization Fund Act of
1819. (21) For the most part, the monies subsidized
the work of missionary groups. By 1825, thirty-two
federally aided Indian educational institutions
reported annually to Congress. (22)

A third pattern of federal educational activity
in the early nineteenth century involved the
establishment of federal agencies with educational
missions. Most became permanent fixtures in the
central government. The Indian Office in the War
Department, which was formally organized in 1824,

supervised the distribution of Indian education
funds, collected demographic and cultural data on
the various tribes, and solicited annual reports
from federally supported Indian schools and
teachers. By the late 1830s, it was a quasi-
independent bureau. In 1839 the Patent Office began
disseminating agricultural data and seeds to the
nation's farmers. Within a decade this exercise in
practical education became the major function of the
Agricultural Division of the Patent Office. In 1849
the Bureau of Indian Affairs and the Agricultural
Division were transferred to the newly created
Department of the Interior. (23) The Department of
Agriculture, established in 1862 as an independent
subcabinet agency, collected and disseminated
information on farming, promoted the science of
agriculture, and distributed practical data,
research findings, and seeds to farmers.
Congressman James Garfield used the Department of
Agriculture Act as a model in framing the Department
of Education Act four years later. (24)

Of the patterns of federal involvement in
education before 1860, institution-building had
initially the least overt impact on the growth of
policy. With modest appropriations and narrowly
defined responsibilities, federal educational
agencies in the early nineteenth century seemed
hardly worth noting. All survived initial periods
of congressional suspicion and several attempts to
abolish them. Their long-term effects were due more
to the growth, increasing permanence, and
"boosterism" of their staffs than to formal
mandates.

All federal educational agencies created prior
to 1860 received assignments to promote basic and
applied knowledge. Here was a fourth type of
federal interest in education. It encompassed
numerous land and coastal surveys, scientific
expeditions, sharing information with states, and
regular population studies, including the decennial
census. The Smithsonian Institution claimed a
singular mission to promote scientific knowledge.
Congress refused to include among its
responsibilities "the increase of the knowledge of

education," as proposed by Henry Barnard and Robert Dale Owen. (25) Nevertheless, during its first two decades of operation, the Smithsonian sponsored studies by several scholars investigating aspects of public education. One of them was Henry Barnard. Even without that connection to the concerns of school people, the Institution involved the federal government directly in broadly focused knowledge-building through its library, museum, laboratory, and research grants.

As a pattern of federal educational activity, knowledge-building proved to be durable and relatively popular. It combined features of federalism generally thought to be mutually exclusive: centralization for the purpose of resource diffusion rather than control. In 1866 Minnesota Congressman Ignatius Donnelly detected a similar mode of activity in federal subsidies for roads, canals, and railways. (26) They struck him as suitable precedents for the duties of the proposed Department of Education, which he interpreted as including the national dissemination of schooling opportunities without the imposition of federal control. He overlooked prospects for a different sort of control. Federal involvement in the regular collection and dissemination of data influenced the construction of standard schedules and forms that in turn affected both how data were organized and which data were worth collecting. These nineteenth-century efforts banked a renewable resource for the subsequent development of quantitative social science, including policy analysis. (27)

Like other war periods in American history, the decade of the 1860s was an interlude of major federal initiatives in education. The Departments of Agriculture and Education were established, the latter in 1867. Abraham Lincoln signed the Land Grant College Act in 1862, and three years later the Bureau of Refugees, Freedmen, and Abandoned Lands began formal operations. Although the Land Grant College Act followed established patterns of federal educational activity, it produced new, egalitarian effects by varying the size of grants according to a

state's representation in Congress. The school
lands ceded to new states offered across-the-board
assistance. Amounts differed by virtue of land
values, not population. Precedents for the
Freedmen's Bureau were more tenuous. It represented
an instance of institution-building and performed
knowledge-building functions. Its educational
mission resembled that of the Bureau of Indian
Affairs, with two major exceptions: it was created
as a temporary agency, and it intruded directly on
local and state policy. After receiving several
extensions, it lapsed in the early 1870s.

Secondary sources agree only on some details of
the bureau's aims and effects and the conditions
within which it functioned. (28) Originally, it had
no formal authority to engage in educational
activity, but it did so nonetheless. As extended in
subsequent legislation, enacted over presidential
veto, it engaged in limited educational work. It
could not pay teachers' salaries, but it could
finance and build schools. Its primary educational
mission was to join private agencies in providing
rudimentary schooling for southern black people,
although its programs did not exclude whites. The
bureau also aided black colleges, most notably
Howard University in the District of Columbia. At
the end, its network of state school
superintendents, agents, and military personnel
encompassed over 2,500 day and night schools, with
almost 3,300 teachers and 150,000 students, and
1,500 Sunday schools with 6,000 teachers and 100,000
students. It had served approximately one-tenth of
the school-aged southern black population.

Controversy over the agency began in Congress
with the original proposal for a bureau of
emancipation. The Republican-controlled House
approved it by a slim margin. The debates focused
on basic questions. Was the bureau constitutional?
Was it necessary? Could it be effective? Was it
part of a strategy to enlist black voters in the
Republican Party? With regard to some of the
bureau's advocates, the answer to the last question
was yes. The constitutional issue became academic.
The bureau's effectiveness was determined in large

measure by events and agencies beyond its control. These in turn indicated the extent to which it represented a necessary federal initiative.

The bureau confronted black demand for schooling. It did not engineer the phenomenal and unexpected clamor for learning that swept among southern black people of all ages as the Union army moved South. The secondary sources agree on that point too. (29) In addition, northern and southern white leaders, for a complex variety of reasons, identified education as necessary to equip blacks for a more independent status. (30) However, there was little talk among northern whites about social equality and much disagreement over full citizenship for black people. The goals were more modest: literacy and basic morality. Would the southern states adopt and pursue them? The answer was no, in part because they lacked the resources to do so.

There were four million black people in the postwar South. Approximately five percent were literate in 1865. Few had the skills and means to earn more than a limited living. The southern economy was in shambles, farms were in disrepair, and major cities in ruins. Beyond the physical destruction were equally debilitating psychological wounds. The damage was pervasive and multidimensional.

Postwar destruction, however, failed to explain the South's policy regarding schools for black people. Most southern and border states lacked a prewar tradition of tax-supported systems of public education. Schools for rural and low-income students were rare; for black students, they were typically illegal. There was little evidence that the attitudes reflected in these traditions had been changed by the war. The Freedmen's Bureau represented in part an attempt to do so. The strategy merged federal resources with philanthropy and payments by black families. In no case did it entail full federal funding of schools. The effort ceased not because it succeeded or failed, but because both private and federal support became unavailable. The result, W. E. B. Dubois argued bitterly, was southern victory on the question of

education   policy. (31)   Public   schooling   for
southern blacks became a function of state and local
governments that had at best ambivalent commitments
to the needs and aspirations of black people for
education.   Separate and unequal school systems
followed predictably.

In   the   1860s   several   federal   initiatives
responded to the problem of inequality in education.
Save for the land grant colleges, they amounted to
an interlude.   With rhetorical flourish but no
mandate, the Department of Education was viewed by
friend and foe as capable of exerting at least
indirect   pressure   on   states   and   communities,
especially in the South, to make schooling more
commonly available.   The Freedmen's Bureau launched
a frontal assault on southern education policy.
Controversy over both efforts centered on questions
of control and political ideology: even under the
extreme conditions left by the Civil War, was
education a federal interest?   Although no one
suggested it should be the only or primary strategy
in   Reconstruction,   the   answer   remained   that
education defined as schooling constituted at best a
temporary federal concern.

Early nineteenth-century federal educational
activities   lend   themselves   to   several
interpretations.   If   policy   implies   intent,
apparently no federal education policy emerged
during this period. Except as a negative factor,
formal intent was absent.   On numerous occasions,
Congress made clear its opposition to encroachments
on what it viewed as a state responsibility and
right.   Even where intent can be detected, the
diffusion   of   unconnected   federal   educational
activities among a host of responsible agencies or
the temporary, tentative character of the activity
weakened the possibility of any coherent policy
taking shape.   On the other hand, how is one to
understand and characterize the amount and variety
of federal educational activity in the period before
1870? Beneath talk about the Constitution and the
tradition of states' rights, a nagging suspicion
remains that localism and slavery better explained
congressional reluctance to enter the educational

field directly and with explicit purposes. Perhaps the only entrance was through the back door; the example of the Freedmen's Bureau suggests as much.

A second interpretation admits the existence of policy but denies its history. At various points, federal educational activities surfaced, but they did not build, evolve, or expand over time. Like a patchwork quilt, their relation to each other, while functional, was superficial and arbitrary. Viewing these myriad involvements, one could conclude that there was less here than met the eye. The use of land grants to encourage states and localities to establish schools, for example, began with the nation's founding. Not until the late 1850s in the debate over the first land grant college bill did Congress confront the notion that without sanctions such incentives lacked the power to direct educational development toward national interests. There was no reason for it to do so. The need for sanctions implies controversy, reluctance on the part of some to observe national priorities. Regarding education, national goals were absent except in the form of general statements on which there was wide consensus. Aside from Indians themselves, few disagreed with the proposition that native Americans ought to be pacified. After a flurry of doubt and complacency, Congress endorsed federally controlled service academies. When it finally arose, controversy focused on equity, that is, universal free public schooling, long an issue within states and local communities but in the late 1850s and 1860s new and troublesome with regard to federal roles in education. Universal public education, it was acknowledged at the time, implicitly challenged the distribution of power in American society. It also placed an unequal financial burden on the states and on different counties within states. If this inequity of capability constituted a national problem, Congress did not address it directly.

The Civil War brought the federal interest in education into open debate. It culminated, sharply and dramatically, a train of seismic disruptions. With each shock to national stability came, among other responses, federal involvement in education: during and after the Revolutionary, 1812, and Mexican Wars, following economic crisis and an outbreak of Indian wars around 1820, before and during more severe economic dislocations in the late 1830s, and then during the long march toward the Civil War. The pattern suggests a third interpretation of federal interest in education, namely that it resulted not so much from initiative, planning, or the visions of statesmen, as from panic. Such an interpretation helps explain the fitful, undeveloped character of federal involvement in education during the first half of the nineteenth century. As responses to war and national crisis, federal education strategies served reformist expectations that were programmed for failure. They confirmed education's inability to produce immediate results or to function as an engine of social change. Also, coming on the far side of crisis, federal involvement in education typically coincided with economic reversals that deprived it of high-priority status and funding.

These political and economic complexities prevailed in the 1860s. Dependent on philanthropic agencies for part of its funding, the Freedmen's Bureau suffered the inability of voluntarism to serve public goals. Educational needs in the South were clear, if complex and enormous. Meeting them required money for staff, supplies, equipment, buildings, and military protection and, in light of the last point, solid commitment in Congress to guarantee schooling for black people. Neither was forthcoming, but a search for causes fails to turn up satisfactory villains. The most useful question regarding federal educational effort during Reconstruction may not be whether it failed or succeeded but whether, given the structure and organization of the effort, an educational goal was actually pursued.

The story admittedly did not end in 1870. Sixty years later, Herbert Hoover appointed a National Advisory Committee to study federal relations to education. In 1931, amid yet another national calamity, the committee of "fifty-two citizens engaged or interested in education" submitted a comprehensive report on federal educational activity. (32) Appended was a startling list of federal involvements in education. By 1931 all three branches of government, including ten Cabinet departments, five federal commissions, and several independent agencies engaged in education-related work. Surprised at its discovery, the committee complained that in the mid-nineteenth century both the "policy and procedure" of federal relations to education shifted markedly. The finding adds yet another interpretation of federal educational activities in the nineteenth century, a "sleeper" effect that circumvented the absence of intent. Such incrementalism retained the possibility of federal involvement while limiting prospects for planning. The effectiveness of subterranean, indirect approaches also suggests that popular opposition to federal roles in education might not have been as durable as some political leaders argued at the time. Perhaps W. E. B. DuBois and Henry Steele Commager were correct. Missing from Washington in the late 1860s, they thought, were nerve and imagination. (33)

If federal involvement in education moved through a formative period in the early nineteenth century, setting prepolicy parameters for subsequent activities, state education policy followed roughly parallel fits and starts. The two levels of government matured concurrently. That point holds particular relevance for education policy, given congressional insistence on the states' responsibility for developing public schools. For their part, state legislatures seemed to waiver on the question of the locus of responsibility. Informed by a variation on the Calvinist work ethic, state policy initially required local districts to support their own schools. Wide discrepancies in the quality and quantity of schooling available in a state resulted. By midcentury, comment by governors and other political leaders indicated growing awareness of the material and symbolic costs to the states of unequal local education. Although the sources of the pressure for state school tax reform apparently differed by state, legislatures began enacting systems of school finance, some in response to constitutional mandates, others in response to general constitutional commitments to support state systems of "thorough and efficient" schools. Attempting to soften the effects of unequal local wealth on schools, the plans experimented with tax formulas that combined local and state resources. Similar efforts to balance local and state control occurred in the areas of teacher training and certification, length of school year, and curriculum. Most state legislatures, however, seemed reluctant to establish structures of regulation. One reason was cost; another was that regulation seemed to be an inappropriate way to build support for schools. There was talk of compulsion, and other forms of enforcement and state systems of school supervision appeared, but they tended to be staffed and maintained locally rather than centrally in the offices of state school superintendents.

In various forms issues over the control, organization, and finance of public schools reached the legislatures of almost every state over the course of the nineteenth century. They frequently received detailed consideration in the annual reports of state school superintendents and on occasion resurfaced after initial solutions had been formulated. (34) State school officers sought each other's advice, corresponded about developments in their respective states, and lobbied state legislatures for action on the school finance question especially. The debates focused in part on ideological imperatives, familiar arguments about the social benefits of public schools, but they often included detailed analyses of local inability to support schools at state-required minimum levels. (35) More was at stake here than who paid for schools. The debates pitted rural agricultural areas against industrialized cities, with the latter in some states agreeing in effect to subsidize schools in less wealthy districts in return for a measure of home rule. The conflicts, apparently heated, suggest that opposition to public schools, particularly state systemization and supervision, may not have been precisely that. It may have reflected also an amalgam of limited local resources and an unsettled public philosophy of education. If such basic policy matters remained problematic within the states, the lack of consistent and coherent development of federal involvement in education during the nineteenth century becomes more understandable.

These alternative interpretations argue the need for a policy analysis research agenda that emphasizes the political history of federal and state education policy. Beyond the obvious fact that such issues occupy the visible horizon in the 1980s, large and seductive knowledge gaps require attention. Although not necessarily related, issue-oriented contemporary preoccupations and scholarly interests converge at several points. Both are served by rigorous conceptualizations that unwrap education's relation to the forms of power and explain changing, conflicting perceptions of its value as an "internal improvement." Both benefit from assessments of the real weight of constitutional arguments in the context of constitutional pragmatism at the federal level especially. Research on nineteenth-century state and federal educational activities provides deep background for twentieth-century developments. But that is likely to be its least significant contribution, given the probability of finding that indeed the times have changed. Capturing the ambiguous origins of state efforts to regulate schools satisfies more than curiosity, however. It reconstructs the reasons why some groups tried to circumvent local political processes and conditions with appeals for state or federal intervention and thus displays education policymaking as a process of political accommodation. Comparative public policy studies place state and federal involvement in education in the context of governmental institutionalization. Case histories of selected legislation and legislatures lay grounds for matching intents with long- and short-run results, including those that are nonquantifiable, of public

investments in education. Analyses of voting
records and election returns combined with
demographic studies penetrate the rhetoric of
congressional and legislative debate and help
isolate connections among seemingly unrelated pieces
of legislation. Such research efforts perform
double duty in opening different approaches to
actual, as opposed to romanticized, public
philosophies, particularly in tracking persistent,
transitory, widespread, or recurring controversies
over education policy. They shed light on local,
state, and federal political interactions in the
nineteenth century and enable policy analysts to
test the assumption that with regard to education,
localities functioned in relative isolation from
nonlocal political phenomena. The research
possibilities invite the collaboration of historians
and political scientists in ways of knowing the
multiple sources, forms, and effects of education
policy. They also address contemporary policy
problems, if only by offering to reduce the
likelihood of uncalculated recycling of old
solutions.

NOTES

1. See Aaron Wildavsky, Speaking Truth to
Power (Boston, 1979), pp. 15-19, 35-36; Richard F.
Elmore and Milbrey W. McLaughlin, "Strategic Choice
in Federal Education Policy: The Compliance-
Assistance Trade-Off," in Policy Making in
Education, ed. Ann Lieberman and Milbrey W.
McLaughlin, Eighty-first Yearbook of the National
Society for the Study of Education 1 (1982):
173-94.
2. Richard J. Light and David B. Pillemer,
"Numbers and Narrative: Combining Their Strengths
in Research Reviews," Harvard Educational Review 52
(February 1982): 1-26. See also any issue of The
Public Historian, a journal of public history that
began publication in 1979 under the sponsorship of
the National Council on Public History and the

Society for History in the Federal Government.

3. For political science materials that discuss educational involvement in the context of other federal activities, see William H. Riker, Federalism (Boston, 1964); Daniel J. Elazar, The American Partnership (Chicago, 1962); S. Rufus Davis, The Federal Principle (Berkeley, 1978). Some of the most useful studies of federal education policy have been produced by economists and political scientists. See, e.g., Joel S. Berke and Michael W. Kirst, Federal Aid to Education: Who Benefits? Who Governs? (Lexington, Mass., 1972); Eugene Eidenberg and Roy D. Morey, An Act of Congress: The Legislative Process in the Making of Educational Policy (New York, 1969); Frederick M. Wirt and Michael W. Kirst, The Political Web of American Schools (Boston, 1972). Historical studies that emphasize the modern period include Rufus E. Miles, Jr., The Department of Health, Education, and Welfare (New York, 1974); Joel Spring, The Sorting Machine: National Educational Policy Since 1945 (New York, 1976); Timothy D. W. Connelly, "Education for Victory: Federal Efforts to Promote War-related Instructional Activities by Public School Systems, 1940-1945," (Ph.D. dissertation, University of Maryland, College Park, 1982). For topical histories, see George N. Rainsford, Congress and Higher Education in the Nineteenth Century (Knoxville, 1972); Gordon C. Lee, The Struggle For Federal Aid: First Phase (New York, 1949); Edward G. Bourne, The History of the Surplus Revenue of 1837 (New York, 1885); Barbara Finkelstein, "Uncle Sam and the Children: History of Government Involvement in Child Rearing," Review Journal of Philosophy and Social Science 3 (Winter 1978): 139-53.

4. Many of the sources for a comprehensive history are cited in National Advisory Committee on Education, Federal Relations to Education (Washington, D.C., 1931). Americo D. Lapati, Education and the Federal Government (New York, 1975), includes a comprehensive, if highly interpretive history. Also see Sidney W. Tiedt, The Role of the Federal Government in Education (New

York, 1966); Goerge B. Germann, <u>National Legislation Concerning Education</u> (New York, 1899); Spring, <u>Sorting Machine</u>.

    5. Ballard C. Campbell, <u>Representative Democracy: Public Policy and Midwestern Legislatures in the Late Nineteenth Century</u> (Cambridge, Mass., 1980); Olan Kenneth Campbell, "An Analysis of Provisions of State Constitutions Affecting Support of Public Schools," (Ed.D. dissertation, Duke University, 1954).

    6. <u>Congressional Globe</u>, 35th Cong., 2d Sess., 28 (1859), p. 718.

    7. Ibid., p. 720.

    8. See, e.g., John Eaton, <u>National Aid to Education</u> (Washington, D.C., 1879), pp. 6-10.

    9. Howard Cromwell Taylor, <u>The Educational Significance of the Early Federal Land Ordinances</u> (New York, 1922); Germann, <u>National Legislation</u>, pp. 13-22, 31-44.

    10. Henry Barnard, "Education and Educational Institutions," <u>Eighty Years' Progress of the United States</u> (New York, 1861), 1: 351-54.

    11. Daniel J. Elazar, "Federal-State Collaboration in the Nineteenth-Century United States," in <u>American Federalism in Perspective</u>, ed. Aaron Wildavsky (Boston, 1967), p. 205.

    12. Ibid., p. 210.

    13. See correspondence between the Indiana and California state school superintendents in State of California, <u>Annual Report of the State Superintendent of Public Instruction</u>, 1859, pp. 15-24.

    14. State of California, <u>Annual Report of the State Superintendent of Public Instruction</u>, 1861, pp. 26-27.

    15. Eaton, <u>National Aid to Education</u>, pp. 12-23; Fletcher Harper Swift, <u>Federal and State Policies in Public School Finance in the United States</u> (Boston, 1931), pp. 28-35; Germann, <u>National Legislation</u>, pp. 51-52; Bourne, <u>History of the Surplus Revenue</u>.

    16. Eaton, <u>National Aid to Education</u>, p. 32.

    17. Ibid.

    18. Elazar, "Federal-State Collaboration," pp.

206-7.
    19. Ibid., pp. 204-6.
    20. See Stephen E. Ambrose, Duty, Honor,
Country: A History of West Point (Baltimore, Md.,
1966), pp. 12-13; Sidney Forman, West Point: A
History of the United States Military Academy (New
York, 1950), pp. 15-35.
    21. U.S.,   Statutes at Large,   3:   516-17.
    22. Evelyn   C.   Adams,   American Indian
Education: Government Schools and Economic Progress
(New York, 1971), pp. 27-46.
    23. U.S. Congressional Globe, 30th Cong., 2d
Sess., 18 (1849), pp. 513-17, 542-43, 669-80.
    24. Ibid., 39th Cong., 1st Sess., 36 (1866),
pp. 2966-68.
    25. Donald R. Warren, To Enforce Education:
A History of the Founding Years of the U.S. Office
of Education (Detroit, 1974), pp. 47-54.
    26. Ibid., p. 82.
    27. Gene M. Lyons, The Uneasy Partnership:
Social Science and the Federal Government in the
20th Century (New York, 1969); also see A. Hunter
Dupree,   Science   and   the   Federal   Government
(Cambridge, Mass., 1957) and Mary O. Furner,
Advocacy   and   Objectivity: A   Crisis   in   the
Professionalization of American Social Science,
1865-1905 (Lexington, Ky., 1975).
    28. See, e.g., George R. Bentley, A History of
the Freedmen's Bureau (New York, 1974); W. E. B.
DuBois, Black Reconstruction in America: 1860-1880
(Cleveland, 1964); Leon F. Litwack, Been in the
Storm So Long (New York, 1979); Paul Skeels Peirce,
The Freedmen's Bureau (Iowa City, 1904).
    29. See Litwack, Been in the Storm So Long,
pp. 450-501; Bentley, History of the Freedmen's
Bureau, pp. 1-29; Thomas L. Weber, Deep Like the
Rivers: Education in the Slave Quarter Community,
1831-1865 (New York, 1978).
    30. Peirce, The Freedmen's Bureau, pp. 1-2;
DuBois, Black Reconstruction, pp. 637-69.
    31. DuBois, Black Reconstruction, pp. 660-67.
    32. National Advisory Committee on Education,
Federal Relations to Education, pp. 424-26; also pp.
117-23.

33. DuBois, <u>Black Reconstruction</u>, p. 637; Henry Steele Commager, "Review of <u>Rehearsal for Reconstruction</u>," <u>New   York   Times   Book   Review</u>, September 13, 1964, p. 6.

34. In the period after 1865 southern and border states typically rewrote constitutions adopted during Reconstruction. Maryland, for example, acquired new constitutions in 1864 and 1867, but the state school system, mandated initially in 1864, survived the change. See Philip Perlman, <u>Debates of the Maryland Constitutional Convention of 1867</u> (Baltimore, Md., 1923); also see Campbell, "Analysis of Provisions."

35. See, e.g., State of Maryland, <u>Second Annual Report of the State Superintendent of Public Instruction for the Year Ending June 30, 1867</u>. Superintendent Van Bokkelen compared the taxable wealth and school tax rates of each county and Baltimore City to demonstrate the necessity of a state school tax.

9

THE USES OF PAROCHIALISM COMPARATIVE AND CROSS CULTURAL STUDY

Harold Silver

Bulmershe College of Higher Education, Reading, England

There <u>are</u> benefits to being parochial, and American history of education <u>is</u> profoundly parochial. There are ways of suggesting that this latter judgment is not true, but none of them is convincing.

It can be pointed out, for example, that from the beginnings of a serious interest in the history of education in the United States there was an awareness of the European roots of American institutions; that C. F. Thwing, for instance, from his earliest contributions to the history of American universities, written in the 1900s, was concerned with the French, German, English, and Scottish influences. Up to the recent past, in the work of Jurgen Herbst and Carl Diehl this can be shown to have been the case. It can be argued that in the increasing concern of American historians of education with the history of the family and childhood, they have responded to the appeals of Bernard Bailyn and Lawrence Cremin to understand the wider social structures inherited and adapted by early colonial America. It also can be pointed out that in recent decades notable American historians of education have written about historical phenomena elsewhere, notably in Britain, including Michael B. Katz's work on official British education reports from the late nineteenth century to the 1960s, and Carl Kaestle in a comparative examination of elite attitudes toward schooling in early industrial England and America. Lawrence Stone has written about European literacy and schooling. Sheldon Rothblatt has relentlessly disentangled strands in English university education, and Robert Berdahl has explored the history of its administration. (1) The History of Education Quarterly has made determined and distinguished efforts to be international in scope.

American history of education profoundly influenced the early development of comparative education, although the basis of comparative education in historical studies of national systems virtually ground to a halt in the 1960s. In various ways and with different emphases and intentions, Robert Ulich, R. Freeman Butts, Henry Perkinson, and Fritz Ringer have written about the West, about civilization, and about Europe.

None of this, although convincing, answers the charge. Much of it relates to the world before the United States, or to the origins and roots of American institutions. Some of it is concerned with the world outside, but is in a sense parochial also, concerned with discrete events and situations, and suggesting little or no relevance to the historiography of education in the United States. If nineteenth- or twentieth-century Canada or Europe creeps into the American picture, hardly any of the resultant American writing is concerned with how historians outside the United States view their own or the American past, or with how such concerns might illuminate the history of education in the United States. Occasional articles in the History of Education Quarterly and occasional sessions at conferences of the History of Education Society, the American Educational Research Association (AERA) or elsewhere, do not basically alter the picture of the insularity of American history of education, and particularly of its historiography. There are sporadic exceptions, when historians discover, say, an Edward Thompson (and even then only his Making of the English Working Class), but generally speaking the literature of American history of American education does not draw on the historical problematics of the great elsewhere. That the United States may not be unique in this respect does not alter the argument.

There are benefits. The most important is undoubtedly that American historians of education have been able to tangle with political science, with sociology, with anthropology, with other kinds of history, and to test theories and assumptions against the hard edge of American experience. In approaching the social and political sciences in the 1960s and 1970s, many historians, whether in established traditions, or in the expanded frameworks set by Bailyn and Cremin, or in more radical "revisionist" or other molds, found themselves continually forced back into historical activity. They had to look at the historical evidence regarding education (whatever its definition) in Chicago or St. Louis, New England or the South, rural America or New York City. Historians found that they were still--despite, and conceivably even because of, entanglement with theory and ideology--trying to understand Philadelphia or the history of childhood, the historical relationship between ethnicity and class, the onward march of the public school. The weakness of parochialism is in the narrow range of definition or conceptual machinery that it encourages. The benefit of parochialism is that it makes it more difficult to lose sight of the pursuit of historical realities, especially the diversity of individual experience. The work of David Tyack and others in the late 1970s and early 1980s on truant officers, school superintendents, the "take off" of public education in rural and urban America and the nature of leadership in American public education, has emphasized the differences as much as the patterns. Kaestle and Vinovskis, in their study of nineteenth-century Massachusetts education, have done the same. The stress in the work of Grubb and

Lazerson on the complexities of the history of vocationalism and of the youth-work relationship has been similar.   Donald   Warren's   History, Education, and Public Policy is a collection that speaks to greater diversity of approach and intention than many publications of the previous decade. The growing emphasis on the experience of education speaks to the same diversity through the work of historians like Barbara Finkelstein, Geraldine Joncich Clifford's search for biography and autobiography, and an increased interest in the early American childhood experience of home and school. As in the work of Joseph Kett, the same is true of the experience of adolescence, school, and religious conversion.

The benefits of all this are obviously those of attention to transcommunity, transcultural experience within the American nation at different stages of development, a process extended since the 1960s to the problems raised by the reinterpretation of the educational history of the American poor, black, minority, and female. It may appear eccentric or harsh to call this range of work "parochial" when the United States is such a multi-cultural and multinational nation. Nevertheless, in the overwhelming majority of the published work, the frontiers of the research and of emphasis have been the frontiers of the United States. The contours of methodology have been overwhelmingly those of the United States, however radically those contours have changed since the early 1960s.

A variety of issues might be seen to surface. To what extent is the parochialism label an accusation or merely a recognition of the inevitable? In what ways might a cross-national, cross-cultural, or comparative educational history prove more attractive or feasible? Can sporadic or systematic concern with the history of other people's education, with their interpretation of their own history and education, have implications for educational historiography generally? Does not cross-cultural history inevitably become some kind of sociology or theory, concerned only with models and paradigms? Is not the real implication of the

accusation of national parochialism a recognition
that historians must concern themselves exclusively
or mainly with that level of unit or conceptual
analysis which their methodology can cope with--the
city, the cultural group, the state, the nation? Is
the role of historians beyond that perhaps to help,
to service the comparative, sociological and other
enterprises where their contribution is useful and
acceptable, and occasionally to synthesize as best
they can? What future is there for a comparative
social history of education?

The past relationship with comparative
education colors the question and the discussion.
Comparativists have on occasion seen themselves as
the inheritors of the historical exercise,
continuing--as Kandel put it--"the study of the
history of education and bringing that history down
to the present." They have grappled with problems
of cause and influence and borrowing across nations,
and with problems of juxtaposition and analysis,
what Bereday described as "the preliminary matching
of data from different countries to prepare them for
comparison." Such juxtaposition and comparison have
been pursued historically as well as with regard to
contemporary analysis of systems. Historically, the
comparative exercise has been one of determining,
portraying, and analyzing national educational
character or characteristics. A range of American
and European comparativists in the early twentieth
century scrutinized national structures,
legislation, and institutions, in pursuit of
concepts that would permit cross-national
comparisons--devising or adopting a conceptual
machinery that included "national psychology,"
centralized and decentralized systems, and
totalitarian and democratic states. From Michael
Sadler to Vernon Mallinson in Britain the search for
national character suggested patterns of
characteristic behavior. Mallinson, one of the last
spokesmen of the tradition, described the components
of national character as those "forces of cultural
continuity which determine the social behaviour of a
nation as a whole." In his search for the
fundamental, for the foundations of educational

systems, Kandel in the United States pursued "those forces that determine the character of an educational system." (2)

From the 1960s the nature of comparative educational scholarship changed amidst widespread expressions of relief and congratulation. Brian Holmes in Britain talked of the "transfer of attention from descriptive studies of national systems to analyses of problems," with the "methodological objective of replacing the names of systems and countries by the names of concepts and variables." Harold Noah in the United States graphically described how R. V. Winkle, Professor of Comparative Education, asleep from 1959, awoke in 1970 to a new style of work which had ousted the dominant forces of Kandel, Hans, and Lauwerys. We are not concerned here with the nature and problems of comparative education, but with the importance that this change represents, as a movement away from a certain kind of history, "from 'country characteristics' to 'problems,' from problems to the specification of relationships and formulation and testing of theories," away from the comparison of data toward a social science attempt to explain and predict rather than simply to identify and describe. (3) Comparative education, whatever fresh difficulties and confusions it was to face in defining problems and producing explanations, had abandoned its commitment to a history of national psychologies.

The new comparative education broke with a historical past at exactly the moment when American history of education plunged into its successive phases of historical revision. The new versions of history of education also discarded various cumulative traditions and conceptual frameworks. It is understandable, given the motivations to revise and to reassess, that American historians were preoccupied with the American and with Europe as largely pre-American. Some slight attention was paid to the nature of U.S.-Canadian educational relationships. At points where history has come closest to ideological debate, non-America has been largely used as supporting historical evidence, for example, the parallel roles of European pioneers of intelligence testing or the similarities of European education in relation to social stratification or corporate capitalism.   It is true, as we have suggested, that the History of Education Quarterly, the History of Education Society, the AERA, and others have presented historical concerns with education in other countries.   American scholars, including research students, have in recent years probed aspects of Latin American, African, European, and other educational pasts in new ways, but the emphasis has been most often on detailed investigation, which has been little concerned with its own historiography or with implications for American historiographical discussion.

It can, of course, be argued that educational historians in other countries, listening to the American debates of the 1960s and 1970s, were aware of a tradition and a profession that had approached new frontiers, that were at the cutting edge of historical controversy.   Historiographically, therefore, the rest of the world has in a sense had more to learn from American educational historians than Americans from others.   European and other historians, listening to the signals from Bailyn and Cremin, from Michael Katz's first books, from Roots of Crisis, from Schooling in Capitalist America, from Diane Ravitch's critique of the revisionists, from David Tyack's The One Best System, have been listening to historiographical reappraisal as well as focusing on American historical content.   Historians of education in other countries may be less parochial for that, and may have assumed perhaps that critical historiography was a short-lived American aberration, having more to do with American politics than history of education.   In Europe, a cross-cultural, comparative history of education has been no less sparse than in the United States, although Europe-wide and international encounters among educational historians have taken place. Whatever purposes European seminars or international conferences may have, the production of cross-national or cross-cultural history does not seem to be one of them. The directions of American history of education cannot, however, be determined by the weaknesses of other people's condition.

What is it that American historians of education may be said to have evaded outside the United States? The answer cannot be located in lists of "relevant" historical moments or texts elsewhere, as any such list may be belied by the scholar who has in fact taken or is taking an interest in some piece of Japanese, French, Islamic, British colonial, or other history. It is, of course, valuable for American scholars to be engaged in such historical tasks, but this does not necessarily point to any work that is in any sense cross-cultural. The argument here is not for a new, even a more advanced, form of juxtaposition. Nor is it merely a suggestion that Americans should be more familiar with specific, recent developments in history of education elsewhere, such as recent European work on the history of literacy or particular types of educational institution or impact or enterprise.

The notion of "cross-cultural history" or a "comparative social history of education" raises questions about what historians have to say to one another about education, about their definitions of the territory, about the strengths and weaknesses of their traditions, about their methodologies. Without such a starting point, cross-national history of any kind in this field must remain imprisoned in two basic difficulties: the reduction of the exercise to a persistently cumulative, nonanalytic level; or the temptation to analyze on the basis of concepts which have little or no foundation in historical analysis and debate. American and other historians in the 1960s and 1970s discovered how intractable their vocabularies were, how elusive was the machinery with which they attempted to order their perceptions of rediscovered and reevaluated past realities. They went through a multitude of interpretations based on such concepts as modernization and industrialization, bureaucracy, social control and centralization, only to find that the concepts proved troublesome and would not stay

still. One of the most instructive and attractive
features of American history of education in the
past two decades has in fact been the explicitness
of its concerns. Some of those concerns may have
seemed less relevant or acute to historians in some
other countries with older or better established
radical or Marxist traditions. But the American
reactions to and debates about them have provoked
fresh reflection on what "history" of "education" is
about. In the United States and elsewhere
historians have developed a need to hold and an
interest in holding dialogue with social and
political scientists grappling with the same
conceptual difficulties. At the same time, the
historian's difficulties and enterprise return
something to social science debate. A prerequisite
of cross-cultural history across frontiers therefore
has to be sustained dialogue among historians, not
only about the cross-cultural meanings and
possibilities, but also about cross-disciplinary
experience.

A second prerequisite is to identify useful
focuses of historical attention within this
framework, and to understand the processes of
historical interpretation involved. At one level
this is concerned with the changing meanings of
concepts. For example, "cultural transmission" was
a concept used in the United States by Monroe in the
1930s and Kandel in the 1950s, within their
historical-comparative framework. (4) The same
concept has also been central to the work of Pierre
Bourdieu and European sociologists since the 1960s.
The concept, the traditions, and the intellectual
basis of the analysis is an important frontier of
historical research in education, whether it be a
concept borrowed from social science literature or
one which, like industrialization, has become a
stock feature of "common sense" historical
vocabulary. An example of this conceptual basis of
comparative historical analysis would be that of
"accountability." The history of accountability in
United States education has to do, for example, with
relations between school and community, with the
testing movement, with changes in the direction from

which political pressures come, including increasingly the federal involvement with education since the early 1960s. The English version of such a history might include variants, although enormously different ones, of all of these, but it would relate directly to the existence of channels of public accountability that do not exist in the United States, including the emergence of a nationwide public examination system from the mid-nineteenth century, the roles of Her Majesty's Inspectorate over nearly a century and a half, and the relationship between local government and school governing bodies, including those of church schools. At this level of conceptualization, historians in a cross-cultural field would find themselves exploring not just parallel and juxtaposed traditions or data, but also different perceptions of educational and political relationships. The exercise in this case would be not the comparativist's interest in elucidating problems and issues, but a historical interest in describing and analyzing how processes converge conceptually and diverge in the social complexities of apparently common phenomena. The pursuit would not be national character and structures, but historical processes, as perceived by participants, as negotiated into historical statements.

Another example would be that of the different national experiences of institutions or processes that have common historical origins. The British and American social science movements of the second half of the nineteenth century both derive from an initiative taken in London in 1857, and for several decades had organizational and ideological affinities and relationships. In this case the cross-cultural interest to historians lies in the processes of transmission, interpretation and adaptation, the meaning of the relationship, as well as the divergent or parallel characteristics of the two national movements. The creation of sociological associations in the United States and in Britain, both in the mid-1900s and after the earlier social science movement had lost its momentum and identity, suggests similar questions, with the added interest of seeing how the two movements domesticated third-party inputs, such as that of Durkheim. Because the nineteenth- and twentieth-century developments in both countries were concerned with the definition of social institutions (including education) and with directly educational activities and concerns, it is historically helpful to disentangle their relationships to quite different emergent patterns of educational provision and control.

These prerequisites of cross-cultural history across frontiers must, therefore, suggest an extremely self-conscious historiography. An area such as the history of adolescence would indicate how self-conscious the rudiments of this history already are. Selwyn Troen's analysis of the American definition of adolescence in the first two decades of this century is explicitly described as an economic interpretation. The work of Joseph Kett and of John Gillis indicate how widely the historical net has to be cast in order to produce explanations of the emergence of a socially accepted category, including the conception of when childhood ends, what society wants from or owes to the child at that point, the changing nature of religious experience and authority, the emergence and nature of youth movements, changes in schooling, employment, the onset of puberty, the family, and attitudes toward vocational elements in curricula. (5) These and many other elements in such a history point both toward major social and cultural differences and toward profoundly controversial ground on which historians of many kinds have done battle. Cross-cultural analysis therefore becomes concerned in this way with the details of small-scale relationships, not just the larger patterns of past approaches.

Examples such as this indicate ways of attempting not just cross-national, comparative history, but the cross-cultural elements in such history. The emphasis could bring history of education closer to anthropological definitions suggested by Bailyn in Education in the Forming of American Society. Cross-cultural interests obviously go beyond institutional patterns into related areas of experience and explanation. Such interests include the social construction and acceptance of symbols, or what Margaret Mead discusses in terms of "images." Her educational images include different types ("expectations" might be a suitable word) of teachers in different eras and settings. The teacher, the schoolhouse, the student, however, are for historians more than types or images; they also represent varieties of expectation or experience shaped and conditioned in different ways. Numbers, argued E. H. Carr, count in history--citing a million discontented peasants as being historically important, where a single one is not. (6) Cultural history, however, cannot be dominated by the composite, by the known outcomes of scale. It is not concerned solely with images, socioeconomically defined groups, patterns of class relationships, the statistics of mobility. It is concerned with varieties as well as uniformities of experience, with teachers as well as the image of the teacher, the biographical reconstruction of schooling as well as its relationship to the social order. This sense of variety and individuality is difficult to hold in view when history of education is pulled toward the grand scale--the cross-national explanation of capitalism, the role of the school, the mechanisms of control. A historical approach to cultures and subcultures is pulled in both directions, toward patterns and theories, and toward the individual biography in specific settings. A cross-cultural history that leans on individual perceptions of the educational condition, as well as on cross-frontier resonances of larger dimensions, has yet to begin to be constructed. Here again, it is necessary to underline the critical historiography that would have to initiate such an exercise. If the purpose is to do more than anthologize, historians will have to debate the cultural complexities they wish and would be able to investigate.

The kind of concept that suggests all these levels at which comparative historical analysis might take place would be that of "reform." Reform historically points toward patterns of national policymaking, legislative and institutional change, and at that level is already strongly represented in the literature. Second, it points toward communities and experience, the declared and undeclared motivations of reformers, and the processes and agencies of change and resistance to change. At this level there are patchy and often fumbling attempts at description and analysis, often without clear targets and merits beyond superficial biography and local or institutional history. Third, it points to the most recent and difficult of the levels of historiography--that of ideology and of the conflicting bases of interpretation. At this level the attempt has often been to demythologize, to dispel accepted assumptions, to suggest the sociohistorical construction of categories and issues and purposes--whether elevating the actors to manipulative, conspiratorial positions, or relegating them to the role of puppets of underlying, larger forces. The history of reform motivation is perhaps the most complex and difficult kind of educational history, and for that very reason could perhaps benefit most from a new, comparative historical approach, supplementing and challenging untested and often untestable macrotheory and macrodiagnosis. The nature, elements, and boundaries of educational reform are the kind of research territory that could prove most profitable if subjected to rigorous cross-national scholarship and confronting the methodological and ideological problems it must inevitably raise.

Extensions of and debates about social and cultural history only recently have begun to intrude upon the history of education. The "cross-cultural" and "comparative social" dimensions of historical research will need to benefit from those intrusions if they are to become serious fields of analysis and research. A historical extension of this kind begins, therefore, with glances back at an older historical, comparative education, at anthropological and other social science debates, at national uniformities and diversities, and at the historiographical issues that the very intention provokes.

NOTES

1. Michael B. Katz, "From Bryce to Newsom: Assumptions of British Educational Reports 1895-1963," International Review of Education, (1965), 11: 287-302; Carl F. Kaestle, "Between the Scylla of Brutal Ignorance and the Charybdis of a Literary Education: Elite Attitudes towards Mass Schooling in Early Industrial England and America," in Schooling and Society: Studies in the History of Education, ed. Lawrence Stone (Baltimore, Md., 1976); Lawrence Stone, "Literacy and Education in England 1640-1900," Past and Present (1969), 42: 69-139; Sheldon Rothblatt, The Revolution of the Dons: Cambridge and Society in Victorian England (London, 1968); idem, Tradition and Change in English Liberal Education: An Essay in History and Culture (London, 1976); Robert O. Berdahl, British Universities and the State (Berkeley, Calif., 1959).

2. I. L. Kandel, The New Era in Education (London, 1954), p. 46; George Z. F. Bereday, "Reflections on Comparative Methodology in Education 1964-1966," in Scientific Investigations in Comparative Education, ed. Max A. Eckstein and Harold J. Noah (London, 1967), pp. 5-8; Vernon Mallinson, An Introduction to the Study of Comparative Education, 4th ed. (London, 1975), p. 263. (Originally published 1957); Kandel, New Era, p. 45.

3. Brian Holmes, "General Introduction," in Relevant Methods in Comparative Education, ed. Reginald Edwards et al. (Hamburg, 1973), pp. 8, 15; Harold J. Noah, "Defining Comparative Education," in Relevant Methods, p. 109; ibid., pp. 109-12.

4. Paul Monroe, A Text-Book in the History of Education (New York, 1935), p. 758; Kandel, New Era, p. 22.

5. Selwyn K. Troen, "The Discovery of the Adolescent by American Educational Reformers, 1900-1920: An Economic Perspective," in Schooling and Society; Joseph F. Kett, Rites of Passage: Adolescence in America 1770 to the Present (New York, 1977); John R. Gillis, Youth and History: Tradition and Change in European Age Relations 1770-

Present (New York, 1974).

     6. Margaret Mead, The School in American Culture (Cambridge, Mass., 1962); E. H. Carr, What is History? (London, 1964), p. 50. (Originally published 1961.)

10

THE GEOGRAPHIC IMPRINT
REGIONAL STUDY

Irving G. Hendrick
University of California, Riverside

While there has been no dearth of regional historical studies of education, the precise identity of regions, much less the significance of regional differences, is illusive. Geologists and geographers may decisively agree on what constitutes a region; historians do not. The nature of a region varies with the needs, purposes, and standards of the user. Most frequently it refers to fixed geographic regions of the United States, but some scholars have preferred to think of natural, cultural, and service regions, which are not always in identifiable geographic areas. Historians, not unlike journalists, sometimes speak simply of western views, in contrast presumably to eastern views.

New England alone among the geographical regions has enjoyed a fixed or agreed-upon identity. It always contains Connecticut, Maine, Massachusetts, New Hampshire, Rhode Island, and Vermont, while the specific composition of the South, Midwest, and Far West changes. (1) Texas is sometimes identified with the South, sometimes with the West. California is sometimes identified as part of the Far West, sometimes as a separate region. Most historians of California emphasize the uniqueness of that state's experience, but some argue that its history is typical of western and American experiences. (2) Earl Pomeroy, for one, has contended that California, Oregon, and Washington have more in common with the East than with the heartland states of the Midwest, owing primarily to the centrality of urban and commercial development on the Pacific coast. (3)

Regional definitions in France, by contrast, are generally more clearly delineated. (4) There linguistic and religious differences have produced regional distinctions not apparent in the United States, where transportation, communication, commerce, and a common language have brought the several regions relatively close together. While the Midwest and the Far West are widely perceived to be distinct regions of the United States, one might not expect a middle-aged, middle-class, Republican, Lutheran, cotton farmer from the central valley of California to hold significantly different educational values from a middle-aged, middle-class, Republican, Lutheran, corn farmer from Iowa. Indeed, while their views of education may be nearly identical, the California farmer's attitude and perceptions may differ markedly from those of the Oakland shipyard worker who lives barely 200 miles away.

Yet, when one turns from individual to group behavior, the significance of region becomes more apparent. The conclusion one must draw, it seems, is that regional distinctions become important mainly when a cluster of social and economic conditions and values are concentrated in a particular place. C. Vann Woodward and the late David M. Potter, both prominent historians of the American South and the Civil War, have maintained that the appropriate sphere of historical investigation is the group and its experience. (5) In the case of the South, it is plain that a group identity exists special to that region. Similarly, while Iowa farmers may constitute a force potent enough to shape educational policy in that state,

California farmers have not been in as dominant a position in a state of more diverse character.

The larger national focus attended to by historians in recent decades has tended not to emphasize the seemingly infinite variations of national life. At the same time, the long-term emergence of a national culture, attributable to education, travel, communication, intermarriage between persons of different regions, and so on, has not been accompanied by any convincing evidence that regional differences are diminishing. Like other interpretative modes for understanding American ways, regionalism has been the subject of scholarly faddism, but, unlike most other trends in historical study, it has been sustained through the years by romantic and nostalgic impulses, including a fair amount of myth, legend, and self-interest. (6)

Preferences, of course, change over the years. (7) Urban history and social history have enjoyed considerable popularity of late, while regional studies have occurred mainly in the context of something else. Rarely, however, are the categories exclusive. Regional, local, and even urban history all involve the study of population behavior, and, not infrequently, wind up as social history. David Tyack's George Ticknor and the Boston Brahmins, a story of a mid-nineteenth-century Boston intellectual, may be interpreted as essentially intellectual history, social history, nineteenth-century American history, history of higher education, or even as part of New England's regional history. (8)

The usefulness of a regional interpretation of history rests on the de Tocqueville-like belief that democracy needs the help of social institutions mediating between the central government and the individual. Beyond that, an awareness of regional variations is important for comprehending what is happening to the nation's population and its institutions. The regional idea, as was ably pointed out by Louis Wirth over thirty years ago, owes its scientific vitality to a naturalistic and empirically verifiable theory for the interpretation of history. (9) It affords a check on other theoretical explanations by keeping the investigator's mind fixed on the physical conditions of existence. The effort to define a great synthesis of American culture well may be frustrated by regional differences. It is hard to define the American character, or American education, when regional differences tend to overwhelm the similarities. Nevertheless, by itself, a regional interpretation that singles out the interconnections between the human habitat (region) and the complex fabric of ideas, social arrangements, and interpretations, is merely a one-factor theory. Taken alone it will furnish only a one-sided, and hence distorted, picture of social reality. (10)

Even historians who have no intention of writing regional history find regional differences compelling enough to address. Those working with data from colonial America, for example, have found it impossible to discuss educational developments of the period without distinguishing between events in New England and elsewhere. (11) During colonial times distinctions of a regional nature were more apparent than those of any other sort.

When a particular mix of social, religious, economic, and political factors come together in unique ways in particular places, conditions are right for the productive study of regional history. Although Frederick Jackson Turner is known primarily for his "frontier thesis," an interpretation that attributed America's strength and character to its constantly expanding march westward in conquest of new horizons, he is also properly credited with identifying an important methodological approach. It was he who first called attention to the study of population as a key for understanding the evolution of American society. (12)

The stream of regionalism has always run deep in the American character. Until the present century the most vivid manifestations of that consciousness were expressed through an explicit assumption of sectionalism. Before 1780 American leaders in the Continental Congress had already divided the Indian department and military districts into northern, middle, and southern sections. Over the succeeding century sectional and regional conflict helped to validate the perception of differences. Early in the present century some writers in the South and West complained of regional imperialism, asserting that their areas had been exploited through the economic and cultural dominance of the North or the East. (13) Easily the most vivid example of sectional differences was the Civil War. The unique economic and social impact of slavery was enough to assure distinct regional differences between North and South, and the full extent of those differences extended quite clearly to education. In the absence of knowledge concerning unique regional events and characteristics, any attempt to comprehend the development of common school education in the South would be a delusive exercise.

Relatively few recent studies have focused on the theory or methodology of regional study. None has focused explicitly on education. The major recent book on the general topic is Raymond D. Gastil's   Cultural Regions of the United States, which does include a section on the relationship of regional cultures to educational performance. (14) Two classic volumes from the 1930s represent the most comprehensive discussion of regionalism, as well as the most vivid illustration of an actual regional study. These include Odum and Moore's American Regionalism, published in 1938, and Odum's Southern Regions of the United States, published in 1936. (15) The latter includes a highly detailed analysis of southern life and institutions, which is still unmatched. Probably the most notable volume discussing regional studies between the late thirties and the early eighties was a collection of essays edited by Merrill Jensen in 1952, Regionalism in America, which ignored education completely. (16) Though intended primarily as a popular volume, the Congressional Quarterly's recent book, American Regionalism, contains much contemporary information on the population, politics, and economy of nine geographic regions. (17) Although historical and educational considerations are not ignored, they are not central to the volume.

As Gastil pointed out, there are regional differences in culture and behavior that influence educational performance. Regionally concentrated factors of family background, educational and achievement values, and teacher quality (as opposed to methods) are all perceived as determiners of educational performance. Regional patterns of life, it may be assumed, influence whether or not the population is isolated or not, and whether or not towns, schools, and churches are developed. These factors in turn influence the quality and extent of formalized education.

One is able to observe that the presence of towns, schools, and churches worked to produce an educated population in New England. They also worked well in a part of the West, that is, Utah and southeastern Idaho, where poeple of New England background predominated during the key period of first effective settlement. Gastil has suggested that in considering what influence regional cultural differences have on education, it is convenient to consider regional variation on two levels: (a) the level of minimum basic education, and (b) the level of elite or professional education. Data concerning literacy levels and school attendance constitute two sets of easily available information on regions. One can determine, for example, that in 1900 all states with an illiteracy level above 10 percent, and in 1960 above 4 percent, were in the South, while all states with illiteracy levels under 4 percent in 1900 and under 1 percent in 1960 were in a broad belt from Iowa to the Pacific Northwest. (18)

Basic differences in population characteristics and in the southern region's economy go far in explaining the unique realities and problems there. Relatively detailed data describing the educational level of the population by geographic regions give us a vivid clue as to how regional conditions have changed. While the American character and condition can also be explained in part through city versus country, black versus white, and industrial versus rural economy comparisons, it is clear that something important is lost if regional differences are ignored. As sociologist Nathan Glazer observed, "one should be as undesirous of having the distinctive Mormon region, for example, disappear into a homogeneous American mix, and lose its remarkable combination of high fertility, low infant mortality, high education, and highly developed nongovernmental self-help institutions, as of seeing a variant of some food disappear because it was being replaced by something similar but hardier and better adapted to long distance transportation and lengthy storage." (19)

Assuming that regional differences do exist, historians must resist the temptation to attribute one region's history to the nation as a whole. For all of its pioneering programs, New England is not the nation. Conditions unique to other regions helped to determine the nature and quality of schooling provided in those places. A sometime tendency of educational historians to generalize for the nation on the basis of data collected and analyzed from the industrial Northeast received a stiff rebuke from Wayne Urban in his History of Education Society presidential address in 1981. Acknowledging his own preference for using examples from the southern region, he asserted that some "work which we consider of national significance is merely regional in character, a phenomenon that some of us have correctly called Massachusetts Myopia." (20)

Regional history probably includes both the best and the worst of historical writing, simply because there is so much of it. The occupational hazards of regional historians most often are parochialism and descriptive essays devoid of interpretation. Their most commonly identifiable strength is an abundance of data. When characterized by volume of studies produced, regional study includes an overwhelming proportion of descriptive essays on some aspect of education in a single region. No special mode of analysis or theoretical orientation is common to such studies, other than the application of the traditional historical method. Like local history, regional history is the type most frequently pursued by persons with antiquarian interests. When the past is no longer relevant to the present, occupation with the past becomes antiquarianism. While not without value to the human spirit, antiquarian interest is not history, and it is rarely important for understanding contemporary education. Antiquarians are, on the other hand, likely to be close to their sources and thoroughly acquainted with them.

A less notable, but important, function of regional history is in supplying needed information for identifying significant policies and practices. Thus, while chronicling local and regional events may be more the work of the antiquarian than the historian, the latter should not malign those who provide some of the building blocks of history. Few colonial historians, for example, would deny the importance of the American Antiquarian Society's Early American Imprints. (21)

One special advantage of regional study lies in the rich collection of manuscript and documentary evidence maintained by numerous local and regional historical societies. In 1975 there were 3,964 historical societies and agencies operating in the United States, plus another 342 in Canada, many with libraries and historical journals. (22) It is the driving force of local and regional interest that keeps most of the historical societies operating. Except for the National Archives, most libraries, archives, and repositories of documents are almost by definition local or regional entities. Even the National Archives has been decentralized into regional centers throughout the United States. Numerous historical societies have collected and preserved documents essential for the productive study of educational history. One society in particular, the Massachusetts Historical Society, has published more of the basic documents on early American history than any other organization in the country. John L. Sibley's monumental three-volume Biographical Sketches of Graduates of Harvard University is one such resource. (23)

Most regional historical studies of education

are not justified on a firmly held and defined
theory of regionalism. Rather, it is simply that
drawing information from a single region makes the
historian's task manageable and permits pursuit of
the topic in some depth. The typical regional study
is primarily descriptive, focused on a single state,
firmly rooted in original sources, and published in
a   state   or   regional   history   journal.   The
History of Education Quarterly, easily   the   most
prominent history journal devoted exclusively to
topics in education, could not begin to publish the
number of history of education articles appearing in
state and regional history journals each year. (24)

To a limited extent, the relationship between
events in one state and those in another become
evident when looking at even a single state. The
founding of Michigan's state school system, for
example, involved a combination of unique and shared
or borrowed qualities. The system's outline was
taken   from   Massachusetts,   but   the   actual
constitutional provisions for education were more
comprehensive, enough so to allow Michigan to lead
the nation in establishing the legal precedent for
initiating and maintaining publicly supported high
schools.

The legal model of Michigan in turn had an
impact beyond the borders of that state, into
Kansas, for example. Wayne E. Fuller's "School
District 37: Prairie Community," a story of the
one-room school on the sod house frontier of Kansas
gets at an important part of that history. (25)
Data for the study were obtained from records
located in the Kansas State Historical Society and
in the Register of Deeds Office in the county seat
of Osborne County. Though focused on a particular
district in a single state, the insights one is able
to draw concerning the one-room school are probably
generalizable to much of the Midwest and even
beyond. It can happen on occasion that historians
working with data exclusive to a particular region
can develop a substantially new interpretation of
general significance. One such interpretation was
offered by Bernard Bailyn in The New England
Merchants in the Seventeenth Century in which he

suggested that it was the merchants, rather than the clergy, who were the prime movers of the fundamental changes within colonial society of that era. (26)

Comparative regional studies hold greater potential for yielding insight into national issues than do studies of a single region. Occasionally, that insight has been enriched by social science theory and method as well as regional historical data, as with sociologist Charles E. Bidwell's article "The Moral Significance of the Common School: A Sociological Study of Local Patterns of School Control and Moral Education in Massachusetts and New York, 1837-1840." (27)

While the larger significance of regional study does not become apparent until comparisons of policies and practices are made across regions, focus on a single region is justified for securing detailed knowledge concerning the structure of institutions and the relationships between institutions and individuals. Still, insight into the uniqueness of a particular region is not established until cross-regional comparisons are made. Unfortunately, while there are many regional studies, there have been few attempts to compare regional characteristics in American education, or to explain the impact of these characteristics on the general quality and conduct of the nation's schools. Correcting for these shortcomings, utilizing the considerable body of regionally collected resources coupled with a more effective utilization of data analysis techniques developed by social scientists, constitutes an agenda for the future.

With few exceptions, regional history has suffered more from an overreliance on the safe chronicling of events than from misinterpreting them. Population data, including level of schooling attained, literacy rates, and age at leaving school should be analyzed on both a local and regional basis. In pursuing this work, educational historians need to be conscious of relationships between education and other social phenomena and the role of educative agencies other than schools. They need not, however, apologize for focusing on the school as an institution.

In defining a research agenda for regional study, it would be useful at first to concentrate on several categories of questions relating to the institution of schooling, and another set of questions focusing on the results of education, primarily schooling, for individuals and the society. Concerning the school as an institution, it would be helpful to learn how public schools in the several regions resolved conflicts between group claims, for example, religious, socioeconomic and racial, and public claims concerning the responsibilities of citizenship.

Essential to comprehending the meaningfulness of state school laws are studies, both single state and regional, concerning the extent to which enforcement was realized. Compulsory attendance laws, for example, were essentially meaningless in the absence of enforcement, but enforcement itself produced an entire set of new problems. Although studies of state school systems have fallen from favor in recent decades, studying them to determine regional patterns could yield a number of insights, including a clearer perspective on who stood to gain from the development of centralized systems.

The financing of education, including higher education, is an example of a field where an abundance of information is available for cross-regional studies. What, for example, has stimulated the substantial unevenness in the quality of public and private universities across the several regions of the nation, and what has been the impact of those differences on the social and economic development of the region?

One area in which a state or regional approach would seem to be the only approach possible concerns the effectiveness of various state regulatory boards and commissions, which control the establishment of curricula, the adoption of textbooks, and the licensure of teachers. In California, for example, it well may have been that the firm resolve of state school officials to implement "progressive education" from the 1920s through the 1940s helped to set the stage for an unusually strong reaction against that theory during the 1960s and 1970s. The fate of teachers, including inquiry into their preparation and the conditions under which they work, is another area well suited to regional study, as is the study of state teacher organizations, which exist presumably for the advancement of the teacher's cause and for public schooling in general.

There are also national educational concerns that can best be examined on a regional basis. One might explore, for example, the extent to which the states had standardized curricula as a result of the influence of national textbook publishers. Similarly, it would be valuable to learn the extent to which certain textbooks became a dominant influence on the curriculum of various regions.

Apart from a host of questions relating to society's stake in education are questions concerning the interrelationship between the public and private purposes of education, including the impact that school and family relationships had on literacy and school attendance. While the influence of eighteenth-century private and church-related schools has been studied in some detail, relatively little is known about the role of private schools during the past 100 years. Both their role and the extent of their use varied appreciably from region to region.

Some of the most important questions of those that are framed in local and regional settings concern the effects of schooling on the lives of citizens. Of special interest is the nature of schooling in the several regions and its effect on racial, ethnic, and other minority groups of the population. (28) Much more can be learned through a study of biographical data, employment records, and oral history accounts.

Regardless of the topic pursued or the data reviewed, the essence of a study's regional character cannot be finally determined until cross-regional comparisons are made, which reveal either the presence or absence of regional uniqueness. In its narrowest and purest form, regional history can be justified only in terms of unique regional qualities. Historians focusing on regional study, like their colleagues approaching the past from other perspectives, are forced to realize that in history there are no final victories, no absolutes, no finally defined truths. There are only approximations and interpretations of truth, which serve to extend our grasp of the past. Regional study has contributed--and continues to contribute--much of the diverse detail that serves to qualify, define, and explain the national character.

NOTES

1. Geographic regions of the United States identified by the Editorial Research Reports include New England, The South, Rocky Mountain West, Great Lake States, Middle Atlantic States, Pacific Northwest, California, The Plains States, and Washington, D.C. American Regionalism (Washington, D.C., 1980). Gastil, on the other hand, divided the nation into thirteen regions: New England, The New York Metropolitan Region, The Pennsylvania Region, The South, The Upper Midwest, The Mormon Region, The Interior Southwest, The Pacific Southwest, The Pacific Northwest, Alaska, and the Hawaiian Islands. Raymond D. Gastil, Cultural Regions of the United States (Seattle, 1975).

2. See Gerald D. Nash, "California and Its Historians: An Appraisal of the Histories of the State," Pacific Historical Review, 50 (November 1981): 410. The entire issue of that number is devoted to western state historiography.

3. Earl S. Pomeroy, The Pacific Slope: A History of California, Oregon, Washington, Idaho, Utah, and Nevada (New York, 1965), p. 95.

4. Detail concerning French regions is found in Pierre Goubert's essay, "Local History," in Historical Studies Today, ed. Felix Gilbert and Stephen R. Graubard (New York, 1972), pp. 300-19.

5. C. Vann Woodward, The Burden of Southern History, rev. ed. (Baton Rouge, 1968); David M.

Potter, "The Historian's Use of Nationalism and Vice Versa," American Historical Review, 67 (July 1962): 924.

6. See Laurence R. Veysey, "Myth and Reality in Approaching American Regionalism," American Quarterly 12 (Spring 1960): 31-43.

7. For a comprehensive discussion of contemporary trends in historical scholarship, see Michael Kammen, The Past Before Us: Contemporary Historical Writing in the United States (Ithaca, 1980).

8. David B. Tyack, George Ticknor and the Boston Brahmins (Cambridge, Mass., 1967).

9. Louis Wirth, "The Limitations of Regionalism," in Regionalism in America, ed. Merrill Jensen (Madison, 1952), pp. 381-93.

10. Ibid., pp. 381-82.

11. For example, see Lawrence A. Cremin, American Education, the National Experience, 1783-1886 (New York, 1980), pp. 150-63.

12. Frederick Jackson Turner, The Frontier in American History (New York, 1931); idem, The Significance of Sections in American History (New York, 1932). Turner's emphasis on regionalism was shared by other early twentieth-century historians, as was his interpretation that the origin of American uniqueness and greatness was attributable to westward expansion. See Richard M. Andrews, "Some Implications of the Annales School and Its Methods for a Revision of Historical Writing about the United States," Review 1 (Winter-Spring 1978): 171-73.

13. Western journalists promoted a lively interest in regionalism for forty years prior to the Civil War. Probably the most prominent historian to emphasize unique western qualities and problems after Turner was Walter Prescott Webb. See his The Great Plains (Boston, 1936); Divided We Stand (New York, 1937); The Great Frontier (Boston, 1952).

14. Gastil, Cultural Regions, pp. 116-27.

15. Howard W. Odum and Harry E. Moore, American Regionalism (New York, 1938); Odum, Southern Regions of the United States (Chapel Hill, N.C., 1936).

16. Merrill   Jensen,   ed.,   _Regionalism   in America_ (Madison, 1952).

17. Editorial   Research   Reports,   _American Regionalism_ (Washington, D.C., 1980).

18. Gastil, _Cultural Regions_, p. 118.

19. Ibid., p. x.

20. Wayne J. Urban, "History of Education: A Southern Exposure," _History of Education Quarterly_ 21 (Summer 1981): 133.

21. Clifford K. Shipton, ed., _Early American Imprints_ (Worcester, Mass., 1955-).

22. Donna   McDonald,   comp.,   _Directory: Historical Societies and Agencies in the United States and Canada_, 10th ed. (Nashville, 1975).

23. John   Langdon   Sibley,   _Biographical Sketches of Graduates of Harvard University_ (Boston, 1933).

24. All geographic areas of the United States are rich in state and regional history journals. A few examples from the South alone include _The Alabama   Review_, _Arkansas   Historical   Quarterly_, _Florida Historical Quarterly_, _Georgia Historical Quarterly_, _Journal of Southern History_, _Maryland Historical   Magazine_, _North Carolina   Historical Review_, _South Carolina Historical Magazine_, _Virginia Magazine of History and Biography_, and _West Virginia History_.

25. Wayne E. Fuller, "School District 37: Prairie Community," _Western Historical Quarterly_ 12 (October 1981): 419-32.

26. Bernard Bailyn, _The New England Merchants in the Seventeenth Century_ (Cambridge, Mass., 1955).

27. Charles   E.   Bidwell,   "The   Moral Significance of the Common School: A Sociological Study of Local Patterns of School Control and Moral Education in Massachusetts and New York, 1837-1840," _History of Education Quarterly_ 6 (Fall 1966): 50-91.

28. An example of the careful study needed, utilizing both historical and social science methods, is D'Ann Campbell, "Was the West Different? Values and Attitudes of Young Women in 1943," _Pacific Historical Review_ 46 (August 1978): 453-63. On the factor of optimism, for example, Campbell found that is was the high proportion of educated

people living in the West that made western attitudes different, while on personality and morality factors, there was a western regional effect.

11

EDUCATION AND THE CITY
URBAN COMMUNITY STUDY

James Sanders
College of Staten Island, City University of New York

Serious study of the American urban educational past has been with us for over a decade. But despite a much-heralded beginning and the publication of a dozen or so impressive scholarly books, it does not appear to have jelled into one of educational history's readily identifiable subdisciplines. Practically no discussion of its unique nature has taken place; and, based on analysis of what has thus far been produced, one would be hard put indeed to venture a definition, much less identify present trends or suggest a likely and desirable future. In part urban educational history's amorphous condition stems from a failure to consciously and reflectively nurture its roots in urban history generally; but in part the ambiguity also results simply from the confusion reigning in urban history itself. To understand this situation one has to look first at the nature, development, and present condition of urban history, and then consider urban educational history as an aspect of that phenomenon. Only then can some patterns come into focus and a rational agenda for future research be laid out. The following pages

will attempt to do just that--to look first at the
development and present condition of urban history
as a discipline, then at the development of urban
educational history as an aspect of that discipline,
and finally make some projections for the future of
research in urban educational history.

After a faltering start in the 1950s, the study
of urban history came into its own during the
sixties and early seventies. Prompted perhaps by
the revelation of the 1960 census that
three-quarters of the United States population then
lived in urban communities, and by the painful
awareness that urban problems had come to dominate
the public consciousness, American social historians
turned increasingly to the city as the focus of
interest. Urban history quickly became the glamour
stock of the scholarly publication world in American
history, and any new book with "urban" or "city" in
its title was sure to attract attention. American
colleges and universities scrambled to hire at least
one sample of this newly attractive commodity coming
out of graduate history departments--a specialist in
urban history. (1)

But, as with any new disciplinary focus, urban
history's remarkable rise was also accompanied by a
period of considerable confusion and debate. The
confusion resulted largely from a lack of clarity
over just what constitutes the study of urban
community. In the wake of guidelines suggested by
Arthur Schlesinger's seminal 1949 article on "The
City in American Civilization," the first modern
urban historians focused on urbanism as a unique
factor in the American experience. Richard Wade,
for example, argued in one book that the frontier
cities dominated the nation's westward movement and
life on the frontier, and in yet another that in the
South urbanism and slavery as an institution had
become incompatible even before the Civil War.
These and other urban studies dealt with urbanism as
what has appropriately been called "process"; that
is, they looked at ways in which the urban
experience itself, as distinguished from nonurban,
affected the lives of Americans both inside the city
and out. In this approach, only the historian who

focuses on those aspects of the American experience
that are uniquely urban--the urban process--can
properly be called an urban historian. (2)

In contrast, possibly because of the magic then
associated with urban history, numerous other
studies called themselves urban histories when in
fact they used the city merely as a convenient
"site" for researching issues that were not uniquely
or often even peculiarly urban. The examples are
legion, and even justly celebrated works like
Stephan Thernstrom's studies of Boston and
Newburyport used these two cities not primarily to
analyze an urban issue but as convenient locations
to look at an issue that is not specifically urban
at all, namely, occupational mobility. Use of the
city in this way has led to considerable confusion
over the proper scope of urban history. Does choice
of the city merely as a convenient way to narrow the
focus of investigation or to carve out a manageable
data base constitute urban history? This issue of
urban history as process versus urban history merely
as site remains unresolved. (3)

More fundamentally, continuing discussion and
debate has focused on differences between the
so-called "new" urban history and the "old." (4) At
the surface this argument has centered largely on
the question of method, with the "new" history
dealing heavily and sometimes exclusively in
quantitative methodology and the "old" dealing often
exclusively with the more traditional historical
sources that provide material for so-called
narrative history. But beneath the methodological
differences lie more substantive issues. The
recourse to quantitative methods was prompted in
part by the desire to study the past of the "common
man," who left few if any written records and whose
life could only be recaptured in numbers duly
recorded in census data, financial statements,
employment registers, and the like. Thus, the
desire to write urban history from "the bottom up"
led almost inevitably to the use of numbers. The
more traditional urban historians do not generally
quarrel with this, since they also embrace the quest
for understanding the past of the common man.

But they often do quarrel with a further step the quantification movement has taken: the attempt to use quantification techniques to test and to apply sophisticated contemporary sociological theory to the past. This attempt has focused on several research areas. One deals with urban ecology, spatial configurations in relation to urban life, which is of minor concern here. Another became preoccupied with questions related to equality of opportunity in American life, focusing primarily on the issue of social mobility, mainly occupational mobility. While the study of other, less cosmic urban issues went on without fanfare, the study of social mobility, possibly because it dealt with an issue of such central concern to Americans and because it used such an arcane methodology, received a share of attention over the past decade disproportionate to its quantity, and, some say, its importance. Its place in the sun now seems threatened by the investigation of modernization theory, testing the thesis that industrialization and urbanization have radically alienated human life and the familiar institutions that supported it. But, whether under the guise of mobility or modernization, the sociological approach to urban history has not been readily accepted by many historians.

Thus, the differences between the "new" and the "old" urban history have not been resolved. Argument over the use of quantitative techniques has distilled into the question not of whether they have a place in urban history, but how big a place. More fundamentally, differences remain over the application of social science theory to the study of urban history. Some argue that history studies unique events, and consider the attempt to explain the urban past according to laws of human behavior to be mere scientism rather than science, and thereby a detraction from the properly humanistic character of historical study.

Meanwhile, as with all glamour stocks, the glamour of urban history itself has partially faded. It is difficult, after all, to stay glamorous forever. At least part of the declining lustre can be traced no doubt to the directions briefly outlined above, partially to the failure in defining the proper scope for urban history, but particularly to the preoccupation with quantification techniques and their use to test social theory. Unlike the literary products of the earlier urban histories, the newer studies, especially those most lionized within the profession, became progressively less readable and less understandable even to historians. Neither the quantitative methods nor the theories they were used to test seemed to interest the literate, interested reader. Ironically, the very attempt to write the history of the common man resulted in history intelligible only to very uncommon men. (5)

Then, too, urban history has faded somewhat in the face simply of new interests in the general field of social history. Increasingly, the study of American social history has turned to ethnicity, women, the family, labor, and to some extent childhood. Often enough these areas of research have used the city as site, but the urban aspect has taken second place to the dominant interest in family or women or labor and the like. In fact, the urban base of the study sometimes appears incidental, merely providing a convenient parameter for the main event. At other times, issues intimately related to urban environment as such do emerge--the question of whether urban life served as a liberating force for women, for example. (6)

Thus, both because of persistent theoretical differences about its nature and because of newly emergent interests, urban history has endured confusion and, especially more recently, partial eclipse. These same developments, though appearing under sometimes different guises, can be discerned in one of urban history's offshoots--urban educational history.

Educational history was just beginning to struggle for some true degree of scholarly legitimacy in the years when urban history came into its own. Educational historians were not slow to ride the new wave. And understandably so, since developments in contemporary urban education were prompting urgent questions about the past. Revelations of declining achievement, mushrooming absentee and dropout rates, explosive confrontations over racial and ethnic differences, concern about bureaucratic, impersonal control, and the like, aroused not only desire for solutions but questions about how things had gotten that way. Thus, both because of urban history's general popularity and the pressing practical need for more understanding of the urban educational situation, urban educational history shared in urban history's glamour. (7)

The urban educational histories of this period fell vaguely within the urban process framework, though neither exclusively nor very self-consciously. Thus, for example, some historians saw the development of antebellum urban public education in the context of a characteristically urban struggle, reflecting the effort to provide services and impose controls that had not been necessary in rural America. Others placed educational developments in late nineteenth-century cities within the framework of urban political and social reform. Several authors dealt with racial, ethnic, and religious diversity related to education which was not unique in the city, but certainly had special emphasis there. Yet, within educational history there was little or no discussion of possible unique features that might conscitute urban educational history as opposed to nonurban. In this sense urban educational history shared the confusion of urban history generally, though with less self-consciousness. (8)

The debate between the "new" and the "old" urban history also largely bypassed the urban educational historians. Or rather, the debate took on a different form. For one thing, quantification played much less of a role; the distinction between historians who count and those who do not was never sharply drawn. The question of applying contemporary social theory to the past, though, did take on a unique cogency. Concern over the question of equal opportunity in American society preoccupied much of educational history during this period, just as it did in the "new" urban history. But it took less the shape of occupational mobility studies and more the investigation of the school as an instrument of social control versus individual liberation. In fact, equality of opportunity provided the background for the major ideological debate during this period as historians argued over whether urban public school systems had been altruistically created to elevate the urban under class or devised simply to train the new urban proletariat into quiet submission and prepare them for their appointed role as the drones of the urban beehive. The argument escalated into a pitched battle between the "revisionists," with their ideological assumption of a public school conspiracy against the children of the common man, and the "traditionalists," with their assumption that the public schools represented an innocent expression of the American dream in its purest form. The debate has ended in a stalemate for the protagonists and boredom for the less ideological bystanders. Like the mobility studies, it has left the average interested reader no longer interested. (9)

In the meantime, as the glamour of urban educational history has somewhat faded along with its parent, urban history, an interesting new development has taken place, again paralleling that within urban history itself. After the earlier spate of activity focusing on the development of educational institutions and programs in specific cities, much of the recent work that deals with education at all deals with it as part of the new interest in the history of women, the family, ethnic minorities, and the like. Thus, the study of Italian acculturation in Buffalo or Polish acculturation in Philadelphia might include a section on education. Or a book on the experience of women in cities might include analysis of their educational opportunities and experiences. Or one might hear a prominent historian of the family call for exploration of the "relationships between the family and other urban institutions--social welfare agencies, labor unions, educational institutions--all of which are critical for understanding of the urban process." Thus, increasingly one finds the study of education in works not clearly or primarily identified as educational research. (10)

This, in broad outline, summarizes the past and present state of urban educational history against the background of developments in urban history generally. It also provides a solid base and an intellectual framework for suggesting the following future directions.

First, in the effort to keep urban educational history not only in the mainstream of American history where it has only recently found acceptance, but to help it contribute something of lasting value to the study of urban history, educational historians must more consciously focus on those issues that deal with the relationship of human behavior to the urban environment, that is, those issues having to do with the urban process itself. Urban educational history has to become more self-consciously urban. While the use of the city simply as the site for the study of some educational issue can certainly be justified and may have its value, it does not in itself advance the understanding of how the urban environment itself affected and was affected by educational issues. This latter constitutes the hard core of urban history; and to date not many of these issues have been looked at, nor a sufficient number of case studies examined, to draw any significant conclusions.

It is not the purpose here to offer a comprehensive list of topics to be researched, but to stress the need for continuing research on the urban process related to education. The following examples merely illustrate some of the uniquely urban educational issues that ought to be investigated more fully in the coming years. The initiation of urban educational systems, for example, in antebellum America in many respects constituted just one aspect of the struggle to provide newly needed urban services. In many ways the urban public school emerged as one piece with the creation of sewer and water systems and police and sanitation departments, which were needed to make the new urban way of life viable. Likewise, the great educational reforms of the late nineteenth and early twentieth centuries were merely one aspect of the progressive urban reform that shook American cities to their foundations. We still know little about such fundamental issues of urbanization in the United States. The tension between the American ideal of community control and the development of urban educational bureaucracies is still imperfectly understood either in past or present. Regarding political organization, the historic drive for urban autonomy versus state control as it applied to education has been studied little, yet could shed much light on present issues. And, perhaps most fundamental, the historic tension between two basic American educational beliefs, that in the neighborhood school versus that in the public school as the common crucible for the nation's immense socioeconomic, ethnic, racial, and religious diversity, begs examination. Only the cities experienced this tension because residential segregation made the neighborhood school and the integrated school mutually exclusive. Other peculiarly urban questions remain virtually unexplored, such as the relationship between suburbanization and schooling, or that huge area having to do with the city as educator, everything from institutions of high culture like museums to the streets themselves. Available evidence indicates that peculiarly urban activities like hawking newspapers and bootblacking may have provided more education for many children than the schools provided. (11)

But, to repeat, whatever the specific topic, the issues that ought to be explored are those that deal with educational developments in some way unique to the city. Only by sharpening the focus in this way can urban educational history hope to develop some degree of coherence and to contribute anything of lasting value to our understanding not only of education but of the city in American history.

This same principle should be applied to the

trends already set in motion by the growing interest in ethnicity, women, the family, and probably even the worker. Here urban as process and urban as site easily become confused, though each of these areas provides ample and important opportunity to study the urban process. In one sense, to study the acculturation of Italians in New York, for example, might seem to use the city simply as a convenient parameter. Much easier, after all, to look at Italians in a single location than in the entire United States. Yet, studying the Italians in New York provides a basis for comparing their adaptation in Boston, or San Francisco, or Chicago, or even Buenos Aires. Out of such comparisons might come unexpected conclusions. To cite one example, it is clear that the Irish immigrants adapted to American life, including educational opportunity, quite differently in Boston than they did in Chicago or New York, which suggests significant differences in the respective urban environments. Pursuit of such differences will contribute to our understanding both of the urban and the educational past. When one turns to the history of women or the family, the possibility of a unique urban dimension becomes even clearer. Thus, studying the education of women in one city might look like using urban as site, and it could be. But if one looks at how urban life itself affected the education of women, then the study becomes truly urban in its dimensions. The questions become: Did life in the city break down the traditional assumptions about the education of women? Did it have a liberalizing effect? Or did it merely set the stage for further feminine exploitation of a different kind, this time in the factories and the marketplace or in the confinement of the nuclear home? Similarly with the family. Did urban life change American family patterns? Did it weaken the family? Did the weakening call forth the greater importance Americans have placed on their schools as a substitute for the lost educational force of the family? Or did the schools become instead a focus for family and community concern and identity in the struggle to hold off the creeping impersonality of the city? (12)

In a word, the recent intense interest in ethnicity, women, family, and the like should be embraced as a healthy trend in urban educational history, even though education plays only a part in the overall study. In examining the adaptation of different ethnic groups to the American city one must ask how they dealt with educational questions. In researching the adaptation of the family to the new urban environment, one must ask questions of education and schooling. In analyzing the developing relationships of women to the urban environment, one essential aspect obviously must be educational opportunity. All this has begun. And the serious inclusion of education in questions not having to do specifically or centrally with education marks educational history's coming of age. The only dubious aspect of the trend is that to keep informed about educational history it will no longer be sufficient to look simply for studies having "education" or "school" in their titles.

These and other aspects of the urbanization process as it related to education should be studied in much more detail, particularly in a variety of cases that extend beyond the already much-studied major cities like Boston, New York, Chicago, Philadelphia, and a few others. Recent trends in American urban history indicate a shift toward the study of smaller cities, southern cities, and western cities. The trend represents a healthy effort to lay the groundwork for a broader understanding of the urban phenomenon. All the world, after all, was not Philadelphia, and certainly not Boston. Much insight about the past of urban education could be gained through the study of these previously neglected urban areas. (13)

The current and, it is hoped, future emphasis on family, ethnicity, and related topics in urban history will also help serve as a needed corrective to the preoccupation with mobility studies that characterized the past ten years and more of urban history. The corrective will come in two ways. The first and obvious one is to broaden the horizons beyond mobility alone. But the second, and probably more important, is to serve as a corrective within

the mobility study movement itself. For the
interest in mobility properly goes on, and
educational historians must continue to attend to it
because of the absolutely essential link between
education and mobility in American thought and
practice. But the experienced shortcomings of
earlier mobility studies have now spawned a new
direction with new sets of questions more fruitful
for history in general and for educational history
in particular.

The earlier mobility studies started from the
assumption that upward social mobility constituted
the universally accepted goal in America. Following
this assumption, any person or group of persons not
moving upward at a rate on a par with others had to
be considered relative failures. Thus, for example,
the Irish of Boston or Newburyport, because they did
not experience occupational mobility at a rate
comparable with others, had to be thought of as not
participating fully in the American dream. And the
only questions left unanswered were the reasons
behind the failure. Why were the Irish less mobile?
Was it because of negative baggage they brought with
them? Because of some hereditary shortcoming? Or
perhaps because of anti-Irish discrimination in the
marketplace?

But without completely discounting any of these
possibilities, the assumptions on which these
studies rested precluded attention to the actual
economic profile painted by the Irish, which pointed
to a different explanation. The evidence indicated
that the Irish had made economic choices that did
not fit the expected pattern. Instead of investing
what money they had in the education of their
children, they bought homes. Instead of entering
the higher risk occupations in the world of
business, they settled for lower paying but more
secure positions in municipal government and civil
service. In other words, they seemed to be making
economic choices not motivated primarily by upward
mobility, but by some other set of values. (14)

Discovery of this fact, which has been found
true of other subgroups in American society as well,
has focused attention on the possibility that upward

mobility has not played the totally dominant role in the American value system that had earlier been assumed. More fruitfully, it has begun to focus on the variant value systems that might have motivated subgroups in American society, influencing their economic decisions, and derivatively their educational choices. The issue opens up yet another aspect of pluralism in American life. What has been exposed here appears to be the persistence of subcultural value systems that modified the dominance of the mainstream culture. That not every group progressed at the same rate does not necessarily indicate inequality of opportunity but simply a difference in the value placed on "getting ahead." Much work remains to be done in this interesting and highly significant area, particularly in its educational applications. (15)

The prospect of research on the attitudes and value systems of subgroups in American society presents yet another kind of challenge and opportunity. The mobility studies of the so-called "new" urban history relied heavily, in fact almost exclusively, on quantitative methods. They could well do so. For as long as one assumed that all Americans shared a like attitude toward "getting ahead," what remained was to count the results. The counting was sometimes difficult because of scarce records, a fact that sometimes led to questionable outcomes even after the development of elaborate methodologies. And the result was a series of highly technical, largely unreadable studies that drew much criticism and cast doubt on the value of quantitative methods in general.

The need now to question the assumption that all Americans shared the same attitudes toward mobility also opens up a rich possibility to forge a marriage of convenience between the powerful quantitative methods developed in urban history over the past decade, and the more traditional use of documentary evidence of a more literary nature. The latter might include methodologies borrowed from other disciplines such as anthropology. Because once differences in mobility, which can only be discovered by quantitative methods, have been established, then possible differences in attitude, which can in the last analysis only be fully documented by other methodologies, must be employed. A fusion of numbers with everything from ethnic newspapers and literature, to immigrant letters, folk songs, sermons, and the like would make for powerful and interesting history. (16)

Still another lesson can be learned, perhaps, from what now appears to be the perceived shortcoming of the earlier mobility studies in urban history and the dead end of the revisionist controversy in educational history. That is the danger of beginning from too fixed assumptions. If one starts from a particular assumption, that all Americans shared the "getting ahead" motive, for example, then not only will the conclusions be unduly influenced by the assumption, but the possibility of fresh insight is impeded. This, of course, is the perennial danger that historians labor under, and it constitutes a basic dilemma. Everyone operates from assumptions. The danger lies in not being sufficiently aware of the assumptions and in accepting them as unimpeachable.

The danger has been compounded in recent years by overindulgence in the ideological underpinnings of historical research in education, particularly in social history. If one begins from the assumption that public schools were created to hold the masses in check, then ample evidence can be found to support that theory. If one begins from the assumption that they were created out of the democratic impulse to give everyone a fair chance, then ample evidence can be found to support that theory too. The problem lies not with which assumption one starts from but with starting from such a fixed assumption in the first place. The tendency drives the "social controllers" and the "equal opportunists" into mutually exclusive positions, and all are then expected to choose sides. Ideological warfare seldom allows any room for compromise. The unhappy result is that truth is sacrificed to a cause, and the richly veined historical records are selectively and miopically mined. The profession now appears to have emerged

from that particular ideological war, out of
weariness if for no other reason.

But the danger of a new ideology that will then
spawn its counter ideology hovers ever in the
foreground. "Modernization" theory seems the most
likely candidate, as the sides are drawn between
those who would explain everything in terms of the
impersonalization brought on by urbanization and the
industrial revolution and those who, perhaps
offended by the totalitarian nature of every new
ideology, look for evidence that in fact
industrialization and urbanization served as
liberating, individualizing forces in releasing the
human race from the tyranny of the clan. In other
words, every ideology creates its counter ideology,
and the two are then driven into opposite positions.
The loser, again, is the richer reality of the
historical truth.

The present situation calls for a bit more
modesty along the ideological front. Research in
the area of urban educational history should avoid
ideological extremes of whatever nature, whether
revisionist or traditionalist, modernist or
antimodernist. Understanding, interpretation, and
explanation should be pursued at a less cosmic
level. What is needed in American urban educational
history for the 1980s are individual urban studies,
conducted piece by piece, with careful analysis and
comparison, but with determined resistance to the
temptation of oversimplified, synthetic
interpretations of the American urban educational
past.

Finally, all the above suggestions for the
immediate future of American urban educational
history appear to fit together in complementary
fashion. First, if educational historians wish to
contribute significantly both to the development of
educational history and urban history as a distinct
field of study, they should concentrate on those
educational issues that have a uniquely urban
aspect. In doing so they will greatly enhance our
understanding of the intricate relationships between
urban life and education. Second, among the
uniquely urban issues, they should not neglect those

raised by the current interest in ethnicity, women,
the family, labor, and childhood. They should
instead pursue the tripartite relationships between
education, the city, and these other issues of
current interest. Third, in pursuit of these issues
they should attend to previously neglected cities
such as smaller ones and those in the South and
West. Fourth, in doing all this they should stick
to their painstaking task, studiously avoiding the
temptation either to simplify the research by
recourse to an ideological starting point or to
overstate the results by spinning a meta theory
based on a single case study.

NOTES

1. Some publishers of scholarly books even
launched urban series, for example, the Oxford
University Press Urban Life in America Series and
the Harvard University Press Studies in Urban
History. Another mark of urban history's coming of
age was the launching of a journal of its own in
1974, the Journal of Urban History. The Journal, in
its articles, book reviews, and interviews with
prominent urban historians, provides the best single
source for documenting the developments in urban
history briefly outlined in this chapter.

2. See Arthur M. Schlesinger, "The City in
American Civilization," Paths to the Present (New
York, 1949), pp. 210-33; Richard C. Wade, The Urban
Frontier (Cambridge, Mass., 1959); idem, Slavery in
the Cities: The South, 1820-1860 (New York, 1964).

3. Stephan Thernstrom, Poverty and Progress:
Social Mobility in a Nineteenth-Century City
(Cambridge, Mass., 1964); idem, The Other
Bostonians: Poverty and Progress in the American
Metropolis, 1870-1970 (Cambridge, Mass., 1973). For
a thorough discussion of the distinction between
urban as process and urban as site, see Theodore
Hershberg, "The New Urban History, Toward an
Interdisciplinary History of the City," Journal of

Urban History 5, no. 1 (November 1978):   3-40.
      4. For a more thorough discussion of this
issue, see the volumes of the Journal of Urban
History; also see Stephan Thernstrom and Richard
Sennett,   eds.,   Nineteenth Century Cities, Essays
in the New Urban History (New Haven, Conn., 1969);
Leo   F.   Schnore,   ed.,   The New Urban History,
Quantitative Explorations by American Historians
(Princeton, N.J., 1975).
      5. These comments are not meant to downgrade
the value of quantitative history, as the author's
own laborious efforts to gain quantitative skills
should testify. But the reporting of quantitative
research in a manner intelligible to the uninitiated
has left much to be desired, and has contributed,
along with other factors such as overindulgence in
theory, to a certain narcissism in American social
history.
      6. See note 10.
      7. While this is not intended to be a
bibliographical essay, the following examples, in
chronological order, illustrate the extent of
concentration on specifically urban educational
issues during the 1970s: Marvin Lazerson, Origins
of the Urban School, Public Education in
Massachusetts, 1870-1915 (Cambridge, Mass., 1971);
Carl F. Kaestle, The Evolution of an Urban School
System: New York City, 1750-1350 (Cambridge, Mass.,
1973); Stanley K. Schultz, The Culture Factory:
Boston Public Schools, 1789-1860 (New York, 1973);
Diane   Ravitch,   The Great School Wars: New York
City, 1805-1973 (New York, 1974); William A.
Bullough, Cities and Schools in the Gilded Age:
the Evolution of an Urban Institution (Port
Washington, N. Y., 1975); Selwyn K. Troen, The
Public and the Schools: Shaping the St. Louis
System, 1838-1920 (Columbia, Mo., 1975); David B.
Tyack, The One Best System: A History of American
Urban Education (Cambridge, Mass., 1975); James W.
Sanders, The Education of an Urban Minority:
Catholics in Chicago, 1833-1965 (New York, 1977);
Ronald D. Cohen and Raymond A. Mohl, The Paradox of
Progressive Education: The Gary Plan and Urban
Schooling (Port Washington, N. Y., 1979); Vincent

P. Franklin, The Education of Black Philadelphia: The Social and Educational History of a Black Community, 1900-1950 (Philadelphia, 1979).

8. Schultz, e.g., saw the development of public schooling in Boston within the urban discipline framework; Lazerson and Ravitch, though from different viewpoints, viewed urban education in Boston and New York in relation to the larger issue of urban progressive reform; Franklin and Sanders dealt specifically with racial, ethnic, and religious diversity in urban populations related to education.

9. Perhaps the best dispassionate account of this controversy can be found in Cohen and Mohl, Paradox of Progressive Education, chap. 8: "Urban Schooling and the Revisionist Perspective," pp. 160-75.

10. Quote from Tamarah Hareven, "Introduction: The Historical Study of the Family in Urban Society," Journal of Urban History 1, no. 3 (May 1975): 263-64. This entire issue is devoted to the history of the family in urban society. Examples of the attempt to explore the relationships between women, education, and the city are Barbara J. Berg, The Remembered Gate: Origins of American Feminism, The Woman and the City, 1800-1860 (New York, 1978); Margaret G. Wilson, The American Woman in Transition: The Urban Influence, 1870-1920 (Westport, Conn., 1979). Examples of urban ethnic histories dealing in part with educational issues are many. Random instances would be Josef Barton, Peasants and Strangers: Italians, Rumanians, and Slovaks in an American City, 1890-1950 (Cambridge, Mass., 1976); John W. Briggs, An Italian Passage, Immigrants to Three American Cities (New Haven, 1978).

11. For an exploratory treatment of the historical relationship between suburbanization and schooling as well as family factors, see John Modell, "An Ecology of Family Decisions, Suburbanization, Schooling, and Fertility in Philadelphia, 1880-1920," Journal of Urban History 6, no. 4 (August 1980): 397-417. Work presently under way by David Nasaw on "Children of the

Streets" illustrates the power of the city as educator.

12. For differences among the Irish see James W. Sanders, "Roman Catholics and the School Question in New York City: Some Suggestions for Research," in Educating an Urban Population: The New York City Experience, ed. Diane Ravitch and Ronald K. Goodenow (New York, 1981). For women and education in the city, see Berg, Remembered Gate; Wilson, American Woman in Transition; Journal of Urban History 4, no. 3 (May 1978), devoted entirely to immigrant women and the city.

13. As examples of this trend, see Stuart Blumin, The Urban Threshold: Growth and Change in a Nineteenth-Century American Community (Kingston, New York) (Chicago, 1976); Clyde and Sally Griffen, Natives and Newcomers: The Ordering of Opportunity in Mid-Nineteenth Century Poughkeepsie (Cambridge, Mass., 1978); Carl Abbott, The New Urban America: Growth and Politics in Sunbelt Cities (Chapel Hill, N.C., 1981); Gunther Barth, Instant Cities: Urbanization and the Rise of San Francisco and Denver (New York, 1975). Another direction the study of urban education might follow is into the 1930s and forties. This was a period marked by declining birth rates and absence of foreign immigration, which provided a breathing space for previously overtaxed urban educational facilities. It has served as a seldom examined benchmark against which many have judged the present malaise, but deserves closer scrutiny.

14. For an excellent analysis of mobility study shortcomings, see Richard W. Fox, "Modernizing Mobility Studies," a book review in History of Education Quarterly 17, no. 2 (Summer 1977): 203-8.

15. For the best exploration to date into this area, see Michael B. Katz's excellent The People of Hamilton, Canada West: Family and Class in a Mid-Nineteenth Century City (Cambridge, Mass., 1975). Also see David Hogan, "Education and the Making of the Chicago Working Class, 1880-1930," History of Education Quarterly 18, no. 3 (Fall 1978): 227-70.

16. See Stephen Olsen, "Yankee City and the New Urban History," Journal of Urban History 6, no. 3 (May 1980): 321-38.

12

NEITHER VICTIMS NOR MASTERS
ETHNIC AND MINORITY STUDY

William J. Reese
Indiana University

A renewed concern with ethnic and minority study during the past two decades has emerged for several reasons. Besides the overall popularity of social history, academicians, like other citizens have recognized the resilience of ethnicity and pluralism and the continuing struggle of racial minorities for civil rights and equal opportunity. During the past decade in particular, an impressive array of articles, monographs, edited readers, and dissertations have altered many of our conceptions of the past. (1)

While suggesting new research strategies and directions in ethnic and minority study in the history of American education, one must simultaneously examine the major themes in the recent literature. For the most part, educational and social historians generally have begun to abandon social control interpretations of the past; some historians, for example, utilize Antonio Gramsci's theory of "hegemony" as an elegant alternative to social control, and other analysts draw upon the social sciences for additional theoretical and practical leverage on historical problems. (2) The current message in ethnic and minority studies of education is that these groups were not simply manipulated by dominant interests or victimized by an omnipotent social or economic system. Rather, ethnic and minority groups often successfully resisted attacks on their culture and preserved their unique values while struggling against a system that was insensitive, if not hostile, to their needs.

"In the 1960s," writes Oscar Handlin, "victimization explained everything: deprivation, failures to achieve, cultural inadequacies, and personal maladjustments, past as well as present--all originated ultimately in the society that corrupted its members." Though Handlin appreciated the greater respect shown by historians for immigrants, Indians, blacks, and other minorities, he chided those who simply glorified their subject and imputed "evil intentions to their individual or group antagonists." Whether or not they interpret ethnic and minority groups uncritically compared to the political establishment, historians have indeed rediscovered the vitality of ethnic and racial groups. Maxine Seller, in a review of the literature on immigrants and education, notes how white ethnics are now seen "not as objects of American education, but as subjects, creators of formal and informal educational institutions in their own communities." Jay Saunders Redding similarly writes that "the Negro is no longer slighted or scorned as a creature of attitudes and actions beyond his comprehension and--frequently--even beyond his concern." (3)

By emphasizing the role of individuals as active forces in shaping the past, historians continue to chip away at social control theories of American history and develop more complex interpretations of social change and educational patterns. For example, the expanding scholarly writing on the family has enormous implications for the history of education. Instead of centering attention on the aims of the schools, which preached the values of conformity and acculturation, Ronald Cohen and John Bodnar suggest the need "to understand and appreciate the attitudes and desires of parents and children. What they thought and did, not just what was done to them, should also be our prime concern." (4)

Though much research still needs to be done, a considerable amount of work has already proceeded in this direction. For example, Bodnar has completed extensive research on the Slavic immigrants of Pennsylvania, who rejected the excessive "materialism" associated with public education during this century. Resisting the integration of their children into a secular school system, many Slavic immigrants preferred parochial education and familial values that prized morality, Catholicism, and early entry into the labor market. (5) How did such values compare with those of other ethnic groups arriving in America at the turn of the century? At what point did various groups develop more "instrumental" attitudes toward education, as described by David Hogan in his study of Chicago in the early twentieth century? According to Hogan, once home ownership and some economic stability were achieved by various ethnic groups in Chicago, even the children of the foreign born realized that education was a prerequisite for survival and advancement in the American social order. (6)

Many other ethnic groups also saw children as part of the family economy, and we still need to understand how different groups interpreted "success" and "mobility" in different periods of American history. If various groups sought different ends in American society, the schools--which provided a path to that world and its values--obviously meant divergent things to them. Some historians have accused educators of tracking immigrants and blacks in disproportionate numbers into inferior educational programs, thereby systematically limiting their opportunity. That criticism is sound but incomplete, because it ignores how parental values--based on religious ideals, economic circumstances, or notions on the superiority of work versus prolonged schooling--also determined the future of many children. The relationship between family, schooling, and economy remains one of the genuinely murky areas of educational history. (7)

Historians often deal with extreme cases of school success and school failure in their analyses of ethnicity in education. The contadini, it is regularly noted, came from an oppressive, backward, rural past where state involvement in education was weak and resented; hence, Italian children ordinarily faced tremendous difficulties in the American schools. Eastern European Jews, on the other hand, long oppressed in Europe but heirs of a tradition that prized scholarship and learning, eagerly embraced state-sponsored schooling in this country. Even when authors note that neither all Eastern European Jews succeeded in the schools nor all Southern Italians failed, the use of extreme cases ignores the wide range of ethnic group experiences that fell somewhere between these groups. Studying the extremes, of course, amply demonstrates that there has never been a single "immigrant" experience. (8)

Michael Olneck and Marvin Lazerson have analyzed the divergent school performances of different ethnic groups, but more elaborate studies of various groups would greatly enhance our comprehension of ethnic life and schooling in the past. (9) This would require full attention to the role of the family, the church, the ethnic press, voluntary associations, and all other components of community life, including perceptions on the value of education. Although some fascinating articles have already appeared on the subject, more knowledge is welcome on the educational attitudes and school attainment of the Greeks, Hungarians, Latvians, Lithuanians, Koreans, Japanese, Chinese-Americans, and numerous other immigrant groups. Even though Hispanics form the largest growing minority segment in the United States, we lack comprehensive histories of the education of Puerto Ricans or Mexican-Americans. The education of ethnic and minority girls and women has been almost totally ignored. (10) What familial and cultural factors determined school success or failure? How much responsibility did schools have for adult status compared to the family, or to the current economic and political structure?

The study of the black family is a particularly inviting and significant research subject. From the insights of Herbert Gutman's The Black Family in Slavery and Freedom, 1790-1925, scholars now recognize that the black family was neither destroyed nor especially disorganized as a result of the slave experience. (11) Assuming the importance of family life in school attendance and performance, what accounted for the major changes in the black family following the inauguration of the New Deal? Was the federal government (as conservatives argue) responsible through its welfare programs for undermining the black family, just as state and local governments (as conservatives forget) were responsible through their policies of undermining integrationist efforts throughout the twentieth century? The tragedy of black education is that historically black Americans had strong desires for educational success that never matched their actual school experiences; white ethnics, on the other hand, had divergent attitudes yet often more desirable outcomes. (12) Exactly how did government policy at all levels contribute to this anomalous situation for black Americans?

Exploring how ethnic and black Americans shaped their own lives and communities is also a welcome trend in minority group studies. John Blassingame and others have stressed black influence in shaping the antebellum slave community. Thomas Webber has similarly analyzed the ability of the family to survive the travails of slavery. Jacqueline Jones's examination of the Northern teachers who served as missionary teachers in Georgia after the Civil War may help to reorient educational research on the Reconstruction period; her work demonstrates that few black children were actually taught by these schoolmarms and that blacks themselves built and taught in their own schools to help assure cultural and community survival. Emphasis therefore must be placed not only on the work of philanthropic foundations, missionary groups, and government policies affecting black education, but more research must be done on black voluntary associations that had educational, social, and political implications in local communities both in the North and South. Perhaps Robert Engs's analysis of Hampton, Virginia, and Vincent Franklin's study of Philadelphia augur a new and desirable trend. (13)

While blacks in Philadelphia as elsewhere fought for integrated schools, the issue divided localities in serious ways. Black teachers, for example, often opposed integration for fear of losing their jobs; and other Afro-Americans apparently shared W. E. B. DuBois's famous assertion that black children in integrated schools were crucified, not educated. (14) But if school integration was a devisive issue in black communities (a subject that assuredly merits more research) the problem of assimilation versus cultural isolation also divided ethnic communities. The black and the white ethnic situations were never fully comparable, of course. Blacks were forcibly segregated by law and custom, denied the right to move easily into new neighborhoods, and became segregated to a degree unknown by white ethnics, who often never faced the enduring poverty, political impotence, and lasting discrimination that stymied the progress of black Americans. Still, black as well as white ethnic leadership faced divided constituencies, who saw merits both in assimilation and segregation. We need more studies of how different leaders in different settings and time periods responded to these schisms in local ethnic and minority groups. (15)

Thomas Sowell, who has repeatedly debunked the notion that segregated facilities inevitably produce inferior education, not only highlights the academic excellence of segregated black institutions like Dunbar High School but recently has also suggested that many nonblack minority groups have performed admirably in segregated settings. Hardly a brief for segregation, Sowell's work challenges the idea that segregation necessarily means inferior schooling. Japanese and Chinese Americans, for example, have been treated shamefully in our past yet performed extremely well in their segregated public schools, achieving high levels of academic success and social mobility as adults. Writing from an entirely different political perspective, Irving Howe notes in his epic tale of the Eastern European Jews, World of Our Fathers that New York City Jews in the early 1900s never complained about Jewish concentration in particular neighborhood schools. Inclusiveness helped to build a community that nurtured things Jewish. (16) Blacks, of course, unlike white ethnics, were forcibly segregated in most regions of the nation and faced inferior schools and dim prospects for employment even when they had educational qualifications equal to white competitors.

Unfortunately, studies of ethnic and minority leaders in education who faced these conditions tend to center on a few famous individuals. Black leadership is often limited to discussions of Frederick Douglas, Booker T. Washington, W. E. B. DuBois, and the legal activists who built the pathway to the Brown decision; the full range of black leadership that must have emerged in many communities has not been integrated into black or educational historiography. (17) Ethnic leadership also has not been examined sufficiently. Leonard Covello's inspiring work in the New York City schools is a staple of the history of American education. But what of the many male and female ethnic leaders of other groups in our past? Such studies needn't degenerate into celebrationist biographies of "men of achievement," like early county and urban histories. Rather, a complete examination of various types of ethnic leadership will enrich our understanding of the men and women who represented various community constituencies, who taught and administered in the schools, and who helped shape policy on language instruction and many other subjects. (18)

Analyses of educational innovation at the community level formed the heart of the new history of education during the past two decades, and they will undoubtedly continue to illuminate ethnic and minority study. We have little comprehensive knowledge about the ethnic leaders and clientele who participated in immigrant-controlled language schools, evening schools, and other community institutions that preserved cultural values as well as introduced newcomers to life in America. Studies are needed on the way in which ethnic communities responded to the teaching of their native language in the public schools, the extensiveness of that teaching in different communities, and the effects that it had on personal and community development. (For the more recent period, historians will want to analyze the effects of the Lau decision and the fate of black English in the schools.) Little is known, for example, about the actual impact of the many language schools and folk schools sponsored by Koreans, Japanese, Lithuanians, Poles, and so many other ethnic groups in the twentieth century. Was their influence pervasive, short-lived, and significant, and were they effective supplements to public education? (19)

Historians also must become more sensitive to the many tradeoffs that immigrants consciously made to help reap whatever economic benefits may have existed for them in America. If slaves could easily put on ole Massah, so too could immigrants. How many immigrants nodded their head in apparent approval at the most asinine and insulting adult education and citizenship lecture at the evening school? Did various groups perceive the bias of "Americanization" programs in the schools as sharply as we do today? How many children as well as adults simply drew selectively from their public educational experiences, learning enough to cope with their new environment and ignoring the racist or ethnocentric barbs that accompanied their learning experiences? Educators and social commentators have long praised the role of the school in integrating millions of immigrants into the American mainstream. But we should be sensitive to another perspective: the immigrants were not simply pieces of clay molded by their environment, but acted upon it too. Maxine Seller's research, for example, shows that the vast majority of immigrant adults at the turn of the century never attended evening schools and that those who did attended sporadically. (20)

Whether or not one studies white ethnics or other minority groups, numerous questions remain about the role of the school in their lives. Besides examining the issues of academic performance, assimilation, integration, and family-based values, historians still need to evaluate the effectiveness of many school programs. With the expansion of social services in education, for example, schools were used as social centers, school playgrounds were established, school lunch programs became common, and counseling and guidance networks joined rapidly expanding vocational programs. (21) How well did these programs serve different communities? Did particular ethnic groups, for example, use the schools as social centers more than others? Did children receive any lasting nutritional benefits from programs initiated under the National School Lunch Act? Did any of the new social service programs contribute to the well-being of children? (22)

Often the study of particular social services can provide insights into immigrant culture. When the schools inaugurated medical and dental inspection at the turn of the century, many contemporaries regarded this as part of the general expansion of the role of the modern school. Yet the phenomenon was viewed critically by some groups who condemned the state for intervening in private affairs. Although little research has been completed on the subject, school boycotts were common in particular communities that tried to establish compulsory vaccination; modern science clashed with traditional notions of family responsibility for health and medical care. In one celebrated event, Jewish parents in New York City rioted when they learned that school physicians were removing children's adenoids without parental permission; the children, they heard, were having their throats slit! (23) How common was parental resistance? Did minority youth benefit from school health inspection, health instruction, or in places where it was systematically available, sex education classes? Did native born, foreign born, and black youth and their parents respond differently to the expansion of public surveillance and regulation of children's health?

In essence, one needs to know what tradeoffs occurred in the schools and local communities: whether different immigrants believed that learning English was worth the value of a better job or citizenship; whether attention to health practices was worth the invasion of privacy; whether vocational programs (even those leading to semiskilled positions) were preferable to joining mom in the mill or dad in the mine; whether the schools promoted "success" and "mobility" in terms set by various groups who converged upon the schools.

In this regard, the relationship between vocational programs and economic mobility must be reassessed. The IQ test and its historical evolution have been studied extensively over the past decade, and its racist and ethnocentric basis exposed. (24) But we need to inquire into how vocational programs did or did not lead to greater opportunities for youth, measured against the alternatives some poor children faced at particular points of their lives. If narrow vocational tracks separated youth from their college-bound peers, did they ever open new economic opportunities for those who were not academically inclined or who had been improperly tracked into programs because of their race or class backgrounds? Were guidance counselors fully aware of the class biases implicit in the entire tracking system? How did the vocational curriculum change over time, tie its programs to a changing industrial society, and deal with various student constituencies, boys as well as girls? (25)

While the recent history of education of ethnic and minority groups has dealt with mass education and the common school, other educational institutions, both formal and nonformal, have always transmitted values, skills, and sentiments to students. Alternative educational institutions like Socialist Sunday Schools, folk schools, working men's colleges, and the like offered instruction for

at least some citizens with unique social
perspectives. (26)   For others,   church-related
Sunday schools, youth groups, peer associations,
athletic leagues, reading groups, soapbox lecturers,
newspapers, the radio, and other forms of
association and communication had educational impact
on many individuals, though that impact varied from
group to group in different places over time and is
often difficult to measure. (27) By the same token,
other nonschool institutions like juvenile courts,
detention centers, and houses of refuge must be
investigated because they regularly dealt with
immigrant and black wayward youth.   Historical
investigations on the procedures used to diagnose
mentally handicapped children in the schools would
undoubtedly illuminate racial and ethnic
biases. (28)

Another vital research area is the education of
immigrants and their children in institutions of
higher education. The role of the City College of
New York in promoting the interests of Jewish
children is legendary and well documented in the
literature.   There are also significant studies
carefully documenting trends in the history of
college admissions of minorities. (29)   Still,
considerable research must be undertaken on the
education of ethnic groups in secondary and higher
education for different historical periods; this
would include not only high schools and junior
colleges but also business schools, "beauty"
colleges, trade schools, and secretarial schools, as
well as traditional liberal arts colleges and
universities.

What has been the rate of college and graduate
school attendance for various groups of second- and
third-generation immigrants? For example, have the
Slovaks of Pennsylvania, so carefully studied by
some historians for the early twentieth century,
seen their grandchildren attend higher education in
increasing numbers? Have unskilled Slavic miners
and factory workers, now retired, seen their
grandchildren earn advanced degrees, or is the rate
of educational advance greatly exaggerated by some
analysts?   Have the grandchildren of Italian

immigrants--who had such negative feelings toward public education--differed in their attitudes toward higher education compared to other ethnic groups?

Black colleges and universities have received considerable attention in the history of education for many years. There are many histories of individual colleges and universities. There is still a pressing need, however, for a comprehensive analysis of the history of these institutions, of their students, curricula, professional schools, schools of education, and the like. Richard Kluger, in his magisterial analysis of the historical background of the Brown decision, has demonstrated how black universities produced some of the leading legal minds of this century. Again, without reducing the history of black colleges and universities to a compendium of men and women of achievement, how did these various schools contribute to the formation of the professional black elite of modern America? How did segregated as well as integrated forms of higher education school the talented tenth? How has integration in higher education affected the black students in previously elite, all-black schools, and what is the fate and role of such schools of higher learning in the contemporary world? (30)

Comparisons of white ethnic and black students in education have long been popular. When the history of modern education is written, it will be interesting to compare the fate of separate programs like women's studies, ethnic studies, and black studies, all of which now compete for increasingly scarce funds in the university budget. (31) Disputes over whether blacks are indeed the last immigrants to the city will also undoubtedly continue. At this point, however, historians have continually revealed the power of racism in shaping the black experience: government policies undermined the black family, discriminatory hiring practices limited black mobility, and housing policies segregated blacks and hence promoted all-black schools in many regions of the nation even after the Brown ruling. Historians will probably investigate myriad reforms in completing the history of modern black education: affirmative action, magnet schools, busing, and the overall effort to integrate school systems as well as classes within individual schools. (32)

One final point on research in ethnic and minority studies in education relates to class analysis. Historians clearly must try to reconstruct the world as earlier participants experienced and understood it, yet much can still be learned by exploring the class dimensions of ethnic and minority lives. That adult blacks vis-a-vis other groups generally have never enjoyed a reasonable distribution across the occupational spectrum has had obvious social, political, economic, and educational consequences. To what extent do discrete categories like "ethnicity" and "race" obscure the fundamental role of class in shaping the lives of millions of Americans throughout our past? To what degree are "racial" and "multicultural" problems in the schools fundamentally class problems, given the fact that the racially and culturally different often are also poor? How have the lives and educational experiences of ethnic and minority groups fit into the larger structural patterns in American society?

Because current interests shape historical writing so directly, it is impossible to predict accurately the future direction of ethnic and minority studies in the history of education. Generally, however, one can probably expect more social analyses of ethnic and racial minorities themselves, investigations of their families and cultures, studies of churches, voluntary associations, and other mechanisms of education and socialization within subcommunities. Historians will continue to document the survival and resilience of groups who have resisted integration into the melting pot and the frustrations of those who cannot escape segregated settings. Although the reemphasis on the strength and vitality of ethnic and racial groups has undermined simplistic writing on social control, hopefully the pendulum will not swing too far in the other direction. Ethnic and minority groups were not islands unto themselves; rather, they interacted with and were shaped by definite political forces, economic structures, and ideological beliefs that transcended their own narrower communities. If ethnic and minority group members were not victims, they were rarely masters.

NOTES

1. The historiographical literature on ethnic and minority study in education is vast. The citations contained in the following notes list only a small part of the total source materials. Furthermore, most of the citations are deliberately drawn from materials published during the last decade.

2. See, e.g., Michael B. Katz, "The Origins of Public Education: A Reassessment," History of Education Quarterly 16 (Winter 1976): 381-406; Harold Entwistle, Antonio Gramsci (London, 1979); Kenneth Teitelbaum and William J. Reese, "American Socialist Pedagogy and Experimentation in the Progressive Era: The Socialist Sunday School," History of Education Quarterly 23, forthcoming.

3. Oscar Handlin, Truth in History (Cambridge, Mass., 1979), p. 397; ibid., pp. 401-2, where he writes: "If the immigrants were no longer sinister undermen, or the Negroes childlike savages, or the Indians barbarians, then they were saintly victims, whose difficulties stemmed from the evil intentions of individual or group antagonists"; Maxine S. Seller, "The Education of Immigrants in the United States: An Introduction to the Literature," Immigration History Newsletter 13 (May 1981): 1; Jay Saunders Redding, "The Negro in American History: As Scholar, As Subject," in The Past Before Us: Contemporary Historical Writing in the United States, ed. Michael Kammen (Ithaca, 1980), p. 292.

4. Ronald C. Cohen and John Bodnar, "Ethnicity and Schooling in the United States: The Twentieth

Century," Review Journal of Philosophy and Social Science 3 (1977): 111-12; Seller, "Education of Immigrants," pp. 1-8; Bernard J. Weiss, ed., American Education and the European Immigrant: 1840-1940 (Urbana, Ill., 1982), p. xvi. Also see Ronald D. Cohen and Raymond A. Mohl, The Paradox of Progressive Education: The Gary Plan and Urban Schooling (Port Washington, N.Y., 1979).

5. John Bodnar, "Materialism and Morality: Slavic-American Immigrants and Education, 1890-1940," Journal of Ethnic Studies 3 (Winter 1976): 1-20; idem, "Schooling and the Slavic-American Family, 1900-1940," in American Education, ed. Weiss, pp. 78-95. Compare these essays with Timothy Smith's classic article, "Immigrant Social Aspirations and American Education, 1880-1930," American Quarterly 21 (Fall 1969): 523-43; M. Mark Stolarik, "Immigration, Education, and the Social Mobility of Slovaks, 1870-1930," in Immigrants and Religion in Urban America, ed. Randall M. Miller and Thomas Maryck (Philadelphia, 1977).

6. David Hogan, "Education and the Making of the Chicago Working Class, 1880-1930," History of Education Quarterly 18 (Fall 1978): 227-70.

7. Pertinent critical "revisionist" interpretations, written from a wide range of perspectives, include the following: Michael B. Katz, Class, Bureaucracy, and the Schools (New York, 1971); Joel H. Spring, Education and the Rise of the Corporate State (Boston, 1972); Clarence Karier, Paul Violas, and Joel H. Spring, Roots of Crisis (Chicago, 1973); Colin Greer, The Great School Legend (New York, 1972); Samuel Bowles and Herbert Gintis, Schooling in Capitalist America (New York, 1976). In addition, examine C. H. Edson, "Immigrant Perspectives on Work and Schooling: Eastern European Jews and Southern Italians, 1880-1920" (Ph.D. dissertation, Stanford University, 1979).

8. For a sampling of excellent writing on the education of Jews and Italians, see the following: David B. Tyack, The One Best System: A History of American Urban Education (Cambridge, 1974), pp. 229-55; Selma C. Berrol, "Education and Economic

Mobility: The Jewish Experience in New York City, 1880-1920," American Jewish Historical Quarterly 65 (March 1976):71; idem, "The Open City: Jews, Jobs, and Schools in New York City, 1880-1915," in Educating an Urban People: The New York City Experience, ed. Diane Ravitch and Ronald Goodenow (New York, 1981), pp. 101-15; Patrick J. Gallo, Old Bread, New Wine: A Portrait of the Italian-Americans (Chicago, 1981); Leonard Dinnerstein, "Education and the Advancement of American Jews," American Education, ed. Weiss, pp. 44-60; Salvatore J. La Gumina, "American Education and the Italian Immigrant Response," ibid., pp. 61-77. Also see Diane Ravitch, "On the History of Minority Group Education in the United States," Teachers College Record 78 (December 1976): 213-28.

9. See Michael Olneck and Marvin Lazerson, "The School Achievement of Immigrant Children, 1900-1930," History of Education Quarterly 14 (Winter 1974): 453-82; idem, "Education," in Harvard Encyclopedia of American Ethnic Groups, ed. Stephen Thernstrom et al. (Cambridge, 1980), pp. 303-19. For an earlier assessment, see David K. Cohen, "Immigrants and the Schools," Review of Educational Research 40 (February 1970): 13-28.

10. An introduction to the education of these various groups would include the following: Andrew T. Kopan, "Greek Education in Chicago: The Role of Ethnic Education," in Ethnic Chicago, ed. Melvin G. Holli and Peter D'A. Jones (Grand Rapids, 1981), pp. 80-139; Josef Barton, Peasants and Strangers: Italians, Rumanians, and Slovaks in an American City, 1890-1950 (Cambridge, 1975); Antania Kucas, Lithuanians in America (Boston, 1975), pp. 205-18; Bong-youn Choy, Koreans in America (Chicago, 1979), pp. 272-73; Roger Daniels, "Japanese Immigrants on a Western Frontier: The Issei in California, 1880-1940," in East Across the Pacific, ed. Hilary Conroy and T. Scott Miyakawa (Santa Barbara, 1972), p. 82; Stanford Lyman, Chinese Americans (New York, 1974), pp. 83, 119, 177-78; Philip A. Lum, "The Creation and Demise of San Francisco Chinatown 248 Historical Inquiry in Education Freedom Schools: One Response to Desegregation," Amerasia

Journal 5 (1978):59-73; Kal Wagenheim, A Survey of Puerto Ricans on the U.S. Mainland in the 1970s (New York, 1975); Thomas P. Carter, Mexican-Americans in School: A History of Educational Neglect (Princeton, N.J. 1970); Rudolfo Acuna, Occupied Americans: A History of Chicanos (New York, 1981); and the special issue of Aztlan 8 (1977) on the education of Chicanos. On immigrant women, see Maxine S. Seller, "The Education of Immigrant Women: 1900 to 1935," Journal of Urban History 4 (May 1978): 307-30.

11. Herbert Gutman, The Black Family in Slavery and Freedom, 1750-1925 (New York, 1976).

12. This observation is reiterated by Vincent P. Franklin, who asserts that "the beliefs and values of blacks in American cities about education resembled those of the East European Jews, and yet the occupational distribution of blacks in these cities, especially before 1915, tended to be closer to that of the Southern Italians." See "Continuity and Discontinuity in Black and Immigrant Minority Education in Urban America: A Historical Assessment," in Educating an Urban People, ed. Ravitch and Goodenow, p. 62.

13. John Blassingame, The Slave Community (New York, 1972); Thomas L. Webber, Deep Like the Rivers: Education in the Slave Quarter Community, 1831-1865 (New York, 1978); Jacqueline Jones, Soldiers of Light and Love: Northern Teachers and Georgia Blacks, 1865-1873 (Chapel Hill, N.C., 1980), cf. Robert C. Morris, Reading, 'Riting, and Reconstruction: The Education of Freedmen in the South, 1861-1870 (Chicago, 1981); Robert Francis Engs, Freedom's First Generation: Black Hampton, Virginia, 1861-1890 (Philadelphia, 1979); Vincent P. Franklin, The Education of Black Philadelphia: The Social and Educational History of a Minority Community (Philadelphia, 1979). For important work on philanthropy and black education, see James Anderson, "Northern Foundations and the Shaping of Southern Black Rural Education, 1902-1935," History of Education Quarterly 18 (Winter 1978): 371-96.

14. Franklin, Education of Black Philadelphia; Tyack, One Best System.

15. See the useful collection of essays in John Higham, ed., Ethnic Leadership in America (Baltimore, Md., 1978).

16. Thomas Sowell, "Black Excellence: The Case of Dunbar High School," The Public Interest 35 (Spring 1974): 3-21; idem, "Assumption vs. History in Ethnic Education," Teachers College Record 83 (Fall 1981): 37-71; Irving Howe, World of Our Fathers (New York, 1976), p. 275, where he writes: "In the years between, say, 1900 and 1914 there were sporadic efforts by Jewish groups to pressure the Board of Education with regard to overcrowding of schools, released time for religious training, and the teaching of foreign languages; but we have no record of major objection to the racial homogeneity of a given school or district." Also see Berrol, "The Open City," p. 105.

17. Most valuable studies of black leadership in education include Louis Harlan, Booker T. Washington: The Making of a Black Leader, 1865-1901 (New York, 1972); Richard Kluger, Simple Justice: The History of Brown v. Board of Education and Black America's Struggle for Equality (New York, 1975).

18. On Covello, see Tyack, One Best System; Francesco Cordasco, ed., Studies in Italian American Social History: Essays in Honor of Leonard Covello (Totowa, N.J., 1975).

19. For a sampling of the literature on ethnic schools, see John N. Hawkins, "Politics, Education, and Language Policy: The Case of Japanese Language Schools in Hawaii," Amerasia Journal 5 (1978): 39-56; Efraim Inbar, "The Hebrew Day School--The Orthodox Communal Challenge," Journal of Ethnic Studies 7 (Spring 1979): 13-29; Lloyd P. Gartner, ed., Jewish Education in the United States: A Documentary History (New York, 1969); Raymond A. Mohl and Neil Betten, "The Immigrant Church in Gary, Indiana: Religious Adjustment and Cultural Defense," Ethnicity 8 (March 1981): 1-17; Zinta Sanders, "Latvian Education in the United States: Antecedents and Development of Supplementary Schools," Journal of Ethnic Studies 7 (Spring 1979): 31-42; Joshua Fishman, Language Loyalty in the United States (London, 1966). Also see L. Ling-Chi

Wang, "Lau v. Nichols: History of a Struggle for Equal and Quality Education," in Counterpoint: Perspectives on Asian Americans, ed. Emma Gee (Los Angeles, 1976), pp. 240-63; and the special issue on Black English in the Journal of Negro Education 43 (Summer 1974).

The trend in many graduate schools away from extensive foreign language requirements for doctoral degrees is unhealthy from the standpoint of ethnic and minority study. As quantitative methods became more fashionable in recent years, many students avoided serious language training. This only weakens any researcher's examination of the history of ethnic and minority groups in education.

20. Maxine S. Seller, "Success and Failure in Adult Education: The Immigrant Experience, 1914-1924," in History, Education, and Public Policy, ed. Donald B. Warren (Berkeley, Calif., 1978), pp. 197-212. For a comprehensive analysis of Americanization programs in the schools, see Robert A. Carlson, The Quest for Conformity: Americanization Through Education (New York, 1975).

21. See, e.g., William J. Reese, Case Studies of Social Services in the Schools of Selected Cities, Final Report to the National Institute of Education (Washington, D.C., 1981).

22. On early school lunch programs, see William J. Reese, "After Bread, Education: Nutrition and Urban School Children, 1890-1920," Teachers College Record 81 (Summer 1980): 496-525. On playgrounds, see Cary Goodman, "(Re) Creating Americans at the Educational Alliance," Journal of Ethnic Studies 6 (Winter 1979): 1-28; relevant sections of Spring, Education and the Rise; Paul Violas, The Training of the Urban Working Class (Chicago, 1978).

23. Selma Berrol, "Public Schools and Immigrants: The New York City Experience," in American Education, ed. Weiss, pp. 36-37.

24. The testing movement has captured the attention of many histories. One recent analysis is by Paula Fass, "The IQ: A Cultural and Historical Framework," American Journal of Education 88 (August 1980): 431-58.

25. For divergent perspectives, see Donald Spivey, Schooling for the New Slavery: Black Industrial Education, 1868-1915 (Greenwood, Ill., 1978); Arthur Wirth, Education in the Technological Society (Scranton, Pa., 1972).

26. See Richard J. Altenbaugh and Rolland G. Paulston, "Work People's College: A Finnish Folk High School in the American Labor College Movement," Paedagogica Historica 18 (1978): 237-56; Rolland G. Paulston, Other Dreams, Other Schools: Folk Colleges in Social and Ethnic Movements (Pittsburgh, Pa., 1980); Paul Avrich, The Modern School Movement: Anarchism and Education in the United States (Princeton, N.J., 1980); Teitelbaum and Reese, "American Socialist Pedagogy."

27. Lawrence Cremin has pioneered the examination of the nonschool dimension of the history of American education. His most recent contribution is American Education: The National Experience, 1783-1876 (New York, 1980).

28. See especially Steven Schlossman, Love and the American Delinquent: The Theory and Practice of "Progressive" Juvenile Justice, 1825-1920 (Chicago, 1977); David Rothman, Conscience and Convenience: The Asylum and Its Alternatives in Progressive America (Boston, 1980). Also examine Cecile Frey, "The House of Refuge for Colored Children," Journal of Negro History 66 (Spring 1981): 10-25.

29. Dinnerstein, "Education and the Advancement," pp. 44-60; Marcia Graham Synott, The Half-Opened Door: Discrimination and Admissions at Harvard, Yale, and Princeton, 1900-1970 (Westport, Conn., 1979); Harold S. Wechsler, The Qualified Student: A History of Selective College Admission in America (New York, 1977).

30. Although the literature is vast, examine Frederick Chambers, "Histories of Black Colleges and Universities," Journal of Negro History 57 (July 1972): 270-75; Rutledge M. Dennis, "DuBois and the Role of the Educated Elite," Journal of Negro Education 46 (Fall 1977): 388-402; two essays by James D. Anderson, "The Hampton Model of Normal School Industrial Education, 1868-1900" and "Northern Philanthropy and the Training of the Black

Leadership: Fisk   University,   a   Case   Study,
1915-1930," in New Perspectives on Black Educational
History, ed. Vincent P. Franklin and James D.
Anderson (Boston, 1978), pp. 61-111; Kluger, Simple
Justice;   James   M.   McPherson,   The Abolitionist
Legacy: From   Reconstruction   to   the   N.A.A.C.P.
(Princeton, N.J., 1975); Raymond Wolters, The New
Negro on Campus (Princeton, N.J., 1975).

    31.   See   John   W.   Blassingame,   ed.,   New
Perspectives on Black Studies (Urbana, Ill., 1971);
Lawrence P. Crouchett, "The Development of the
Sentiment for Ethnic Studies in American Education,"
Journal of Ethnic Studies 2 (Winter 1975):   77-85.

    32.   The literature comparing blacks and white
immigrants includes the following: John J. Appel,
"American   Negro   and   Immigrant   Experiences:
Similarities and Differences," American Quarterly 18
(Spring 1966):   95-103; Nathan Glazer, "Blacks and
Ethnic Groups: The Difference and the Political
Difference It Makes," in Key Issues in the Afro-
American Experience, ed. N. Huggins, M. Kilson, and
D. Fox (New York, 1971); Timothy Smith, "Native
Blacks and Foreign Whites: Varying Responses to
Educational Opportunity in America, 1880-1950,"
Perspectives in American History 6 (1972):   309-37;
Vincent Franklin, "Historical Revisionism and Black
Education," School Review 81 (May 1973):   477-86;
idem,   "Continuity   and   Discontinuity";   Stanley
Lieberson, A Piece of the Pie: Blacks and White
Immigrants Since 1880 (Berkeley, Calif., 1980).   On
the history of integration since 1954, see J. Harvie
Wilkinson III, From Brown to Bakke (New York, 1979).

13

LOOKING AT GENDER
WOMEN'S HISTORY

Ellen Condliffe Lagemann
Teachers College, Columbia University

More often than not, women's history is thought of as the history of women. It is that, of course, but it is also much more. It is the history of institutions and movements in which women, and often men, have been involved, and it is the history of ideas, as those ideas have shaped and been shaped by attitudes, values, circumstances, and behaviors directly and indirectly related to gender. Women's history grew out of an interest in recovering an overlooked aspect of human experience, and it is not only and should not always be approached as the study of a female "sphere."

Implicit in women's history is a possibility for promoting greater awareness of the need to develop more accurate and encompassing histories of all people and for identifying the kinds of questions that must be asked if such histories are to appear. The general revisionist potential of women's history has been recognized by feminist scholars. The queries they have raised concerning traditional canons of historical method show that. In their calls to reappraise assumptions having to do with periodization, categories of social

analysis, and theories of social change, scholars in
women's history have drawn on what was learned
during the late 1960s and early 1970s: first, that
women had been important in history, if relatively
invisible in traditional interpretations of the
past; second, that a concentration on activities and
achievements within public domains had been largely
responsible   for   the   seemingly   historical
insignificance   of   women;   and   third,   that
fundamentally new perspectives would need to be
developed if fuller and more balanced accounts were
to emerge.   Hence, if the promise implicit in
women's history is to be realized, a central task
for historians during the 1980s will be to develop
the kinds of theoretical constructs that can make
the study of differences between women and men not
an incidental or isolated historical problem, but an
integral element of all historical work. (1)
     Although important knowledge gaps still exist
about   the   historical   experience   of   women,
educational history must now go beyond efforts to
examine the ways in which women have been educated
and involved in educating others.   In recent years,
women's colleges and academies have been studied, as
has   the   participation   of   women   as   students,
teachers, and administrators in higher education and
schooling more generally.   The role of women in
Sunday schools and other educationally oriented,
benevolent organizations has begun to be examined.
The educational experience of individual women and
groups of women has been approached through life
histories,   and   the   educational   opportunities
available to women, not only in institutions of
schooling, but also in work settings and churches
and via networks of acquaintance developed within
families, schools and colleges, churches, jobs, and
through the media have been at least initially
described.   However important the continual amassing
of such monographic knowledge may be, therefore, it
is not to the special characteristics of education
as it has been experienced and influenced by women
that educational historians must now primarily
attend.
     The future development of women's history will

require a more direct response to feminist historical critique. It will require more searching study of the theoretical premises that have diminished the visibility of gender in history. Only if data gathering is more self-consciously and purposively combined with general methodological rethinking and revision will new categories for synthesis eventually be defined. Many kinds of studies will be important, and research in new source materials will be needed, but review and reinterpretation of what is and is not already known about relationships between gender and education may be of particular value. Specifically directed toward further isolating and understanding the methodological shortcomings that have limited historical writing, such review and reinterpretation, indeed, may be the most fruitful way for the concerns of women's history and educational history to be combined. (2)

Two of the many theoretical issues that might be highlighted in this way are already familiar to educational historians. The first has to do with tracking and appraising the influence of educational institutions, the second with conceptualizing views of education that are not school centered. Neither issue will be addressed directly here, but through brief examples, both can be suggested as means for illustrating the degree to which the problems involved in fully incorporating women into educational history are inseparable from the more general and well-recognized problems that face the field.

One such example, having to do with the matter of institutional influence, outreach, or boundaries, is evident in the literature on medical education. In comparison to preparation for other professions, medical education has been well studied, with particular attention having been given to the development of medical knowledge in the early twentieth century and to the impact of the medical curriculum advocated in the 1910 Flexner report on medical education and almost universally adopted across the country by the 1930s. Interestingly, however, at least one intriguing, if small, point seems to have been overlooked in this research, and it is just this kind of point that could be identified through review and then related to possible methodological sources for its neglect.

During the nineteenth century, nutrition was a part of analytical chemistry and biochemistry. During the early twentieth century, however, it increasingly became associated with agriculture, on one hand, and home economics, on the other. Chemistry, but not nutrition, was stressed in the Flexner curriculum, partly no doubt for reasons indirectly and subtly related to both gender and social class. Abraham Flexner asserted in his report that a "doctor is first of all an educated man." Granted the familiarity of such rhetoric in an earlier, less gender-conscious age, two questions still need to be asked. Would nutrition, as a "farmer's science," be of value to such an educated man? And, more important here, would nutrition, as a "feminized science," be of value? Apparently not. The relationship needs further study, but it certainly would appear that the transferral of nutrition to peripheral, low-status departments within the university was a factor in its relative insignificance within medical training. (3)

So far as I am aware, gender connections directly relevant to the medical curriculum have not been examined, although recent work in the history of higher education has laid the groundwork for their explication. Any number of studies have indicated that gender was a primary factor in the development of collegiate and university social structures: in the composition of student bodies and faculties, in the establishment and development of separate and coordinate women's colleges, and in the designing of (different) rules and regulations for male and female students within coeducational institutions. In addition, recent work has shown that views of gender were involved in the definition of university and collegiate curricula: views of woman as leisure companion and educated mother leading to art and child study, views of woman as "sexless scholar" leading to Latin and Greek, and views of man as responsible citizen leading to

self-definition through course election. Implicitly
as well as explicitly, therefore, historians have
already pointed to the importance and possibility of
analyzing gender as an ingredient in the complex
meshing of social and intellectual structures that
connected students and faculty to fields of study,
and, in turn, defined the nature and status of
knowledge domains, partly as a result of the social
attributes of the people they drew. (4)

One matter that recent work seems not so
clearly to have identified for further study,
however, is the extension of gender influence, via
its role within the university, throughout the rest
of society. Again, the relative unimportance of
nutrition within the medical curriculum is
intriguing in that regard. Nutrition was thought to
have little to do with pathology. Its marginal
place within the medical curriculum that was
standardized early in the twentieth century
reflected and reinforced an emphasis within medicine
on pathology; and pathological as opposed to
holistic views of health supported public reliance
on doctors, at the same time that they diminished
public recognition of the importance of (female)
homemakers in the maintenance of health.
Presumably, therefore, in this instance (and no
doubt in others) gender-related curricular
developments within the university not only
contributed to diminishing respect for traditionally
female activities, but also profoundly influenced
attitudes toward and delivery systems for health
care.

That university curriculum decisions have been
far-reaching in their influence is not surprising.
But even within existing research on university
spheres of influence there is relatively little
substantive material available, and, perhaps more
important, there are even fewer conceptual tools
that are helpful in delineating the full and two-way
implications of the university's relationships with
the culture and society that sustains it. When
considering the methodological problems that have
obscured the historical significance of gender, one
might not be inclined to think of conceptual tools

having to do with the boundaries of the university. And yet, if one were to pursue the sort of full review that would be necessary to flesh out the points suggested above, it does seem likely that the relative underdevelopment of such conceptual tools would present itself as a problem. (5)

If reviews were undertaken of work relevant to still evident shortcomings in our understanding of definitions of the university, they also might lead from educational history and educational theory to larger problems in social history and social theory, and from there to more fundamental sources of historical bias. Limitations in the analytical concepts historians have brought to investigations of the influence of universities may be related, for example, to the still common tendency to study institutions as concrete, bounded "things," rather than as more or less formally structured contexts that organize human thought, behavior, and social interaction. Should that, indeed, be the case, one of the methodological blinds that has obscured the various roles universities (and other institutions) have played in the formation and transformation of "social realities" would also become recognizable as a factor that has obscured the social dynamics involved in the impact of gender in and on society. Teasing out those methodological problems that have limited analysis of the ways in which educational institutions have and have not been conductors of gender-related attitudes and values could thus contribute to the understanding, and, where necessary, the revision of both the broad and more specific theories that are inevitably involved in all kinds of historical research. And, needless to say, it is also likely that, in the process, there would be gains in knowledge about the social circumstances that have defined the experience of both sexes as well as the role of education in social change. (6)

As was indicated earlier, the second issue that may exemplify the value of methodologically attentive restudy has to do with how one defines education within the context of historical research. More specifically, it has to do with the consequences, perhaps especially but not exclusively, for an understanding of women's history that may derive from approaching education in traditional, school-centered ways. Many new studies in the economic, political, and social history of women have included important material and fresh insights about education, although few of them have emphasized these data or presented and analyzed them in terms of education. By reinterpreting such studies, using less institutional and more process-based views of education, one may begin to examine the consequences of the school-bound definitions of education that scholars often derive from works in educational history and then extend to other contexts. Consider what even a schematic reinterpretation of three recent studies might show. (7)

Linda Kerber's Women of the Republic explores how women created a place for themselves, however marginal and constraining, within the political structures of the new nation. The study includes intelligent and useful information on literacy and schooling, but, reanalyzed from the perspective of education as a process of deliberate growth or change, the whole book becomes highly relevant to the history of education. The centerpiece of Kerber's work is an analysis of the impact of different kinds of literature, styles of behavior, and discussions of character in tutoring and crystallizing collective and individual visions of female capacity. Kerber's book deals with schooling, but more important in terms of the perspective suggested here, it also deals with the larger processes of public and private teaching and learning that laid the groundwork for subsequent familial, school, church, and media curricula specifically directed at women. Although written as an intellectual history of the ideology of "Republican Motherhood," Women of the Republic can thus be seen as a treatise concerning the educational impact of the American Revolution on women. (8)

Ellen Carol DuBois's Feminism and Suffrage, which deals with the antislavery movement's radicalizing effects on women, can also be reconceived in terms of educational process. Arguing that "what American women learned from abolitionism was less that they were oppressed than what to do with that perception, how to turn it into a political movement," DuBois's account can be read as a description of the stimuli for that lesson: the people, events, and arguments that caused women first to recognize, question, and analyze their disenfranchisement, and then to develop the tactical skills necessary for political organization. Furthermore, because the political awakening DuBois describes could not have occurred without private reflection and peer instruction concerning the personal and social meanings of "womanhood" and "citizenship," her book can also be read as a case study in education as the continuous and cumulative individual and collective reinterpretation of ideas. Reexamined in this way, Feminism and Suffrage illuminates both the political significance of the early suffrage movement, as was intended, and, as was not intended, the educational significance for women of participation in politics within public realms. Further analyzed, it might even suggest that in more ways than are known, female exclusion from public politics was also exclusion from "public education." (9)

Focusing on Eleanor Roosevelt and the women who were her colleagues in planning and administering the New Deal, Susan Ware's Beyond Suffrage is still another example of a book in which education becomes more important when one focuses on teaching and learning regardless of institutional context. In Beyond Suffrage, Ware treats close friendships among members of a self-conscious network of politically active women and indicates, but does not explicate, the instructional as well as the emotional and practical functions of such friendships. More interesting, she suggests the degree to which these women self-consciously modeled themselves on the preceding generation of "Great Pioneers" (Jane Addams, Florence Kelley, M. Carey Thomas, and Julia Lathrop, among others); and, in exploring the differences in self-definition and group consciousness that separated Eleanor Roosevelt's generation and the next, she points to fundamental differences in educational experience. Eleanor Roosevelt's generation was inducted into public life via the sponsorship and tutelage of peers and was sustained thereafter by continuing collegial exchange; the next generation was prepared for public roles more formally and narrowly and with less continuing support and reinforcement via professional training. The purpose of Ware's study was to document the role played by women in the New Deal and the continuance of political activity among women after 1920. But, when the unmined sideline of Beyond Suffrage is emphasized, the book also documents the importance of education as an enabling process that has helped to define what women have and have not been able to do. (10)

Taken together and reinterpreted in this fashion, these three books should suggest that recent work in women's history abounds with material concerning the nurturance of talent, the training of skill, and the development of self-concept in and among women--in other words, with data concerning what it is that education is meant to do. Further, the very possibility of reanalyzing these studies should also suggest that, because such data have not tended to square with known and established approaches to the study of education, their significance for educational history has gone largely unexplored. It would seem, therefore, that there is an unfortunate disjunction between accumulating empirical evidence concerning the relevance of education for an understanding of women's history and the capacity of historians to make that relevance clear; and that this disjunction is a consequence of the greater development of institutional, and especially school-centered, perspectives within educational history, and the lesser development of other kinds of perspectives, including those derived from an understanding of the educational process.

Obviously, it is not certain what would be found through more detailed and voluminous reviewing and reinterpretation, first, in secondary sources to discern relationships that may have been of educational significance, and, then, in primary sources to examine and analyze those relationships. Nevertheless, it does seem likely that such review and reinterpretation would confirm the causative relationships ventured here. After all, however valuable, school-centered approaches cannot allow for the mapping and analysis of the full range of institutional and interpersonal resources to which individuals and groups have turned in search of educational opportunity. And, leaving aside available evidence, even common sense would argue that many of the educational settings and experiences that can only be isolated through such mapping and analysis would have been likely to have been extremely important to women, not only because women have been excluded and steered away from some types and levels of schooling, but also because their interests and aspirations sometimes have encouraged them to search out, design, create, and use opportunities for learning that could not be found in formal institutions of schooling. (11)

In pursuing this issue, educational historians once again could pursue any number of related matters. For example, if school-centered approaches to educational history have indeed contributed to misperceptions concerning the significance and role of education in women's history, then the roots of those approaches might be worth reconsidering. The attention Ellwood P. Cubberley and his fellow "educationists" and historians focused on schools in American history was directly related to progressive educational philosophy and policies. Hence, attitudes toward gender and derived from gender-related social circumstances may have been more influential in the development of progressive educational philosophy and policies than has been fully realized. Certainly it seems plausible that progressive thinking was influenced by male hegemony within school bureaucracies and professional associations of educators and social scientists. And progressive thinking is known to have been influenced by a migration of religious sentiments from the church to the school, which also may have helped to exclude female perspectives. Regardless of whether these hypotheses are true, the point here is simply that consideration of the implications of school-centered studies of education for a full appreciation of what gender difference has meant could lead to interesting work on various theoretical and substantive problems. (12)

Finally, one might also point out that if historians were to discover that education beyond the walls of a school had been of special import to women, that discovery might in turn promote greater interest in examining the organization, the curricula, and the pedagogies that have been used in nonschool educational agencies. Worthwhile and much needed in their own right, such inquiries might have instrumental contemporary value. For policymakers, they could illuminate which educational tasks have and have not always been undertaken by schools, thus adding yet another perspective to discussions of what schools are for. And for educational theorists, they could point out new settings in which to analyze the circumstances that have given rise to teaching and learning, thus adding a new chance to refine what is known about the ways in which psychological and social circumstances combine to promote education. Through this kind of research, the necessity and power that educational historians find in insights derived from the past might become more widely shared.

To suggest these possibilities may seem to venture far afield. When thinking about the research needs of women's history, basic problems in educational history and educational theory are not usually at issue. And yet, during the 1980s, questions having to do with how one studies educational institutions and frames criteria of relevance within this field must be addressed if the concerns of scholars in women's history are to be attended to with the directness they deserve. No doubt, there are other problems that also must be dealt with if the import of education in women's history is to be better understood, if the educational experience of both sexes is to be more fully recovered, and if the categories, assumptions,

and perspectives that have obscured the significance
of gender difference in history are to be
identified, analyzed, and revised. But women's
history challenges and affords educational
historians the opportunity to rethink the
fundamental methodological structures of all aspects
of their craft. Review and reinterpretation
directed toward heightened understanding of existing
and alternative methodologies is for that reason a
logical next step.

NOTES

1. For several examples of statements
concerning the methodological challenge implicit in
women's history see Carl N. Degler, "Is There a
History of Women?" Inaugural lecture, Oxford
University, March 14, 1974 (Oxford, 1975); Gerda
Lerner "Placing Women in History: Definitions and
Challenges," Feminist Studies 3 (1975): 5-14, and
reprinted in The Majority Finds its Past: Placing
Women in History (New York, 1979); Joan Kelly-Gadol,
"The Social Relation of the Sexes: Methodological
Implications of Women's History," Signs 1 (1976):
809-23. A more recent discussion that touches upon
some of these matters is Ellen DuBois et al.,
"Women's Culture in Women's History: A Symposium,"
Feminist Studies 6 (1980): 26-75.

2. Leila Rupp has argued that feminism may be
defined as "a world view" in which gender is seen as
"a primary category of analysis or explanatory
factor for understanding the unequal and unjust
distribution of power and resources in society"
("Reflections on Twentieth-Century American Women's
History," Reviews in American History 9 [1981]:
283). The premises inherent in that "world view"
may or may not have historic validity, but the point
here is that they cannot be confirmed, disproven,
or, as is most likely, refined, until gender as a
"social force" is first made more fully visible.

3. Abraham Flexner, Medical Education in the
United States and Canada, The Carnegie Foundation
for the Advancement of Teaching, Bulletin Number 4,
1910, p. 26. An intriguing recent study that deals
with the history of nutrition is Margaret W.
Rossiter, "'Women's Work' in Science, 1880-1910,"
Isis 71 (1980): 381-98.
4. The best study of women in the medical
profession is Mary Roth Walsh, "Doctors
Wanted: No Women Need Apply": Sexual Barriers in
the Medical Profession, 1835-1975 (New Haven, Conn.,
1977). It deals with the Flexner report, but not
with points raised here.
5. Obviously, there are some studies that are
useful in considering this problem. One place where
this kind of research has been collected is
Alexandra Oleson and John Voss, eds., The
Organization of Knowledge in Modern America, 1860-
1920 (Baltimore, Md., 1979).
6. Among the many works in history and the
social sciences that are relevant here are Peter L.
Berger and Thomas Luckmann, The Social Construction
of Reality: A Treatise in the Sociology of
Knowledge (New York, 1966); Herbert G. Gutman,
Work, Culture and Society in Industrializing America
(New York, 1976); Clifford Geertz, "Blurred Genres:
The Refiguration of Social Thought," American
Scholar 49 (1980): 165-79.
7. Two examples of secondary analysis in
educational history, not dissimilar from the kind of
reinterpretation suggested here, are Lawrence A.
Cremin, "The Family as Educator: Some Comments on
the Recent Historiography," in The Family as
Educator, ed. Hope Jensen Leichter (New York, 1977),
pp. 76-91; idem, "Family Community Linkages in
American Education: Some Comments on the Recent
Historiography, in Families and Communities as
Educators, ed. Hope Jensen Leichter (New York,
1979), pp. 119-40.
8. Linda K. Kerber, Women of the Republic:
Intellect and Ideology in Revolutionary America
(Chapel Hill, N.C., 1980). Another well-known work
that is like Kerber's in that it includes a chapter
on schooling, but can be reinterpreted in its

entirety as a study in educational history, is Nancy
F. Cott, The Bonds of Womanhood: "Woman's Sphere"
in New England, 1780-1835 (New Haven, Conn., 1977).
     9. Ellen Carol DuBois, Feminism and Suffrage:
The Emergence of an Independent Woman's Movement in
America, 1848-1869 (Ithaca, N.Y., 1978). The quote
is on p. 32.
     10. Susan Ware, Beyond Suffrage: Women in the
New Deal (Cambridge, Mass., 1981).
     11. I have developed this point further in
"Education as Exchange: A Perspective Derived from
Women's History," in Educating an Urban People: The
New York City Experience, ed. Diane Ravitch and
Ronald K. Goodenow (New York, 1981), pp. 141-53.
     12. Among the recent works that deal with the
points specifically raised here are Myra Strober and
David Tyack, "Why do Women Teach and Men Manage? A
Report on Schools," Signs 5 (1980): 494-503; Mari
Jo Deegan, "Early Women Sociologists and the
American Sociological Society: The Patterns of
Exclusion and Participation," American Sociologist
16 (1981): 14-24; David Tyack and Elizabeth Hansot,
Managers of Virtue: Public School Leadership in
America, 1820-1980 (New York, 1982).

14

DOMESTIC CYCLES
HISTORY OF CHILDHOOD AND FAMILY

N. Ray Hiner
University of Kansas

It is now impossible to construct an adequate history of education in America or to develop sound educational policy without a thorough knowledge of the history of childhood and the family. The historical scholarship that has been produced in these areas in the last fifteen years is so substantial that it has stimulated a profound reassessment of our understanding of the American past. What began in the 1960s as a small current within the new social history has become a powerful if not dominant force in the mainstream of American historiography. Lawrence Stone observed recently that "there is scarcely any major problem in our lives, or any major dispute about the nature of change in the past, upon which family history does not somehow impinge." (1) And he might have added, any comprehensive understanding of the human family must be based in part on a study of the experience, status, behavior, and influence of children. (2) The reasons for the growing interest in the history of children and the family are too complex to analyze here, but it is certain that the direction of American historiography has been fundamentally altered. (3)

On one level, the increasing influence of childhood and family history should neither surprise nor upset the historian of American education. Competent educational historians have always been aware of the complex relationships among all educational institutions, including the family. Educational historians, more than most, have appreciated the importance of childhood, and since the appearance in 1959 of Bernard Bailyn's Education in the Forming of American Society   few   have questioned his assertion that families are a vital part of American educational history. And yet, the development of scholarship on childhood and the family has been so rapid and so comprehensive, especially during the past ten years, that it may have temporarily overwhelmed our capacity to assimilate and think through its implications for educational historiography.

Even a brief review of the major documentary histories and anthologies that have appeared recently will illustrate the astonishing size and scope of this area of scholarship. In 1974, Robert Bremner (et al.) completed his massive three-volume documentary history of Childhood and Youth in America. This collection updates and greatly expands Grace Abbott's earlier The Child and the State and is therefore heavily institutional in focus. Even so, the great variety and number of the issues affecting children identified in Bremner's work are striking and would themselves constitute a major agenda for future research. Another extensive documentary history that appeared in 1974, Sol Cohen's five-volume Education in the United States, includes types of material on children and the family not available in the Bremner collection. Furthermore, the relationship between the history of education, childhood, and the family is obviously made more explicit in Cohen's work. Philip Greven's Child-Rearing Concepts, 1628-1861: Historical Sources and Wilson Smith's Theories of Education in Early America, 1655-1819 are more restricted in scope, but are still useful and illustrate the close relationship of the history of education, children, and the family. Greven argues convincingly that "the historical background of childhood and the family is vital to any understanding of the history of education, since most education prior to the mid-19th century was primarily informal and domestic rather than institutionalized in schools." (4) This interrelationship is confirmed further by Donald Scott's and Bernard Wishy's just published America's Families: A Documentary History, which includes many documents that relate directly to education and childhood and suggests avenues for future research that cut across all these fields. One cannot review these rich collections without being impressed by how essential a study of the history of children and the family is for an understanding of American society, culture, and education.

The remarkable number of excellent anthologies on the history of childhood and the family that have appeared within the last decade show clearly that this study is well under way. Perhaps the best known and most influential collection of articles on the American family is Michael Gordon's The American Family in Social-Historical Perspective. This volume and the substantially revised edition published in 1978 constitute the best single entree into the complex and growing literature on the history of the family. The 1978 edition includes short but well-selected bibliographical sections. Turning Points: Historical and Sociological Essays on the Family is another excellent volume of essays on family history, several of which are devoted to explicit educational themes. This collection, published in 1978, edited by John Demos and Sarane Spence Boocock, originally appeared as a special issue of the American Journal of Sociology and contains a section in which sociologists critique the essays on family history. Tamara Hareven has also edited several volumes on the history of the family. Among the most useful are Transitions: The Family and the Life Course in Historical Perspective and Family and Kin in Urban Communities, 1700-1930. Hareven, who was instrumental in establishing the Journal of Family History, has been a consistent advocate of the view that the family is not simply a passive and static entity but an active and dynamic institution in its own right. (5) Finally, Allan Lichtman and Joan Challinor edited in 1979 Kin and Communities: Families in America, an uneven, but helpful group of essays originally presented to a symposium on the family sponsored by the Smithsonian Institution.

Two major collections of original essays on the history of childhood have also appeared. The first, The History of Childhood, was edited by Lloyd deMause, founder and editor of the History of Childhood Quarterly (now The Journal of Psychohistory). The chapters by Joseph Illick on seventeenth-century Anglo-American child rearing, and John Walzer on childhood in eighteenth-century America provide a good introduction to the history of childhood in early America. deMause, an energetic, academic entrepreneur, has been criticized severely for his flamboyant style and his psychogenic theory of history, which is explained in the first chapter of this volume. Some (not all) of this criticism seems justified, but deMause has raised significant questions, and his assertion that children and childhood should be at the center of historical inquiry deserves consideration on its own merits. The second major collection of essays on the history of childhood also has a psychohistorical emphasis but is much less controversial than deMause's work. Barbara Finkelstein's Regulated Children/Liberated Children: Education in Psycho-historical Perspective represents an admirable "effort to incorporate an awareness of children into our understanding of modern educational history." (6) A third major anthology, History of Childhood in America: A Thematic Analysis and Handbook, is in preparation. This reference work, edited by Joseph Hawes and Ray Hiner, will contain fifteen original essays designed to assess the entire range of scholarship on the history of children.

One other recent anthology deserves special mention: the impressive and provocative Loving, Parenting and Dying: The Family Cycle in England

and America, Past and Present, edited by Vivian Fox
and Martin Quitt. The book's organization is based
on a systematic comparison of the life cycle in
early modern England and America. This unique
volume has much to recommend it. First, it
represents a level of integration of childhood,
family, and educational history not achieved in any
other single work. Second, the editors' ninety-page
interpretive essay, "Uniformities and Variations in
the English and American Family Cycle: Then and
Now," is an interesting and perceptive synthesis.
Indeed, the extensive notes for this section are
themselves a valuable addition to the literature.
This volume will serve as an excellent companion to
the Gordon and Finkelstein readers.

Even this review of recent anthologies and
documentary histories fails to capture the full
depth and scope of the latest scholarship on the
history of childhood and the family. An enormous
variety of articles have appeared not only in The
Journal of Family History and the History of
Childhood Quarterly but in such periodicals as the
Journal of Social History, The Journal of
Interdisciplinary History, History of Education
Quarterly, The Psychohistory Review, The William
and Mary Quarterly, and American Quarterly.
Furthermore, numerous books and monographs have been
published that either focus directly on children and
the family or devote major sections to them (see
note 22). Perhaps the most efficient way to
approach this larger mass of publication is through
one or more of the comprehensive review essays that
have appeared recently. Articles by Patricia Rooke,
Ruby Takanishi, and Ray Hiner review the
historiography of childhood, and those by Maris
Vinovskis, Lawrence Cremin, Lawrence Stone, and
Daniel Blake Smith discuss the literature on the
family. (7) Major bibliographies are also available
for both fields. (8)

Historians of education should give high
priority to incorporating this new research on
childhood and the family. Although the historiography of education is far more comprehensive and
sophisticated than it was twenty-five years ago, it

is still more narrow and institutional in focus than it ought to be. The continuing emphasis on formal educational processes and institutions is understandable and justified in many cases, but we will not be able to understand even the history of schooling until we have a better grasp of how it is related to what has been and continues to be the institution in which the vast majority of Americans experience the major transitions of human life--the family. Lawrence Cremin demonstrates how much analytical power the educational historian can gain from an awareness of the history of the family in his two recent books on American education in the colonial period and in the nineteenth century. (9) And even Cremin's first-rate work will be subject to revision as our knowledge of the family continues to grow.

If educational historians have been slow to integrate family history into their work, they have been reluctant even to recognize the need to develop a conscious and explicit concern for children and their perspectives. As Barbara Finkelstein has said, historians of education have usually "visualized learners as essentially passive" and too often assumed that what is taught is what is learned. Their histories, she declares,

> proceed as though children were cavernous holes into which are poured status, skills, books, and curricula, and out of which emerge formed human beings. Unwittingly asserting that human beings become only what others intend them to become, they have relegated learners and learning to the back seat of the historical bus. (10)

It should also be noted here that too many family historians, while supporting the proposition that families are not simply passive recipients of social and economic change, have nevertheless tended to ignore the fact that all human relationships are to some degree reciprocal and dynamic and that children are often actors and educators in their own right,

influencing as well as influenced, changing as well
as being changed. Neither family historians nor
educational historians can afford to overlook the
experience, perspective, status, and behavior of
children.

But beyond these theoretical concerns, there
are also compelling substantive reasons why
educational historians should pay close attention to
the burgeoning history of childhood and the family.
The research in these areas has profoundly altered
our traditional conceptions of past childhood and
family life. For example, Bernard Bailyn's notion
that the growing importance of schools in the
eighteenth century was in large measure a response
to the breakdown of the dominant extended family
into an isolated, nuclear form unable to fulfill its
traditional functions has become completely
untenable. It is now widely accepted that the most
common structure of English and American households
has always been nuclear, not extended. This is not
to say that there have been no important family
relationships outside the nuclear unit or that
extended kin networks did not exist (indeed, they
may have become more important in the eighteenth
century than in the seventeenth), but Bailyn's
family disintegration hypothesis can no longer be
justified as an explanation of the growing
importance of schools in the eighteenth
century. (11) Similarly, past efforts to explain
the emergence of compulsory public education in
nineteenth-century America look more and more
deficient because they did not take the family into
account or were based on assumptions about the
family that have now been discredited. Further,
attempts to evaluate the efficacy of schools as
instruments of assimilation and enculturation in the
late nineteenth century must now be based on an
awareness that differences in school achievement and
attendance seem to be related in part to variations
in family life among various ethnic groups. (12)
Finally, our awareness of the complexity of the
educational impact of the Great Depression has been
heightened considerably by the research of Glen
Elder. Through a careful analysis of the life

histories of individuals in Berkeley and Oakland who experienced the Depression as children and adolescents, Elder discovered that the long-range effects of the Depression and the deprivation it often brought were strongly associated with the characteristics of the families in which the individuals lived and the ages of the children during the Depression. (13) Other, similar examples from recent family history that have immediate implications for educational history could be added indefinitely. There is simply no major area of educational history that cannot be illuminated by a better understanding of the family.

An equally long list of relevant examples can be drawn from recent work on the history of childhood. However, it should be sufficient here to identify two major conclusions from this work and discuss briefly their importance for educational history. First, historians of childhood have established beyond question the profound historicity of childhood as an idea and as a social category. Moreover, the development of the modern concept of childhood is linked so closely with the emergence of modern educational ideas and practices that it is impossible to conceive of one without the other. (14) In this sense the history of education cannot be separated from the history of childhood. Even so, it would be a mistake to assume that the experience of childhood is synonymous with childhood as a social category, that children are only inert projections of what adults think they are or expect them to be. The history of childhood in America is replete with examples of how children either consciously or unconsciously resisted the demands of adults and gained some control over the educational process. (15) Any historian who views children only as ciphers of social ideas and processes does not understand children, and any educator who assumes it is possible to gain complete command over a child's education understands neither children nor history.

Thus, one of the first steps in any future research agenda for educational history should be a general review of the history of childhood and the family and a careful analysis of the scholarship

that relates most directly to the research to be
undertaken. Not only will errors of fact and
judgment be avoided by this procedure, but fresh new
questions and topics will be generated that will
broaden and enrich the quality of educational
history.

In completing such a review and analysis the
number of research topics relating to childhood and
the family that deserve the attention of educational
historians will be seen to be enormous. Further,
because new areas of inquiry are constantly
appearing, it is not prudent to insist on a rigidly
defined program for future research. It is
possible, however, to suggest the kinds of topics
where new or additional research would be
profitable.

Perhaps the most glaring anomaly in the
existing literature on childhood and family life is
that although the majority of Americans lived in
rural areas until well into the twentieth century,
most of the published scholarship concentrates on
urban life. This is a serious deficiency, because
the full meaning of what we know about urban
children and families will evade us until we have
the basis for comparison provided by a comprehensive
knowledge of the rural experience. Some of this
discrepancy can be explained by the greater
availability of records for urban areas, but sources
for the study of rural children and families have by
no means been exhausted. (16)

The history of religion in America has
certainly not been neglected, but like many fields,
it is only beginning to be viewed from the
perspective of families and children. Moreover, the
history of religion has itself not been utilized by
educational historians as much as it could be. A
greater focus on the religious experience of
children and families should make this integration
easier. (17)

Ethnicity and gender are relatively new areas
of historical research that offer many opportunities
for the educational historian interested in
childhood and the family. It is now clear that
ethnicity and gender exercised a profound influence

on the educational experience of children and the character of family life, but the precise nature of this influence will not be fully understood until more work is done and more questions are posed that focus on families and children. (18) The new history of women has provided valuable insights that are indispensable in the construction of a comprehensive history of education, but historians of women have not yet made children a central concern of their research. A greater concentration on children and families would further enrich women's history and provide immense benefits to the history of education. (19)

The development of youth culture is another promising area for further investigation that has been grossly neglected. Historians of education have not been as sensitive as they should be to the educational significance (including the unintentional consequences) of requiring, encouraging, and permitting children to spend much of their time with other children. Closely related to this is the history of play which, according to developmental psychologists, reveals a great deal about the essence of childhood as a special way of being in the world. We need to know much more about the history of this phenomenon, including not only how and why adults often tried to promote, control, or eliminate play but also how children experienced it and used it for their own purposes. (20)

Among the many other topics directly relating to children that need more attention from educational historians include latency, adolescence (especially female adolescence), sexuality, orphanhood, child abuse, corporal punishment, political socialization, and children's health. It would be counterproductive to extend this list of research opportunities further, in part because it would reinforce an impression that this essay has no doubt encouraged, namely, that educational historians have much more to learn from historians of childhood and the family than they can offer in return. This would be a serious error, for historians of education have a great deal to contribute to the history of childhood and the

family. Anyone familiar with these fields knows
that in spite of their tremendous vitality, they
both suffer the serious weakness of having not yet
developed an adequate theoretical base. Historians
of the family have at times depended too heavily on
functionalist   modernization   theory,   and   are
experiencing great difficulty in relating the vast
amount of quantitative data they have collected to
important questions about the psychological and
emotional   dimensions   of   family   life.   The
scholarship on the history of childhood is so
fragmented and dispersed that it cannot really be
said to have a theoretical emphasis, although some
of the work in this field does reflect a strong
psychological orientation, occasionally to the point
of   reductionism.   Thus,   efforts   to   integrate
scholarship within and between these fields has had
to proceed on an ad hoc basis. What is needed at
this critical stage in the development of these
fields   is   a   theoretical   perspective   that   is
consistent with the unique character of childhood
and family study but is not bound by the narrow
parameters of either.

Much of this need could be met if historians of
childhood and the family made greater use of an
explicit, comprehensive theory of education when
designing questions and evaluating research on
childhood and the family. Whether they adopt
Lawrence Cremin's definition of education as "the
deliberate, systematic, and sustained effort to
transmit, evoke, or acquire knowledge, attitudes,
values, skills or sensibilities," or, as I prefer,
choose to view it as "the entire process by which
humans develop a sense of self, acquire their
identity, learn the ways of their society, and
transmit   their   culture   from   generation   to
generation," historians of childhood and the family
can gain enormous analytical leverage and greatly
enhance their ability to see the relationships
between their fields and others. (21) By adopting a
comprehensive educational perspective, they will
reduce the conceptual and methodological narrowness
that has too often weakened new areas of inquiry and
reduced their influence. Thus, if the history of

education can obviously be illuminated and enriched
by the new research on childhood and the family,
historians of the family and childhood should also
understand that an educational perspective can be a
vital ingredient in ensuring the future strength and
development of their fields. And if this mutually
beneficial exchange makes it more difficult to
distinguish the history of childhood and the family
from the history of education, then we will have
indeed made progress. (22)

NOTES

1. Lawrence Stone, "Family History in the
1980's: Past Achievement and Future Trends,"
Journal of Interdisciplinary History 12 (Summer
1981): 87.
2. Daniel Blake Smith, "The Study of the
Family in Early America: Trends, Problems, and
Prospects," William and Mary Quarterly 39 (January
1982): 11; N. Ray Hiner, "The Child in American
Historiography: Accomplishments and Prospects,"
The Psychohistory Review 7 (Summer 1978): 15-16.
3. Stone, "Family History," pp. 51-87; Smith,
"Study of the Family," p. 28.
4. Philip J. Greven, Jr., ed., Child Rearing
Concepts, 1628-1861: Historical Sources (Itasca,
Ill., 1973), p. 1.
5. Tamara K. Hareven, ed., Themes in the
History of the Family (Worchester, Mass., 1977), p.
22. I regret that the excellent anthology edited by
Mel Albin and Dominick Cavallo (Family Life in
America, 1620-2000, St. James, New York, 1981), came
to my attention too late to include in the text of
this essay.
6. Barbara Finkelstein, ed., Regulated
Children/Liberated Children: Education in Psycho-
historical Perspective (New York, 1979), p. 1.
7. Patricia Rooke, "The 'Child
Institutionalized' in Canada, Britain, and the
United States: A Trans-Atlantic Perspective,"

The Journal of Educational Thought 11 (August 1977):
156-71; Ruby Takanishi, "Childhood as a Social
Issue: Historical Roots of Contemporary Child
Advocacy Movements," Journal of Social Issues 34
(1978): 8-28; Hiner, "Child in American
Historiography," pp. 13-23; Maris A. Vinovskis,
"From Household to Life Course: Some Observations
on Recent Trends in Family History," American
Behavioral Scientist 21 (November-December 1977):
263-87; Lawrence Cremin, "Family-Community Linkages
in American Education: Some Comments on the Recent
Historiography," Teachers College Record 79 (May
1978): 683-704; Stone, "Family History," pp. 51-87;
Smith, "Study of the Family," pp. 3-28.
    8. Gerald L. Soliday, ed., History of the
Family and Kinship: A Select International
Bibliography (Milwood, N.J., 1980); James Wallace
Milden, ed., The Family in Past Time: A Guide to
the Literature (New York, 1977); John J. Fitzpatrick
et al., "A Bibliography of Psychohistory," History
of Childhood Quarterly 2 (Spring 1975): 517-62;
Manuel D. Lopez, "A Guide to the Interdisciplinary
Literature of the History of Childhood," History of
Childhood Quarterly 1 (Winter 1974): 463-94.
    9. Lawrence Cremin, American Education: The
Colonial Experience, 1607-1783 (New York, 1970);
idem, American Education: The National Experience,
1783-1876 (New York, 1980).
    10. Finkelstein, Regulated Children, p. 1.
    11. For a review of the literature on this
issue, see N. Ray Hiner, "Wars and Rumors of Wars:
The Historiography of Colonial Education as a Case
Study in Academic Imperialism," Societas 7 (Spring
1978): 89-114.
    12. For examples of the burgeoning literature
on these topics, see Barbara Finkelstein, "In Fear
of Childhood: Relationships Between Parents and
Teachers in Popular Primary Schools in the
Nineteenth Century," History of Childhood Quarterly
3 (Winter 1976): 321-35; Michael Katz and Jan E.
Davey, "Youth and Early Industrialization in a
Canadian City," in Turning Points: Historical and
Sociological Essays on the Family, ed. John Demos
and Sara Boocock (Chicago, 1978), pp. 81-119; Carl

Kaestle and Maris Vinovskis, "From Apron Strings to ABC's: Parents, Children, and Schooling in Nineteenth-Century Massachusetts," in ibid., pp. 39-80; Michael R. Olneck and Marvin Lazerson, "The School Achievement of Immigrant Children: 1900-1930," History of Education Quarterly 14 (Winter 1974): 453-82; Daniel T. Rogers, "Socializing Middle-Class Children: Institutions, Fables, and Work-values in Nineteenth-Century America," Journal of Social History 13 (Spring 1980): 354-67; Jane Wilkie Riblet, "Social Status, Acculturation, and School Attendance in 1850 Boston," Journal of Social History 11 (Winter 1977): 179-92.

13. Glen H. Elder, Jr., Children of the Great Depression: Social Change in Life Experience (Chicago, 1974); Glen Elder and Richard Rockwell, "The Depression Experience in Men's Lives," in Kin and Communities: Families in America, ed. Allan J. Lichtman and Joan R. Challinor (Washington, D.C., 1979), pp. 95-118.

14. Philippe Aries, Centuries of Childhood (London, 1962); Lloyd deMause, "The Evolution of Childhood," History of Childhood Quarterly 1 (Spring 1974): 503-75; Lawrence Stone, The Family, Sex, and Marriage in England, 1500-1800 (New York, 1977); Randolph Trumbach, The Rise of the Egalitarian Family (New York, 1978); Jean-Lovis Flandrin, Families in Modern Times (Cambridge, 1979); David Hunt, Parents and Children in History (New York, 1970).

15. For further discussion of the nature of childhood as an experience and for illustrations of how children have influenced adults, see Hiner, "Child in American Historiography," pp. 15-21.

16. For examples of recent studies of rural families and children, see D. Clayton Brown, "Health of Farm Children in the South, 1900-1950," Agricultural History 53 (January 1979): 170-87; John M. Faragher, Women and Men on the Overland Trail (New Haven, 1979); David Tyack, "The Tribe and the Common School: Community Control in Rural Education," American Quarterly 24 (March 1972): 3-19.

17. For a flawed but interesting effort to

provide an integrated picture of family, child-rearing, and religion, see Philip Greven, The Protestant Temperament: Patterns of Child-Rearing, Religious Experience, and the Self in Early America (New York, 1977).

18. Leonard Dinnerstein, Roger Nicholas, and David Reimers, Natives and Strangers: Ethnic Groups and the Building of America (New York, 1979); Werner Sollors, "Theory of American Ethnicity," American Quarterly 33 (Bibliography 1981): 257-83.

19. For example, there are several valuable recent articles on childbirth practices, but they concentrate almost entirely on the experiences of the mothers and pay little attention to how these practices may have affected children. See Nancy Schrom Dye, "History of Childbirth in America," Signs 6 (Autumn 1980): 97-108; Janet Bogdan, "Care or Cure? Childbirth Practices in Nineteenth Century America," Feminist Studies 4 (June 1979): 92-99. For examples of recent scholarship that includes more direct concern for children and for discussions of the relationship between the history of women and the family, see Ruth Bloch, "American Feminine Ideals in Transition: The Rise of the Moral Mother, 1785-1815," Feminist Studies 4 (June 1978): 101-26; Nancy Cott, "Notes toward an Interpretation of Antebellum Childrearing," The Psychohistory Review 6 (Spring 1978): 4-20; Barbara J. Harris, "Recent Work on the History of the Family: A Review Article," Feminist Studies 3 (Fall 1975): 159-72; Rayna Rapp, Ellen Ross, and Renate Bridenthaul, "Examining Family History," Feminist Studies 5 (Spring 1979): 175-200.

20. The value of pursuing these questions is illustrated by the following studies: David Wallace Adams and Victor Edmonds, "Making Your Move: The Educational Significance of the American Board Game, 1832 to 1904," History of Education Quarterly 17 (Winter 1977): 359-83; Leroy Ashby, "'Straight From Youthful Hearts': Lone Scout and the Discovery of the Child, 1915-1924," Journal of Popular Cultural 9 (Fall 1975): 775-93; Dominick Cavallo, Muscles and Morals: Organized Playgrounds and Urban Reform, 1880-1920 (Philadelphia, 1981); John Clark, "The

Stoop is the World," Kansas Journal of Sociology 3 (Summer 1967): 99-109; David K. Wiggins "The Play of Slave Children in the Plantation Communities of the Old South, 1820-1860," Journal of Sport History 7 (Summer 1980); 21-39. Also see Erik H. Erikson, Toys and Reasons (New York, 1977); D. W. Winnicott, Playing and Reality (New York, 1971).

    21. Cremin, American Education, p. xiii; N. Ray Hiner, "An Epistemological Framework for Educational Studies," (Unpublished paper, University of Kansas), p. 8.

    22. In fact, this process is well under way. Among the recent works that are difficult to classify because they reflect an integrated concern for education, childhood, and the family are the following: James Axtell, The School Upon a Hill: Education and Society in Colonial New England (New Haven, 1974); Stone, Family, Sex, and Marriage; Greven, Protestant Temperament; Daniel Blake Smith, Inside the Great House: Planter Family Life in Eighteenth-Century Chesapeake Society (Ithaca, 1980); Michael Zuckerman, "William Byrd's Family," Perspectives in American History 12 (1979): 253-311; Peter Gregg Slater, Children in the New England Mind (Hamden, Conn., 1977); Bernard Farber, Guardians of Virtue: Salem Families in 1800 (New York, 1972); Michael Paul Rogin, Fathers and Children: Andrew Jackson and the Subjugation of the American Indians (New York, 1975); Allan Stanley Horlick, Country Boys and Merchant Princes: The Social Control of Young Men in New York (Lewisburg, Pa., 1975); Charles Strickland, "A Transcendentalist Father: The Child-Rearing Practices of Bronson Alcott," History of Chilhood Quarterly 1 (Summer 1973): 4-51; Kathryn Kish Sklar, Catherine Beecher: A Study in American Domesticity (New York, 1973); Joseph Kett, Rites of Passage: Adolescence in America, 1790 to the Present (New York, 1977); Thomas L. Webber, Deep Like the Rivers: Education in the Slave Quarter Community, 1831-1865 (New York, 1978); Faragher, Women and Men on the Overland Trail; Joseph Hawes, Children in Urban Society: Juvenile Delinquency in Nineteenth Century American (York, 1971); Cavallo, Muscles and Morals; Steven

Schlossman, Love and the American Delinquent: The Theory and Practice of "Progressive" Juvenile Justice, 1825-1920 (Chicago, 1977); Glen Davis, Childhood and History in America (New York, 1977); Christopher Lasch, The Culture of Narcissism (New York, 1978).

15

SCHOOLS, WORK AND FAMILY LIFE
SOCIAL HISTORY*

Michael B. Katz and David Hogan
University of Pennsylvania

In the 1840s Horace Mann, then Secretary of the
Massachusetts Board of Education, asked
manufacturers for their views on the value of a
common school education. Those who replied
preferred schooled workers. However, their reasons
had nothing to do with any special cognitive or
technical skills. Rather, workers who had been to
school, said the manufacturers, were more reliable,
honest, punctual, and less likely to strike.
Although early school promoters were eager to win
the support of manufacturers, they had other
objectives, which conflicted with training docile
and deferential workers: they argued that schooling
should promote economic independence and social
mobility by instilling self-control, self-direction,
and a will to achieve. In fact, two or three
decades later employers and other social
commentators began to complain that schools had
destroyed the national taste for manual work and had

*The research in this paper has been supported
by the National Institute of Education, Grant No.
9-0173.

produced a superabundance of unemployable aspirants to white collar work.

Conflicting views about the relation between education and work have been a feature of educational discourse for a long time. What role have schools played in shaping the labor force? Has a link between school and work been forged through the transmission of technical and cognitive skills or by the way schooling has affected personality, values, and habits? For generations employers have complained about the inadequate preparation schools have given to young people. Have these complaints reflected low levels of skill and marginal literacy or a more subtle problem, the development of attitudes that conflict with the organization of work? If the problem lies in habits and attitudes, where have young people learned them? Has there been something about the way school life is organized that transmits a message more powerful than the skills and content that teachers try to impart? Or do the attitudes of young people merely reflect what they have learned in their families, from their peers, and, now, through the mass media? Controversies about the relation between education and work involve not only questions about the impact of schooling on individuals' behavior but also on social processes. What effect has the vocationally differentiated character of secondary education had on equality of opportunity and on social mobility? Although these questions have been asked in one way or another since the early part of the nineteenth century, their answer is by no means clear, and scholars disagree, sometimes quite sharply, on the relations between family background, educational achievement, and occupational attainment in both the past and present.

These are some of the questions that led us to undertake a large project on the relations between the organization of schools, work, and family life in Philadelphia between the early nineteenth century and, roughly, the First World War. The project began in September 1979 and is now in its third and officially final year. Most of our work to date has been the collection of data, particularly the preparation of large, machine-readable files. We are only now starting the analysis of the quantitative data. Nonetheless, we can best illustrate our ideas about the direction that should be taken by research on the relations between education and social structure by discussing the sources we have used and how we have organized the research.

Although we expect our research to contribute to the reformulation of general interpretations about the relations between school, work, and family, its value does not lie entirely, or even primarily, in its theoretical success. As we have thought about the questions we wanted to answer, we have been impressed over and over again by the relative empirical vacuum in which most debate about the historical role of education takes place. Despite the recent interest in the social history of education, ignorance about many basic issues remains monumental, and, as a consequence, we lack the hard demographic and descriptive data on which to build interpretations with confidence. Our project will correct this deficiency for one city, but we remain painfully aware that the task is still in its infancy, and our general message here is to urge historians to get on with the systematic social inquiry into the relations between schools, work, and family life in times past.

There is no lack of models of educational development or of the relations between education and social structure. Hogan has reviewed these critically elsewhere. Here we simply want to begin by pointing to three frameworks that guide our general approach to the issues. First, we assume the existence of systematic relations between schools, the economy, and families. Some of these relations are structural, for example, the way in which pedagogy and classroom management sometimes habituate young people for the workplace. Other links are institutional, as in the use of public schooling to channel students into a differentiated and stratified labor market or as a means of promoting social mobility.

Second, we proceed from the premise that the

goals of schooling often have conflicted: parents, educators, and businessmen often have hoped for different outcomes from the schools. One example is the tension between deference and achievement as goals of mid-nineteenth-century schoolmen. Another is the conflict between citizenship and vocational training that has permeated American education since the Progressive period.

We believe that conflicts among the purposes of schooling have generated continual pressures for change within the system itself. At the same time, conflicts between the organization of schooling and the characteristics of social and economic life have generated other pressures for change. Some of these conflicts have been economic, the apparently anachronistic quality of the curriculum, for instance; others have been social, such as the continuation of racial segregation in a society in which most people are at least nominally committed to integration. Sometimes, too, conflicts arise from the failure of schools to foster family goals. Here a current example is the decreased ability of colleges to assure their graduates a well-paying, high-status job.

The point is that the relations between schools, work, families, and social goals never are static. Sometimes conflicts arise within the system itself, as between the dual goals of schools, and sometimes from the mismatch between schooling and some aspect of economic, social, or family life. Rarely, in fact, do these conflicts exist in isolation. Instead, they overlay and interact with each other at the same time. But--and this is what we wish to stress most--it is conflict that generates pressure for educational change. Change is not the result of smooth, functional adaptations to new circumstances or the result of enlightened, rational planning. Rather, change is a messy process, always embedded in conflict, or better, multiple conflicts fought by shifting coalitions.

Our argument is not that conflicts have no recurring patterns or that they lack relations to social structure. Indeed, the basic and enduring divisions in American social structure always are reflected in educational conflict, because classes ultimately want different things from the schools. The problem is how to conceptualize the connection between social class interests and educational change. This brings us to the third perspective that informs our work.

What needs to be explained is change in both educational organization and education-related behavior. For instance, in the late nineteenth and early twentieth century the shape of secondary education changed dramatically with the introduction of differentiated curricula and junior high schools. At the same time the proportion of young people attending secondary schools increased greatly. Most of this increase, given its size, had to come from the children of the working class. Who changed school systems across the country? Why? Why did working-class children begin to attend more?

It is crude to assume an automatic correspondence between the reasons why school boards across the country changed the nature of secondary education and the reasons that working-class children began to stay longer in school. We are unwilling, without explicit evidence, to believe either that families were reluctantly forced to send their children to school longer or that they passively accepted the new ideology of educational expansion and differentiation. We prefer to assume that ordinary people usually assess their circumstances intelligently and act reasonably. The problem, of course, is that nobody is free to act without constraints, and it is the reasons that people choose as they do among the limited options available that historians should seek to discover.

Institutionally, too, school systems were the product of complex processes of political conflict and negotiation among competing groups. By the turn of the century public educational systems within cities had become bureaucracies. At the state and national level organizations of teachers and administrators actively promoted the interests of their members. Indeed, educators' desires for career opportunities, independence, and security exercised a major influence on the development of

public education during the second half of the
nineteenth century. But at the same time major
economic changes associated with the onset of
capitalism and industrialization, particularly
changes in the organization of work and the
stratification of labor markets and opportunity
structures, profoundly altered the institutional
matrix of educational politics and development. The
new educational options offered to working-class and
middle-class families then grew out of a complex set
of economic and political processes and reflected
compromise rather than the realization of any set of
goals for the structure of public schooling.

The emergence of educational change from
conflict, the interpretation of educational behavior
among ordinary people as an element of a family
strategy, and the alteration of educational
structure as part of both the changed social
relations of American industrial capitalism and the
aspirations of professional educators: these
constitute the general framework in which we
approach our study of the relations between schools,
work, and family life in Philadelphia.

One approach to the research task is to divide
the work according to three issues: structural
developments and characteristics, individual
behavior, and outcomes. We hope to describe and
explain a number of the key structural
characteristics of work and schooling. With work,
we set out to study the rate and nature of
industrial and commercial expansion, changes in
occupational structure, internal characteristics and
control structures of workplaces, skill
requirements, changes in the educational
requirements of jobs, how jobs were learned, and the
relationship between productivity and educational
achievement.

With schooling, we focus on the absolute and
relative rates of growth in school enrollment by
educational level and age cohort, the
differentiation of the educational system into
different types of schools and different kinds of
curricula, the introduction of standardized
curricula and evaluation procedures, the

characteristics of classroom organization and pedagogy, the introduction of extracurricular activities, and teacher training and certification. One research project certainly will not be able to produce definitive or thorough descriptions and explanations of all these characteristics of work and schooling. Indeed, given the nature of the sources and the emphases that have developed during the course of the research, coverage will be uneven, but we hope to be able to say something about most of them, even if it is only to point to promising lines of further study.

The project focuses on the key individual behaviors school attendance and achievement. In particular, we want to connect these with the class origin, ethnic background, and family circumstances of young people and to understand education as one element in the way in which men and women from different backgrounds negotiated their transitions to adulthood. As we shall observe shortly, the project has an extraordinary amount of data with which to study these issues.

It is most difficult to investigate educational outcomes. We would like to know what impact education had on people, especially on their adult occupations. We also would like to be able to enter the debate about the relation between schooling and the structure of inequality, the sources of social and political legitimacy, and the nature of work itself. We have a modest amount of data about the adult occupations of high school students. As for the broader social impact of education, our conclusions will emerge from the interplay between our empirical results and theory.

The project demanded a complex design which permitted shifts among various perspectives and facilitated making links among them. Thus, we divided the actual work into five perspectives: the family economy, the individual life course, the demography of school and work, organizational innovation, and social ecology. By and large each perspective corresponds fairly closely to major data sets.

The Family Economy

All families have a cycle, a structure, and an economy. All go through a series of phases from formation through dissolution. All consist of individuals occupying well-defined statuses. And all must earn the means for their subsistence and allocate resources among family members. The task for historians is to show the interrelations among these three characteristics of families, to trace their changing configurations over time, and to show their differentiation by class, ethnicity, and other factors.

The most common theme in discussions of the family economy is the separation of home and work. In this view the family economy dissolved as place of work and place of residence became distinct. Leading this momentous change was the middle class, which pioneered a new family form focusing on the socialization of children and the celebration of domestic values. There are at least two problems with this version of family history. First, the first people to live away from their place of work were wage-workers, not proprietors or professionals, because in cities laborers and other married wage workers usually lived apart from their workplace. In fact, many businessmen, manufacturers, and professionals combined their place of work and residence even well after industrialization had begun to dominate local economies. Even more, the standard interpretation neglects the fact that all families always must have an economy. All of them must deal with the acquisition and distribution of resources in order to survive. Thus the framework for the study of family history should not be the decline of the family economy but its changing nature over time.

There are several important questions about education that can be studied through analyzing the interrelation between family cycles, structures, and economies. Families have had to balance their needs for income against their desires for consumption. At particular points in family cycles the strain between income and consumption is greatest, for instance, when all children are young. How did families compensate for economic strain at different points in their histories? Did families with young children, for instance, take in boarders or relatives who could provide an extra income? Were families more likely to send older adolescent children to school when there were no more young children in the household or when there were others in the family who could supplement its income? How did a family decide when to forgo the income that an employed child could contribute?

Decisions about school probably reflected broad family strategies about social mobility. For example, in early twentieth-century Chicago, Italians and Poles sought to establish and maintain a culturally defined level of economic welfare through the acquisition of property. Hence, they took their children out of school relatively early and used their income to buy property. By contrast, Jews and Rumanians emphasized the social mobility of individual children, as opposed to the family unit, and kept them longer in school. One consequence is that these two groups had lower rates of home ownership than either Poles or Italians.

Clearly, the family economy mediates the relation between school and work. The notion of work, we must stress, should include activities within the home. Domestic work or housekeeping surely is an important type of work, albeit not rewarded with wages. It is also a form of work with important implications for educational behavior, because the expectations of families for their daughters shaped their willingness to allow them to remain in school. Where daughters were expected to play a major role with housework and child care, they left school earlier. The assumption that a woman's place was in the home, however, did not always curtail the school attendance of girls: in the latter part of the nineteenth century many educators and social reformers, alarmed at what they took to be declining domestic skills among working-class and immigrant women, introduced domestic science into school curricula.

There are important methodological problems affecting the analysis of the relations between family cycles, structures, and economies, especially the definition of the phases of the family cycle. In this project we are using stages, based on the age of the mother, defined by Katz for his study of Hamilton, Ontario, and Buffalo, New York. The sources for tracing the relations between family cycles, structures, and economies are manuscript censuses. In Philadelphia we are using samples of families from 1850 to 1880 federal censuses taken by the Philadelphia Social History Project. To this we are adding a new sample from the 1900 census (which includes number of months each person attended school).

Two aspects of classification that haunt all analyses touching on social structure are the grouping of occupations and the definition of class. Although we do not wish to dwell on these issues here, it is important to stress that our notion of class is distinct from stratification. In our analyses classes are not more or less arbitrary levels in a hierarchy. They are based, rather, on social relations and express the fundamental social groups that derive from the way in which material life is reproduced. As such they are dynamic, constantly interacting with each other.

In the study of class, indeed in the study of occupation as well, one methodological point must be emphasized. On censuses, many men have a simple artisan occupational designation such as shoemaker, tailor, carpenter, blacksmith. It is not possible to tell from the census alone whether they are self-employed or wage-workers. Yet the question is imperative because their status determines their class position. Indeed, in his study of Hamilton and Buffalo Katz found that masters and workers behaved quite differently on various matters, including whether they sent their older children to school. Preliminary results in Philadelphia point to similar patterns. Thus, it is crucial to try to make the distinction, to identify those artisans who own their own businesses. We have done this through the use of city business directories, which, although imperfect, generally are a reliable source for this purpose. The process of identifying masters is time-consuming and tedious, but we cannot overemphasize its importance for the historical study of social structure.

The Individual Life Course
        The human life course is only partly determined by biology. It also is a product of culture and history. Aside from birth, maturation, aging, and death, the shape of human lives has varied not only among cultures but over time within Western culture. Even biological events, such as age at menarche or average life span, vary with historical conditions. For our purposes the most critical phase of the life course is adolescence, which we hold to be a modern invention. The historicity of adolescence is of great importance for two reasons. One is the close connection between ideas about adolescence and the development of schooling. The other is our contemporary habit of accepting adolescence as fixed or almost transhistorical. As a consequence, we tend to think of changing or reforming the institutions through which adolescents pass. We do not, nearly often enough, consider whether the shape of the transition to adulthood itself might be different.
        In a rough sense the history of young people since the seventeenth or eighteenth centuries has had three major stages. The first should be called Youth. In this phase, which lasted well into the nineteenth century, young people lived at home, sometimes attending school, until they began to work. They then left their parents' homes and lived in a series of other households as quasi-family members until they married. This stage of "semi-autonomy" was quite lengthy because young people probably left home around the age of 16, and men did not marry until about the age of 27 and women, on the average, until about 23.
        Adolescence as we know it began with a change in the relation between home and work. In the early industrial period many young people began to live at home during their early working years, remaining with their parents probably much longer than ever before in history, longer, on the average, than

today. The reasons why young people began to stay at home longer are not clear, although the practice was ubiquitous throughout the social structure. Very likely it reflected a combination of structural and cultural influences. Prior to the development of cheap mass transportation at the end of the nineteenth century people had to live within walking distance of their work. When most workplaces were small and scattered, many young people probably had to take work which was not within walking distance of their parents' homes. Later in the century the development of large factories with jobs for young people brought work within walking distance of many more young people's homes, making it possible for them to live with their parents even after they began to work.

But there is more to the story. In the same period writers addressing more affluent parents began to argue against boarding schools and to support local high schools partly on the grounds that young people should live with their parents. Given the support for high school development in these years, it is clear that moderately affluent parents sought a way of educating their children and keeping them at home. Young people who attended school were directly dependent on their parents. Those who worked gave most of their income to their families. Hence, they too remained dependent while they lived at home. Thus, the increased time that children lived with their parents initiated a period of prolonged dependence, which increasingly was reinforced and shaped by age-segregated institutions. This prolonged, institutionalized dependence constitutes the social definition of adolescence that has persisted until our own time. Indeed, the new psychological theories of adolescence, such as G. Stanley Hall's, appeared only after the demographic transition to prolonged dependence was well under way.

Adolescence in the nineteenth century was marked by a relatively long spread between certain key life events, such as starting work and marriage, and by relatively little overlap between them. The key elements in the transition to adulthood--leaving school, starting to work, marrying, establishing a household--all occurred in a reasonably well-defined sequence and were contingent upon each other. Sometime after 1900, however, the spread between the initial age of the various stages in the transition to adulthood began to shrink. And, as the transition became more compressed, it lost much of its sequential and contingent character as events within individual lives often overlapped. However, just when and why the shift occurred and how the timing of changes in the transition to adulthood varied by sex, class, and ethnicity remains obscure. This is a major question, which we are trying to answer through systematic study of the ages at which young people left school, when they left home, where they lived when they moved away from their parents, when they began to work, when they married, and where they lived when first married.

Once again our sources are the manuscript censuses of 1850-1900. With these we can look systematically at the residence, household status, employment, school attendance, and marital status of all young people in the sample. Prior to 1880, unfortunately, we cannot determine the ethnic background (defined as parents' birthplace) of children who did not live with their families. Nor do we know the occupations of the fathers of young people who did not live with their families. Nonetheless, we can chart the most important patterns in the transition to adulthood and show how they changed over time.

Modell et al. measured five key transitions in the life course of young people using the 1880 Philadelphia Social History Project sample of the city's white population and 1970 census data. They examined the interrelation of these key events in terms of five dimensions: prevalence, timing, spread, age congruity, and integration. Their analysis showed important changes during the period, but it could not show exactly when they began or the differences between ethnic groups and classes. Modell, also a member of this project, is refining the measures used in the earlier study and applying them to the 1850-1900 samples. As much as possible his analysis will be differentiated by sex, class, and ethnicity.

The Demography of School and Work

The demography of school attendance is a familiar but still vital issue. A number of historians have made important individual studies of towns, cities, and schools. Katz and Davey examined school attendance during the early industrialization of Hamilton, Ontario, using manuscript census material which they analyzed with both descriptive and multivariate statistics. Davey did an intensive study of school attendance at one key school in the city. Joel Perlman recently finished a major study of school attendance in Providence, Rhode Island. Kaestle and Vinovskis studied attendance in several Massachusetts towns during the middle part of the nineteenth century. All these studies have pointed to important connections between school attendance and social structure, but they disagree about a number of important issues, such as the relative importance of class and ethnicity, the role of family structure, and the relations between attendance and industrialization. In part, these disagreements reflect theoretical differences about the nature of social structure and social change. In part, however, they also reflect limitations of the data bases.

Our data base for the analysis of school attendance is unusually rich. It encompasses a much longer time frame than any previous comparable study; it combines data from various sources; it focuses on one city during its evolution from an early nineteenth-century commercial center to a complex industrial city in the early twentieth century; and it combines both aggregate and individual level analysis.

The aggregate analysis includes school enrollment, average daily attendance, length of the school year, and two measures of educational achievement. The first measure is of changes in the educational attainment of cross-sectional age cohorts at different points in time (what economists call educational stock); the second measure is of changes in the educational attainment of successive natural or longitudinal age cohorts at ten-year intervals. By relating educational attainment to various measures of social and economic change it will be possible to test the major theoretical explanations of the expansion of schooling: modernization theory, status competition theory, social control, and a variety of Marxist positions.

Our analysis of school attendance will ask the obvious questions about the connections between attendance at various ages and at various types of schools, and class, ethnicity, sex, and family structure. We will follow the methods developed by Katz and Davey in their earlier work, adapting them to the Philadelphia data. We will, however, also be able to ask more precise and subtle questions. For instance, Perlman found important links between birth order and attendance in Providence, Rhode Island. Was there a trade-off within families? Was it necessary for some children to work in order for others to go to school? If this was so, was it the older children who worked and the younger ones who attended school? In Buffalo, New York, Stern found a close association between adolescent school attendance and fertility. Families with fewer children sent a greater proportion of their adolescent sons and daughters to school. School attendance and fertility, therefore, were two aspects of a new family strategy. This, again, is an idea that we will test. Even more, by combining records from individual schools with records from the census, we can examine the variation in the student body of different types of schools and ask questions such as: was there anything distinctive about the artisans who sent their daughters to Girls High School? That is, we will be able to look for systematic differences in family strategies within as well as between classes. Where we have information on the internal history of individual schools, most notably the key secondary school for boys, Central High School, we will look for connections between shifts in the demography of the student body and changes in curricula.

Our analysis of school attendance is based both

on the manuscript censuses and on the registers of eleven schools. These registers vary greatly in the information they contain, but in each case they permit an analysis of the basic demographic characteristics of the student body. In some cases, including Girls High School and Central, the records include measures of achievement, either examination scores or letter grades; others have detailed comments about why students left school. We have taken the records from four schools and traced students listed in census years back to the manuscript censuses. This long and arduous task enables us to construct a rich portrait of student family background.

Understanding the links between schooling and employment requires answering several questions about the demography of work. This is the most difficult empirical aspect of the project. Historians only now are beginning to study the labor force of individual firms in detail, and, despite the widespread recent interest among labor historians, little is known about how people were hired, the criteria used in various types of industries, how work was learned, or about promotion and the nature of careers within firms. All these matters are of great historical significance. Work on social mobility in the last decade has made clear that movement between the working class and the business class was limited. No one can now reasonably expect to discover many skilled manual workers moving into white collar or managerial positions. Still, there was a great deal of movement within the working class, not only between but within firms.

One of the ways in which industrialization changed the nature of work was to introduce elaborate ladders within individual firms. Although all the jobs were within the working class, the levels of pay and responsibility among them varied greatly. These firm-level hierarchies held out the prospect of at least a modest career within the world of manual work. But historians know almost nothing about how higher levels were filled. Were workers usually hired from outside the firm? How

often were people promoted internally? What
criteria did education play in the job level that
people attained within the working class? These
questions, which form the next frontier for social
mobility studies, are equally important for our
analysis of the relations among work, schools, and
families.

Because so little data exist about the
demography of the workplace, we have had to devote a
major effort to simply finding relevant information.
We canvassed all the historical archives in the city
and contacted most of the individual firms that have
been in existence in Philadelphia since the
nineteenth century. We found useful data in about
seventeen of them. At the same time we discovered a
great many relevant sources scattered in other
places. These include early theses done in schools
of education that trace students' careers; various
studies conducted by civic and university groups;
reports of factory inspectors and other government
officials; discussions in periodicals; and one
remarkable data set, Gladys Palmer's study of the
Wharton School, which traces the occupational
history and educational background of a sample of
2,500 workers born between 1860 and 1920. In
addition, we are reanalyzing the manuscripts of the
manufacturing censuses between 1850 and 1880 coded
by the Philadelphia Social History Project. Our
project's resources will not permit more than a
preliminary analysis of the firm-level material we
have found. But, taken together, the sources on
work should permit us to start drawing a much more
detailed picture of employment than now exists.

The research we have done points to the
importance of describing the labor market in great
detail. Clearly, it seems that the extent and
nature of job opportunities, more than anything
else, governed the length of school attendance and
shaped the transition to adulthood. Working-class
boys usually left school as soon as they could get
jobs. Whether those jobs were the first steps on a
career within the working class or varieties of
dead-end "boy labor," as described for England by
Gareth Stedman Jones and for the United States by

Joseph Kett, is not at all clear. But the attraction of wage-earning itself is unmistakable.

Organizational Development and Innovation

Our fourth perspective is organizational development and innovation. Who sponsored or opposed educational innovations and why? What was the character of the process of organizational innovation? Did innovations reach their intended clientele? What were the politics of bureaucratization? These are among the basic questions we need to study in order to assess the nature of educational innovation and its relation to work, class, and family.

To answer these questions we are concentrating on six aspects of the process of organizational development and innovation in Philadelphia: the creation of a public school system during the 1830s; the system's expansion and its relation to private and parochial schools; the politics of curriculum change; the timing and significance of pedagogical changes in methods of motivation, discipline, and instruction (including the feminization of teaching); the introduction of structural changes (in particular, graded classrooms and graded schools) and the formalization of procedures (such as promotion and hiring); and the characteristics of school governance, particularly the politics and demography of school boards and patterns of bureaucratization.

Our analysis of innovation by and large proceeds from the obvious sources: school board reports and minutes, newspapers, pamphlets, and other primary sources. What these sources usually do not show is how change took place within individual schools. Fortunately, one superb source, the faculty minutes of Central High School, will enable us to trace the process of innovation in the city's key secondary school over almost a century.

As we have pursued these sources, we have focused on three broad issues. One is the politics of organizational innovation. The question is not only who supported or resisted change but what was the nature of political conflict: ethnic and religious, class, or pluralist, for instance? As we argued earlier, educational change should be understood as the result of compromises between different, often contending, interests. Some, such as the goals of social classes, political parties, or business interests, are external to the educational system. Others spring from within the system and reflect competing modes of authority, structural tensions, or the ambitions and problems of practicing educators. The goals of groups outside the system are easiest to establish; the aims and activities of those within are the hardest. Thus, the importance of the faculty minutes at Central High School lies in their illumination of the way in which educators themselves originated, resisted, modified, or accommodated demands for change.

The question of politics leads directly to another issue: the character of schools as social organizations. Historians have largely ignored the relatively rich theoretical literature on schools as social organizations and have focused exclusively on bureaucracy. But schools are more than bureaucracies. Indeed, in some ways their peculiar organizational history and structure limit the scope of bureaucratization. Schools have unusually complex authority structures because they involve varying mixes of accountability, bureaucratic hierarchy, and professional autonomy. The theoretical literature on schools as social organizations can help historians move toward a more complex and nuanced account of the relations between centralization and bureaucratization. At the same time most sociological theory remains uninformed by history. (The work of Bidwell and Dreeben, however, is a notable exception to this generalization.) As a consequence, most theory gives little sense of how schools as organizations actually develop over time and fails to unravel the complex, shifting relations among schools and their contexts, clients, and staffs.

Finally, there is the question of the structural and institutional links among schooling, the labor market, and the workplace. These assume

various forms: for example, a curriculum which
stresses practical and useful education, classroom
procedures embodying important ideological messages,
vocational guidance, techniques of motivation and
discipline, and so on. Some of these link the
school directly to the workplace, others to the
labor market. Clearly, historians need to
understand a great deal more about both the
organization of work and the history and composition
of the labor market before they can fully grasp the
significance of major developments in the history of
education. No one, for instance, has tried to join
the differentiation of secondary education and the
introduction of vocational guidance to the
stratification and differentiation of the labor
market in the late nineteenth century. Nor has
there been more than the most preliminary work on
the private trade and business schools that have
flourished in cities for more than a century and
have often mediated the transition from public
school to work.

Social Ecology
      By and large, the unit of analysis for most of
our project is either individuals or families. To
some extent, that focus is modified by our concern
with innovation: the way in which change occurred
within the system. However, another important focus
is the individual school. Schools served particular
neighborhoods, and their social and ethnic
composition differed markedly. Today we would
expect schools to be affected by these variations in
their student body. Factors such as overall
achievement levels or rates of absence are two
examples. We also might expect to find variations
in the resources available to different schools.
Despite the Coleman Report, poor people long have
suspected that schools in wealthier districts
receive more money, better teachers, and newer
equipment. Whether this is the case today and to
what extent it happened in the past remain open
issues.
      Modell has asked some of these questions in his
analysis of school expenditures and suburbanization

in late nineteenth- and early twentieth- century Philadelphia. He found surprisingly little association between the social composition of districts and school expenditures. But to fully grasp the connections between social ecology and educational resources it is necessary to gather data that cover a longer time span and incorporate more variables. Within Philadelphia it is possible to construct a year-by-year series showing pupil-teacher ratio, per-capita student expense, the ratio of average daily attendance to total enrollment, and the rate of teacher turnover for each school in the city since the late 1830s. The sources are the annual reports of the Board of Education. Schools then can be characterized in terms of the neighborhoods they serve, and relations between changes in social ecology and educational resources can be studied with great detail over a long time period. We had hoped to undertake this sort of ecological analysis, but it is the aspect of our plans with which we probably will be able to do least in this phase of the work.

There is one important ecological issue which we can, however, study in detail for one year, namely, the effect of neighborhoods on individuals. The issue is the relative weight of family or ethnic values and peer influence on behavior. We start from the observation that the behavior of children of immigrants born in North America differed markedly from that of their children born abroad. This is true, certainly, for fertility and school attendance. The distinctions between people who were born in North America and those who immigrated, even as youngsters, were clear in Katz's study of Hamilton, Ontario, in Stern's work on Buffalo, and they are appearing in the preliminary analyses of Philadelphia. All this points to the importance of early experience in shaping behavior. For example, one might imagine that the school attendance of children of Irish immigrants would be different if they lived in predominantly Irish districts than if they lived in neighborhoods dominated by native Americans. For technical reasons we can ask this question only for 1880, but in that year we will be able to assess the influence of the ethnic composition of each youngster's immediate neighborhood (an area about a block and a quarter square) on his or her school attendance.

Conclusion

Although we are pursuing these issues vigorously, we have few definitive answers now, and this, in a very real sense, is a paper without a conclusion. Rather, it is an exhortation to systematic study and an illustration of issues, data, and approaches that will advance the analysis of the relations among schools, families, and social structure. It would be unrealistic to expect many people to undertake projects of the size and scope of the one described here. Indeed, the recent massive cutback in funding for social science research makes another undertaking of this size almost inconceivable for the immediate future. But large sums of money are not necessary for worthwhile research. Within each of the perspectives we have described important work can be done on a modest scale. The important point is to orient research around a set of common concerns, to set individual studies within a larger frame, and to be self-conscious about method and theory. In that way research in the field can be directed to the areas most in need of study, scholars can learn from each other, and the result can be at least a moderately cumulative increase in knowledge (or more accurately, a cumulative decrease in our vast ignorance) about the interconnections among schools, families, work, and social structure in American history.

Note on Sources

In the interests of space we have not documented the argument in this paper with references to historical and theoretical literature. The earlier work by Katz to which reference is made is found in Michael Katz, Michael J. Doucet, and Mark J. Stern, <u>The Social Organization of Early Industrial Capitalism</u> (Cambridge, Mass., 1982), which also contains references to the relevant historical literature. Chapter one includes a lengthy discussion of class analysis in history. The earlier work of the Philadelphia Social History Project is discussed in Theodore Hershberg, ed., <u>Philadelphia: Work, Space, Family, and Group Experience in the Nineteenth Century</u> (New York, 1981). References to the theoretical literature and a discussion of the issues that it raises is in the grant application for the project described in this paper ("The Organization of Schools, Work, and Family Life in Philadelphia, 1838-1920"), which can be obtained from the National Institute of Education. For a review of the literature on the relationship between education and work, see D. Hogan, "Making It in America" in <u>Work, Youth, and Schooling</u>, ed. H. Kantor and D. Tyack (Palo Alto, Calif., 1982).

Contributors

David L. Angus is Professor of Educational History at The University of Michigan, where he has served since 1966. He was formerly on the education faculty at the University of Massachusetts, Amherst, and at Ohio State University, where he received his doctorate. In recent years, his research has focused on the politics of education in the antebellum and progressive periods. He currently serves as the President of the Midwest History of Education Society.

John Hardin Best is on the faculty of Education Policy Studies at The Pennsylvania State University. He formerly taught at Rutgers University and at Georgia State University, Atlanta. He received graduate degrees in history and in education from the University of North Carolina, Chapel Hill. The major part of his work for publication over the years has been in editing, most recently as Associate Editor of the Encyclopedia of Educational Research, Fifth Edition. He has served as President of the American Educational Studies Association and as Vice-president, Division F, "History and

Historiography," of the American Educational Research Association.

Geraldine Joncich Clifford teaches at the Graduate School of Education of the University of California, Berkeley. She has written a biography of Edward L. Thorndike (The Sane Positivist, 1968) and case studies of the effects of educational research school practice. Her current research analyzes nineteenth-century diaries and personal correspondence for what they reveal about the motivations for conditions of schooling. Professor Clifford has held various offices in the History of Education Society and Division F of the American Educational Research Association.

Sol Cohen is Professor at the Graduate School of Education, UCLA. He is the editor of Education in the United States: A Documentary History (5 volumes; Random House, New York, 1974) and has served as President of the History of Education Society. Professor Cohen's work on the history of education has been published widely in the United States and abroad. For the past several years he has been engaged in a long-term exploration of the "medicalization" of American education, an interprofessional study of the influence of the mental hygiene movement, psychiatry, clinical psychology, and psychiatric social work in American education.

William W. Cutler, III is Associate Dean of the Graduate School and Associate Professor of History and Foundations of Education at Temple University. He earned a Ph.D. in history and education at Cornell University. In 1980 he co-edited and contributed to The Divided Metropolis: Social and Spatial Dimensions of Philadelphia, 1800-1975. He has published several articles on oral history and currently is helping the Girl Scouts of Greater Philadelphia conduct an oral history of their work in the Philadelphia area since 1920.

Barry M. Franklin is Assistant Professor of

Education and Coordinator of Special Education at Augsburg College in Minneapolis, Minnesota, where he teaches courses in curriculum, special education, and urban education. He is especially interested in the history of curriculum, particularly in its historical uses in the social control of deviance. His publications deal primarily with the history of the curriculum and the history of special education. He is at present writing a history of the idea of social control in American curriculum thought. He earned his graduate degrees from the University of Wisconsin and University of Chicago.

Irving G. Hendrick is Professor of Education and Associate Dean of the School of Education at the University of California, Riverside where he has been since 1965. Mr. Hendrick spent one year at the University of Michigan, Flint, after completing his undergraduate and graduate degrees at Whittier College and UCLA. His work in regional history has centered primarily on teacher certification and the segregation of minority groups in California. In addition to close to a dozen articles on these topics, his books with a regional focus include The Education of Non-Whites in California and California Education: A Brief History.

N. Ray Hiner is Professor of History and Education at the University of Kansas. He received his M.A. and Ph.D. from George Peabody College and has completed postdoctoral study at the Menninger School of Pscyhiatry and the Topeka Institute for Psychoanalysis. His research has concentrated on the history of childhood and youth with an emphasis on the colonial period. He is co-editor of History of Childhood in America: Analysis and Handbook, Greenwood Press (forthcoming), and he is currently working on a book-length study of children in the life and thought of Cotton Mather.

David Hogan is an Assistant Professor in the Graduate School of Education at the University of Pennsylvania. He recently completed a manuscript on education and Progressive reform in Chicago and is currently engaged in research on the social and economic history of education in Philadelphia from the Revolution through the 1920s. He was awarded the Henry Barnard Award by the History of Education Society in 1977, and a Spencer Fellowship by the National Academy of Education in 1980.

Henry C. Johnson, Jr., is Professor of History of Education in the Division of Education Policy Studies at The Pennsylvania State University. His recent publications include The Public School and Moral Education (Pilgrim Press, 1980). Professor Johnson is presently researching the history of schooling in Homestead, Pennsylvania, parochial schooling, and scientific thought and secularization in American education.

Michael B. Katz is Professor of Education and History and Director of the Urban Studies Program at the University of Pennsylvania. He is a past president of the History of Education Society and has been a Visiting Fellow at the Institute for Advanced Study and a Guggenheim Fellow. He has written extensively on the history of education and the history of social structure and family organization. His most recent books are with Michael Doucet and Mark Stern, The Social Organization of Early Industrial Capitalism (Harvard, 1982) and Poverty and Policy in American History, forthcoming (Academic Press, 1983).

Herbert M. Kliebard holds a joint appointment in the Department of Curriculum and Instruction and Educational Policy Studies at the University of Wisconsin, Madison, where he has taught for the past twenty years. He has published (with Arno Bellack) The Language of the Classroom and Curriculum and Evaluation, the latter a volume in AERA's Readings in Educational Research Series. He has also published a documentary history, Religion and Education in America. Most of Professor Kliebard's research and writing in recent years has been in the area of history of curriculum, and he is currently at work on a volume tentatively entitled, The

Struggle for the American Curriculum: 1893 to 1958.
One outgrowth of that undertaking appeared in the
January 1982 issue of Educational Researcher.

Ellen Condliffe Lagemann is on the faculty of
Teachers College, Columbia University, where she is
an Associate Professor of History and Education and
a Research Associate in the Institute of Philosophy
and Politics of Education. She received her Ph.D.
in history and education from Columbia University.
She is the author of A Generation of Women:
Education in the Lives of Progressive Reformers and
of Private Power for the Public Good: A History of
the Carnegie Foundation for the Advancement of
Teaching and editor of Nursing History: New
Perspectives, New Possibilities.

Paul H. Mattingly is a member of the Department
of History at New York University and Co-Director of
their new Program in Public History. He received
both graduate degrees in History from the University
of Wisconsin, Madison and has served as Associate
Editor and, since 1971, as Editor of The History of
Education Quarterly. His book, The Classless
Profession: American Schoolmen in the Nineteenth
Century (1975), became the first volume in New York
University Press's Series: "Education and
Socialization in American History." From 1974 to
1979 he received a Spencer Fellowship of the
National Academy of Education to assist his
research.

William J. Reese teaches history of education
and related courses at Indiana University at
Bloomington. He has taught at the University of
Wisconsin, Madison and the University of Delaware
and has published articles in journals such as
School Review, Teachers College Record, Educational
Theory, and the History of Education Quarterly. His
first book, Progressivism and the Grass Roots, will
be published by Routledge and Kegan Paul.

James Sanders is Professor of history and
education at the College of Staten Island, City

University of New York, where he has taught since earning a Ph.D. in urban history and education at the University of Chicago. His research has focused on Roman Catholics as an urban minority group in the nineteenth and early twentieth centuries, with particular emphasis on this group's responses to the development of public education. His major publications in this area include The Education of an Urban Minority, Catholics in Chicago, 1833-1965 (Oxford University Press, 1977) and he is presently completing a book on Catholics and the school question in Boston, for which he received a National Endowment for the Humanities research fellowship. He serves on the editorial board of the History of Education Quarterly and the Board of Directors of the History of Education Society.

Harold Silver is Principal of Bulmershe College of Higher Education, Reading, England. He was a professor in the University of London and other British institutions, after graduating in English and modern languages from the University of Cambridge. His publications include The Concept of Popular Education and Education and the Social Condition, as well as other historical works covering British and American educational and social history. He is co-author of A Social History of Education in England and The Education of the Poor. His latest book, Education as History, with a foreword by David Tyack, is due in 1983. He is currently researching British and American educational policies against poverty in the 1960s/70s.

Donald Warren is professor and chairman of the department of Education Policy, Planning, and Administration at the University of Maryland. Previously he was on the faculty at the University of Illinois, Chicago. He holds graduate degrees from Harvard University and the University of Chicago, where he completed his Ph.D. in the history of education. His publications, including To Enforce Education: A History of the Founding Years of the U.S. Office of Education (1974) and History,

<u>Education, and Public Policy</u> (1978), focus on the role of history in policy analysis. He has served as President of the American Educational Studies Association and the Council of Learned Societies in Education.